Homer

A GUIDE FOR THE PERPLEXED

Homer

AHUVIA KAHANE

B L O O M S B U R Y

LONDON • NEW DELHI • NEW YORK • SYDNEY

Bloomsbury Academic

An imprint of Bloomsbury Publishing Plc

50 Bedford Square
London
WC1B 3DP
UK

175 Fifth Avenue
New York
NY 10010
USA

www.bloomsbury.com

First published 2012

British Library Cataloguing-in-Publication Data

A catalogue record for this book is available from the British Library.

ISBN: HB: 978-1-4411-7946-3
PB: 978-1-4411-0010-8

Library of Congress Cataloging-in-Publication Data

A catalog record for this book is available from the Library of Congress.

Typeset by Newgen Imaging Systems Pvt Ltd, Chennai, India

CONTENTS

PREFACE

This short book appears in the series of *Guides for the Perplexed* whose purpose is to introduce major figures and works to students and general readers and especially, as the series title suggests, to explain challenging and difficult aspects of those works. This has particular significance in the case of Homer.

The *Iliad* and *Odyssey* are first and foremost stories to be read (or listened to) for pleasure. They are widely available in print, in translations into almost every language and in electronic form too. There are dozens of translations in English alone, in verse and prose, in versions that follow the original ancient Greek very closely (e.g. by Richmond Lattimore or Walter Shewring) and in others that take greater poetic liberties (such as Christopher Logue's powerful *War Music*, Madelein Miller's Orange Prize winner, *The Song of Achilles*' or Alice Oswald's haunting *Memorial*). Readers who seek short, practical introductions to Homer and Homeric poetry and answers to basic questions will likewise find an abundance of informed introductions, handbooks, companions and encyclopaedias on the subject that outline important facts, characters, themes and contexts. And yet Homer, the first poet in the Western literary canon and one of its mainstays, demands and richly rewards deeper exploration. His poetry deals with some of the most difficult and long-standing poetic, historical and ethical questions ever raised.

Homeric questions have of course been perplexing and fascinating readers, poets, philosophers, politicians, businessmen (Heinrich Schliemann, the father of Homeric archaeology, was a banker in California during the Gold Rush), beginner students and seasoned scholars for over two and a half millennia – longer than any other literary and historical questions in the classical tradition. The range of creative and reflective responses, artistic and learned, to Homer is vast.

Merely in the last 100 years, almost 15,000 (!) specialist books and articles dedicated to the study of Homer have been written. The number of literary, dramatic, cinematic works, works in painting, sculpture and other media, that relate to the *Iliad* and *Odyssey* is hard, if not impossible, to count. With such bewildering abundance, there is more than one persuasive answer to every question about Homer. It can be difficult to find one's way around, not least since many of the most significant developments in our understanding of Homer's poetry and its background are phrased in a highly technical language. Yet this abundance – perplexing, difficult, resistant to simple solutions – is also what defines the special richness of Homer and the Homeric tradition. To have put it aside would have produced a more convenient but less truthful introduction. What I have therefore tried to do in this book is to present some of the main facts, features and approaches to Homer and to characterize them as plainly as I could without masking the complexity of the questions and the exciting, open, meditative themes that give the *Iliad* and *Odyssey* their beauty and ensure their continuing resonance.

This book was written during a period of leave from my duties as a member of the Classics and Philosophy Department and Directory of the Humanities and Arts Research Centre at Royal Holloway, University of London. I am grateful to the Faculty of Arts for providing additional support and, earlier, to the Department of Classics at the University of Cincinnati, for providing me with a Titus Fellowship, during which I had considered some of the issues of presentation and range of this book. Many friends and colleagues have provided encouragement and advice as this book was being written. However, most of all I would like to thank the many graduate students who had taken my University of London Inter-Collegiate Homer course, and from whom, over several years, I had learned a great deal about Homer.

CHAPTER ONE

The figures of Homeric poetry

A beginning for all time

The *Iliad* and *Odyssey* are among the best known poems in the West and increasingly in other parts of the world, and they are widely acknowledged as the beginning of the Western literary canon. They are good stories, well-loved and deceptively easy to read. The *Iliad* is a tale of war; the *Odyssey* is a tale of the return from war. The two Homeric poems are very different from each other, but their narratives, contents, characters, style and traditions are closely entwined. Together they tell at some length – conventionally, 27,803 lines – a plot which is the West's oldest and most famous point of literary departure. The beginning, we might say, of a very long line.

The first poem, the *Iliad*, deals with a conflict that occupies a central position in the collective memory of the ancient Classical world – the Trojan War. It is a story of countless woes, of spears and shields, chariots and horses, fear and pity, fury and grief, blood and dust. The first word of the very first line of the *Iliad* is *mênis*, 'wrath'. It is the theme of the poem and also 'the first word of European Literature'. It offers a harsh forewarning of things to come. The poem makes a rapid start – as one might expect from the 'first' poem – launching into extended narratives of violence and conflict. By the time we have traversed the poem's 24 books and reached the last words, the tone has changed to one of mourning, pity and lament – reflections on wrath as a destructive force, on death and the past. The last line of the poem rounds off the burial of a hero, Hector, 'Tamer-of-Horses', who was a husband, a son, a friend and the emblem of the city's defence. Without him, the high citadel of Troy will fall.

And indeed, beyond the horizon of the *Iliad*'s last verse lie the inevitable flames of destruction. Western literature here takes its first, dark, measured steps. 'Measured' not only because Homeric poetry is composed in formal, repetitive (and technically complex) metrical verse (each line has the same basic rhythm and involves intricate 'formulae' or set groups of words), but no less because of Homer's meticulously crafted thought and poetics, his studied descriptions of physical violence and extreme emotion and because of the claims made by the poems themselves, not merely to tell a story, but to preserve the 'fame' (*kleos*) of fleeting mortal events. 'Dark', not simply because death lurks everywhere in the poems' past, present and future, but because the *Iliad* is a poem that, above all, acknowledges mortality, tragedy and loss. Modern culture and especially modern popular culture (Hollywood film, for example) sometimes ends its stories with a victory for the 'right side' and the rightful defeat of others, or with a sense of wrong when the 'right side' is defeated. Loss in Homer runs deeper. In the background to the *Iliad* lies the abduction of Helen – a basic act of transgression by a guest (Paris) against a host (Menelaus). It is the cause of the Greek expedition against Troy, the war, and Troy's eventual fall. Yet the poem has no right side, and ultimately, despite many victories and defeats, has within it more pity and grief than triumph. The *Iliad* has many battles and duels in which men kill and are killed. Violence is meted out and revenge is exacted. The poem sings of valour, prowess and martial excellence. Heroes sometimes revel in their strength. Yet the *Iliad* recognizes the inevitable price of violence and its irreparable consequences. It looks death, ineluctable and tragic, straight in the eye, although Homer's piercing gaze is neither morbid, on the one hand, nor 'objective' or detached, on the other. This fateful, finely wrought, meditation on mortality seems well-suited to the burden of the *Iliad*'s place in literary history. The end of life, reflections on the end of life, are often the beginnings of a life in words (what the Greeks called a *bios* and the Romans a *vita*), a history, a narrative. This 'end' that is the *Iliad*, a permanent figure of fragility, is, we might almost say, a natural beginning to a life of the mind.

Homer's second poem, the *Odyssey*, deals with the aftermath of the war. The surface of its tale is more varied and colourful. It follows the homeward path of Odysseus, one of the great heroes of the Trojan War and the wanderer-figure par excellence in the literary tradition of the West. During the 10 years of the war, and 10 more years which the journey takes him, tensions mount back in his palace on the island of Ithaca. His wife is besieged by suitors. His young son is coming of age but is still helpless on his own. The *Odyssey* describes both distant journeys and a painful situation at home. It is a poem of adventure, of monsters, ghosts and far-away peoples and lands, of seduction and intrigue, of recklessness and fidelity, of youth and old age, of memory and elaborate tales, of lies and truth, and, finally, of a homecoming and a reunion.

Compared to the *Iliad*, the first word of the *Odyssey*, *andra* (man) presents an elusive, almost enigmatic theme. As if the poem is asking 'what is a *man*?' The name of the poem is *Odysseia*, 'the tale of Odysseus', and yet, unlike the *Iliad*, the hero is un-named in the first line, which simply speaks of 'the man of many ways', *andra . . . polytropon* (1.1). The hero's name is later revealed (obliquely, in 1.21), but we do not actually meet Odysseus until book 5 of the poem. If one of the *Odyssey*'s themes is the absence of the hero from his home, it is also a theme enacted literally in the hero's absence from the first, substantial part of the poem. Significantly, even when Odysseus has come back to occupy the narrative stage, his name and identity are repeatedly withheld from various characters. The question of naming and identity is central to this work. Not only the *Odyssey*'s first word, but also the poem as a whole, asks 'who is this man, Odysseus?' and 'what is a man?' In typical Homeric fashion, the poem celebrates the multiplicity of possible answers.

The hero of the *Odyssey* is indeed *polytropos,* a man of many 'ways' or 'tropes'. Later in the poem, he is also described as *polymêtis*, 'of many schemes' (2.173, etc.), *polyphrôn*, 'of many minds' (1.83, etc.), *polymêchanos*, 'of many devices' (5.203, etc.), *polyainos*, 'much sung' (12.184), and more. He is a compulsive traveller and teller of tales. He assumes many false identities and invents histories – a means of survival for him, and perhaps for the poem at large as it unfolds its story – and he boasts about his skills of deception. 'I am Odysseus, son of Laertes, who is known to all for his wiles', he says (9.19. See Pucci 1987). The *Odyssey*'s narrative, like its hero, follows many winding paths and it carries us to the far corners of Homer's world. The plot takes place on the seas, at the edges of the world, on faraway islands, in Sparta, Ithaca and more. It leaps backwards and forwards in time. We may well ask who exactly is this 'man of many ways' who has been everywhere and seen so much, and what exactly is his story? The answer is often in the plural. In fact, as the poem itself tells us, other journeys await the hero in the future, after he will have arrived in Ithaca, when his journey and his homecoming are fulfilled and the poem itself has ended (see the words of the ghost of the seer Teiresias to Odysseus in the underworld in the *Odyssey* 11.111–37). This future which lies beyond Odysseus' homecoming and beyond the end of the poem, like the future of Troy which lies beyond the end of the *Iliad*, is not an oversight. It does not indicate the premature ending of the narrative. The 'untold' events are not missing pieces of the poem nor loose strands trailing around the plots. Rather, they are essential reflections of the way the Homeric poems relate to the worlds they describe, the way the poems continue to resonate after the narrative has reached the last line.

Many Homers

The *Iliad* and the *Odyssey*, then, are the beginning of a history and a literary timeline. They have been with the West 'since birth' and are (with some periods away from the limelight, in part, for example, from the middle ages to the Renaissance) a recurrent feature at the centre of its literary scene. Translations and adaptations abound – Homeric poetry is part of the literary furnishings of our world. The texts bear the marks of our histories, and are, despite the vast distance that separates them and us and their distinct character, always familiar somehow. There is, even in today's rapidly evolving world, a certain comfortable fit between the *Iliad* and *Odyssey* and many of our sensibilities and historical perceptions. This fit characterizes some of the ways in which the tradition of the West and today's increasingly wider traditions couch their understanding of song and narrative, as well as of conflict, gender, subjectivity, ethnicity, 'self' and 'other', mortality, heroes, knowledge, survival and the relation of the present to the past. Homer seems to remain a figure of significance, sometimes a point of reference, even as these traditions evolve (in a world of changing values and balances of power, global telecommunications, social networking and more), recreate and even more forcefully resist old categories, binary oppositions, monumental historical narratives and metaphysical completeness and/or coherence. Yet the ease with which we often accept Homer also contains deep-seated complexities. When we look at Homer more closely, we find perplexing features and a multiform essence.

Homer's elusive character can be found in both broad and pointed aspects of the poems. Almost every word in the *Iliad* and *Odyssey* marks it. Thus, to give a brief preliminary example, one of the best known and most common expressions in Homer is *epea pteroenta* which, literally translated, means 'winged words'. This expression first appears at the beginning of the *Iliad*, when Achilles, the hero of the poem, is about to respond to the insulting behaviour of Agamemnon, the leader of the Greek armies, with impulsive, violent emotion. The goddess Athena intervenes, grabbing Achilles by the hair. The hero is amazed, but he instantly recognizes the goddess and her flashing eyes. Then, we are told (*Iliad* 1.201–3),

he uttered winged words [*epea pteroenta*] and addressed her
'Why have you come again, daughter of Zeus of the Aegis?
Is it so that you should see the outrageous arrogance (*hybris*)
    of the son of Atreus?'

The flutter of these 'winged words' and the image they inspire seems to anticipate Achilles' following speech and the wrath which is the theme and immediate cause of events in the poem (1.1: 'Of the wrath of Achilles son of Peleus, sing, Muse'). This strange and distinctive expression, 'winged words', has been haunting readers and scholars for millennia. It 'haunts' the text, too, since it is repeated no less than 114 times throughout the poems, in a wide range of contexts, by speakers who display a wide range of emotions and thoughts. Are 'winged words' just rapid words? Are we dealing with one state of mind or with many? Is the essence of these simple words, *epea pteroenta*, a visual image of movement that cannot be grasped? Does Achilles' verbal response and the flutter of wings have anything to do with this scene's rare and unexpected epiphany – the appearance of a god before a mortal? *Epea*, in Greek, means simply 'words'. But it is also the plural of *epos*, which in other contexts can mean 'epic'. Achilles' pointed, situated yet fluttering and elusive response may thus also hint at a general quality of 'epic' poetry, which is itself a response by mortals to visions of death and eternity and of things that are beyond mortality. Homer's poetry itself, we might say, is a kind of 'winged words' whose resonance is always immediate but difficult to grasp, always something more than its literal meaning and presence. The poet Matthew Arnold in his essay 'On Translating Homer' (1861) famously attributed to Homer the qualities of being eminently rapid, plain, direct and noble. Such qualities may indeed have been achieved in Homer's poetry, yet they are achieved by perplexing and elusive means.

In antiquity, Homer's reputation and legacy thrived unmatched. He was celebrated in key canonical works that looked back to the *Iliad* and *Odyssey* in awe and often also with manifest anxiety. These works included epic poems, for example, Apollonius of Rhodes' *Argonautica* (third century BCE), Virgil's *Aeneid* (first century BCE), Lucan's *Pharsalia* (first century AD) and many others. They also included major works in almost every other literary genre including lyric poetry, tragedy, oratory and rhetoric, history and philosophy. Homer's poetry continues to resonate throughout the literary history of the West, not least in contemporary settings, in key modern works such as James Joyce's novel *Ulysses* (1922), Nobel Prize laureate Derek Walcott's long poem *Omeros* (1990), in widely acclaimed films like the Coen brothers' *O Brother, Where Art Thou?* (2000), Mike Leigh's *Naked* (1994), Wolfgang Petersen's *Troy* (2001), Theo Angelopoulos' *Ulysses' Gaze* (1995) and more (see Hardwick 2003, Hardwick and Gillespie 2008, Graziosi and Greenwood 2007, Hall 2008, also entries on 'reception' in Finkelberg 2010). Yet the continuity of Homer's legacy and his enduring attraction today, as in the past, sees no end to change. There are no rules or set boundaries to Homer's resonance. In the third century BCE, in the Hellenistic age, the epic poet Apollonius of Rhodes took Homer's model and transposed it onto a narrative about an unfaithful hero (Jason) who is marked surprisingly by 'helplessness' (in Greek, *amêchaniê*) and about a woman's (Medea's) vengeance. Hellenistic culture's sense of self-identity embraced both the poetic values and practices of earlier Greek eras and sought to break away from them. In Rome, Virgil took Homer's poems of fighting (the *Iliad*) and far-ranging journeys (the *Odyssey*) and turned their order upside down. In the *Aeneid*, the hero Aeneas and his fellow Trojan survivors first journey to a new home (sailing *away* from the Greek lands rather than, like Odysseus and the Greeks, making their way home *towards* Greece), then fight (*founding* a future city rather than *razing* one to the ground, as in the *Iliad*). In fifth century BCE Athens, the dramatist Aeschylus' tragic trilogy the *Oresteia* picks up and retells the narratives of Agamemnon, Clytemnestra and Orestes. Orestes' story is retold many times in Homer's *Odyssey*, where it is presented as a model for later action. Aeschylus embraces this 'Homeric' model and places it on the stage. Yet he recreates the tales in the image of his own times, giving it a distinctly Athenian civic twist instead of the original aristocratic, heroic colouring. In first century AD Rome, Petronius, 'Arbiter of Elegance' to the emperor Nero, turned Odyssean epic verse and its tales of wandering, heroic adventure, homecoming and fidelity into a novel, mostly in prose, which follows the reckless sexual escapades of a hero named Encolpius, 'In-Crotch' (a roundabout way of saying 'Penis'), in the settings of imperial decadence. Homer's lofty Greek epic verse here plays its part within the pages of a racy Roman novel's prose.

Change is no less part of the later Homeric tradition since the Renaissance, right down to our own times. James Joyce transported the scene of the *Odyssey* from Ithaca and antiquity to early twentieth-century Dublin and canonized Homer within Western modernism: the hero of Joyce's *Ulysses*, Leopold Bloom, and his wife Molly are as close a continuation and as radical a break from Homer's characters Odysseus and Penelope as we wish, just as Joyce's free 'stream of consciousness' English prose is both a stranger to the formal, repetitive flow of Homer's Greek hexameter verse and a bedfellow to its open-ended flexibility (for Homer's language, see further below). At the close of the twentieth century, Derek Walcott's epic *Omeros* took Homer to the Caribbean island of St Lucia, with St Lucians Achílle, Hector and Helen in leading roles (*Omeros* chapter 3, section 1):

> . . . Men can kill
> their own brothers in rage, but the madman who tore
> Achílle's undershirt from one shoulder also tore
> at his heart. The rage that he felt against Hector
> was shame. To go crazy for an old bailing tin
> crusted with rust! The duel of these fishermen
> was over a shadow and its name was Helen.

Who are Achílle, Hector and Helen in these verses? What is the rage that drives Achílle here? One cannot read this poem without remembering that we are in the Caribbean, without confronting contemporary questions of the relations of these islands and the colonial empires and cultures that ruled them. One cannot simply superimpose the heroes of Walcott's poem on the characters in Homer's epic (or vice versa!) any more than one can map modern culture onto a single source in antiquity. Yet without the Homeric provenance the powerful modern perspectives and critiques of Walcott's *Omeros* are lost.

The resonance of Homeric poetry effortlessly crosses over to other forms of art – and life. In *O Brother, Where Art Thou?*, film-makers Joel and Ethan Coen famously set the *Odyssey*'s scene in 'musical' surroundings, and in the American deep south of the 1930s, following the adventures of escaped convict Ulysses (as in Joyce's novel, the Latinized form of the name Odysseus and the name of a famous American Civil War general) Everett McGill. British director Mike Leigh placed the Odyssean hero of his film *Naked* in the dark (but also hilariously funny) late-twentieth-century backstreets of London among its subcultures and underclasses. This Homeric hero is lost in the heart of a modern metropolis and the ghostly 'underworlds' of empty high-rise office blocks. In Wolfgang Petersen's Hollywood blockbuster *Troy*, Brad Pitt portrays a glamorous, blond-haired, bronzed Achilles that nevertheless preserves at least some accurate details (Achilles' hair in the *Iliad* is indeed blond; see 1.197). *Troy* follows the Homeric story, but shows more, perhaps too much of the events of the destruction of *Ilium* (complete with dramatic soundtrack, panoramic Computer Generated Imagery [CGI] and rapid camera action) than the *Iliad* and *Odyssey* combined. Director Theo Angelopoulos placed his version, *Ulysses' Gaze*, in the Balkans and created a meditative arthouse film in search of film and about film. We have not even begun to mention elements of the tradition in other media and genres.

Homer's easy fit in his many different contexts, in our contemporary world and in the past, embodies but perhaps also masks a bewildering diversity and also a flexible potential which, in the end, becomes part of the meaning of the poems themselves. Without this flexibility as somehow inherent to the very idea of Homer, it hardly seems possible that two poems should fit to so many different and sometimes incompatible contexts and that the Homeric poems should have played, and continue to play such vastly resonant roles in literary and cultural history.

The *Iliad* and *Odyssey* themselves seem to bear out this idea. The longer and closer we look at the poems, the more intricate, irregular and perplexing are the figures that appear. We begin to wonder what these poems really are, just as when we stare at a familiar face for a long time, we may find ourselves wondering who or what we are looking at. Already the personalized figure of the poet Homer seems to demonstrate this: His name is known everywhere, yet nothing certain is known about him. Many scholars suggest that he is not a historical person at all (see Porter 2004, Kahane 2005; for antiquity, see, e.g. Graziosi 2002). Who, or what is this 'Homer', then? A fiction? A tradition? A word? A sign? Similar elusive qualities characterize the poems themselves, even in their concrete, material form. In our hands, we hold the books that are the *Iliad* and *Odyssey*. We read these books and have been reading them, as books, for thousands of years. Yet, everything we know about the poems suggests that the *Iliad* and *Odyssey* were not created as texts for reading at all. They are, strange as it may seem, not silent books but living performances. The poems, almost all scholars agree, were composed in societies that knew no writing, or had at least evolved orally for a very long period (see Foley 1991, Bakker and Kahane 1997) in a process that eventually led to the texts we have today which are, undoubtedly written texts. The difference between a performance and a text is significant, of course, just like the difference, for example, between a musical performance and sheet music. What, then, are the Homeric poems? When, and how were the *Iliad* and *Odyssey* written down? How do we even know that the poems were composed without writing? After all, the living voice of Homeric bards and rhapsodes has been silent for millennia. How has the poetry of Homer left the mouths and ears of poets and audiences and entered the book?

We accept the *Iliad* and *Odyssey* as the 'beginnings'. Yet as beginnings they begin by raising some perplexing questions. Other cultural and literary traditions, those that begin with the Old Testament, for example, take a more intuitive first step. The book of Genesis, literally 'The Creation', proclaims its place by its contents (before the creation was the void), by its name and its first

words, 'in the beginning' (*bereshith* in Hebrew). Things are a little
different in Homer. The *Iliad* opens, as the Roman poet Horace
later observed, *in medias res*, 'in the middle of things' (*The Art of
Poetry* 148). Indeed, the story of the *Iliad* only begins towards the
end of the Trojan War around which the poem's events revolve.
The *Iliad*'s narrative is followed by the *Odyssey*, which describes
events that happened after the war. Yet, just as Walcott's *Omeros*
or *O Brother, Where Art Thou?* are not simply continuations of
Homer, so even the *Odyssey* is not quite a sequel. It is not *Iliad II*.
The *Odyssey* is a poem of return. But it is not a poem about 'the
return of the *Iliad*'. Rather, the *Odyssey* is a continuation that
almost seems to make a new beginning and to change (or rewrite)
the poem it follows.

This is more than just a general principle. It touches many of
the basic themes of Homer's poems. For example, in the *Iliad*,
heroes die for fame and glory. It is, we might say, part of the
essence of their being. Yet already in the *Iliad*, in Books 9 and 24
for example, some bold challenges are raised to this purpose of
life. Why, asks Achilles (we shall discuss these matters at length
further below), must heroes fight and die? The *Odyssey* picks up
these themes of doubt with doubled vigour. For example, in the
underworld of the *Odyssey*, the world of dead heroes of the *Iliad*,
Odysseus meets the ghost of Achilles. Odysseus consoles and
praises this spectre of the heroic past. Yet in response Achilles
angrily says (*Odyssey* 11.488–91):

> Don't console me about death, great Odysseus
> I would rather be a farm labourer, slaving for another man
> who owns no land and has not much wealth
> than be king of all the withered dead.

There are, as always in Homer, many ways of interpreting these
verses. But can anyone who knows them read the earlier poem,
the *Iliad*, and its portrayal of heroism, martial excellence and
death as she or he has before? It does not seem unnatural to us
that the West's literary history should begin, not with one (as we
might otherwise expect at the point of beginning), but with two
rather different works. Yet, we cannot take this basic plurality
of the Homeric poems for granted. Homer is not a fact of nature
like a tree or a rock, but a constitutive – and telling – cultural

construct. We must thus recognize the unique shapes and figures of the Homeric tradition.

We do not know precisely what historical circumstances brought about the formation of the *Iliad* and *Odyssey* as two separate poems. Hard historical evidence about the early stages of Homeric poetry is hard to come by. To claim that the poems originated in two different traditions of song as some critics do may be right (indeed, some have split the poems into many traditions of song), but in the absence of evidence outside the poems themselves, this is merely to project the fact that they are two different poems back into an earlier history. Likewise, to say that the two poems are inseparable elements of one tradition is merely to rephrase the fact that they are very similar and have always been associated with the one name of 'Homer'. As for the name, we cannot say with certainty what relation it or the persona of Homer and his many ancient biographies bear to historical fact. Some ancient sources claim that the word *homeros* meant 'blind' (see, e.g. the so-called *Herodotean Vita of Homer* 165) – Homer is, of course traditionally portrayed as a blind old bard; others link it with the meaning of the word *homeros*, 'hostage' in Greek (*Contest of Homer and Hesiod* 29). But what does this mean? No satisfactory answer has been provided. Sometimes the name Homeros was associated with the verb 'to follow' (*Pseudo-Plutarchean Life of Homer* 143–4), perhaps as a pun, since Homer is the first poet in the tradition and followed no one, or perhaps, paradoxically, in tacit acknowledgement that the essence of Homer is a kind of traditional 'following' of one poet after another. The ancients linked Homer's name not to one, but to many birthplaces, including Smyrna, Chios and more, and to many different ancestors (see Graziosi 2002, Kahane 2005). Yet, for the most part, the ancients made no attempt to resolve the question of provenance. Modern scholarship understands this multiplicity by arguing that the ancient *Lives* are narratives that reflect the values and opinions of their times but tell us nothing about a historical figure Homer. Homer, from this perspective, is viewed as a famous tradition of many nameless singers, not as a person. Other modern critics, who do think of Homer as an individual poet, distinguish purely on reasons extracted from a reading of the poems between 'the Poet of the *Iliad*' and 'the Poet of the *Odyssey*'. In other words, the *Iliad* and *Odyssey* themselves – by their very relation to each

other as two separate poems – speak of a multiplicity of figures
of narration. Yet, again, by the position that the poems occupy,
inseparably, in the tradition of the West, they speak of a single,
canonical beginning. How many Homers are there, then? As one
scholar put it recently: 'Fortunately for us, not less than one' (Most
2004: 14).

The *Iliad* and *Odyssey* clearly stand out as unique poems.
But they do not stand alone. We know of many other ancient
epic poems that describe events before, after or around those
described in the *Iliad* and *Odyssey*. Many of these other poems
survive only as summaries and fragments. They were composed
in more or less the same poetic language (which is an artificial
mixture of Ancient Greek dialectal forms) and metre (hexameter
verse), often using similar expressions and phrases. Dating can
be difficult, but it is generally agreed today that these are later
works. Best known among these are the poems in the so-called
Epic Cycle (see Griffin 1977, Burgess 2001), such as the *Nostoi*
('The Returns of the Heroes'), the *Cypria* (describing events
that preceded the *Iliad*, including the Judgement of Paris), the
Aethiopis (describing events after the end of the *Iliad*, including
the death of Achilles), the *Little Iliad* (telling of events after
Achilles' death, and especially the story of the wooden horse), the
Ilioupersis ('The Sacking of Troy') and the *Telegony* ('The Story
of Telegonus'. Telegonus was Odysseus' son by Circe. Searching
for his father, he accidentally kills Odysseus). We also possess
various other important related poems such as the *Homeric
Hymns*, 33 shorter poems that introduce myths surrounding the
Olympic gods. In antiquity, some of the poems of the *Epic Cycle*
and the *Hymns* were at times attributed to Homer, but they do
not seem to have ever had quite the same influence or prestige as
the *Iliad* and *Odyssey*. The state of the actual text, for example,
of the *Epic Cycle*, relative to Homer's poems, illustrates this
well. By and large, cultures preserve (or rediscover, or invent)
those texts that are precious to them. Beginning from the third
century BCE, a canonical text of Homer emerged, which marks
the exclusive prominence of the *Iliad* and *Odyssey*. There are
important differences between a so-called vulgate or common
text of the *Iliad* and *Odyssey* and various scholarly corrections
made already in antiquity. But such differences are the domain
of specialists and text critics. Despite its vast size, the text of

Homer's poems has been and remains remarkably well-preserved as a single, authoritative body of work. In contrast, the weaker status of the poems in the *Epic Cycle* is indicated by their poorly preserved remains. Summaries exist, mostly in the work of the fifth century AD philosopher Proclus. But of the poems in the *Epic Cycle*, we have only fragments. Only ten lines of the *Ilioupersis*, for example, survive, in citations in later works. The relatively low status of these other epic poems and their separation from Homeric poetry underline the unique status of the *Iliad* and *Odyssey*. It also shows us the diversity and range of heroic epic narrative, much of it now lost as independent or complete works, yet some of it, at least, still resonant in the Homeric poems. This resonance, combined with the authority of the *Iliad* and *Odyssey*, generates a kind of monumental poetic *synecdoche*, the rhetorical figure of speech that indicates 'a part that contains the whole'.

The 'project' of Homeric poetry

Multiplicity characterizes the figure of Homer, historical and poetic, and his relation to the historical and poetic character of the poems and to the construction and arrangement of the verse. The question of history itself is of great importance to Homer. The Greeks considered the Trojan War as a historical event. They could point to the site of Troy, and thus acknowledged the historicity of at least the background to Homeric poetry, although they sometimes also cast doubts on the accuracy of Homer's version of events and on occasion, more fundamentally, on the very truth of his poetry. In modern times, the site of Troy in the northwest of Turkey has been excavated extensively and has yielded some spectacular finds, some of them so spectacularly off the historical mark that they cannot be associated with the Homeric Trojan War, if such a war ever existed. Yet some form of historicity or historical resonance is almost always attributed to Homer and detected in the Homeric poems. It seems impossible that the *Iliad* and *Odyssey* should have emerged outside a time, a place and outside historical states of mind and patterns of language. Of course, the extent, nature and dating of historical material in the *Iliad* and *Odyssey* are the subjects of many disputes. The very same facts are often seen as proof positive of historicity of one kind or another, or as indicating nothing certain at all. Strangely, this paradoxical state of affairs makes sense if we consider the purpose of Homeric poetry, as many readers and scholars interpret it, which is precisely to acknowledge moments in time yet transcend them. This transcendence can thus be understood as the essence of Homer's 'poetic project'.

Homeric poetry is an extended meditation on the mortal condition, on the passage of time and on the death of heroes. Yet, as students of Homer often point out, the *raison-d'être* of the poems as it is expressed within the poems themselves lies precisely in their role as acts of remembrance, as special acts that overcome transience. Homer's poetry claims to preserve the memory of past events in words and in song, and in this way to enact the mortal hero's 'undying/imperishable fame' (*kleos aphthiton*, cf. e.g. *Iliad* 9.413). Crucially, this contradictory combination of death and transcendence, of finitude and what is beyond finitude, also underlies Homeric poetry's sense of its own value and place in the world as more than merely pleasing entertainment. Heroic poetry is entertaining, of course, and inside the *Iliad* and especially the *Odyssey*, singing is portrayed as the typical entertainment. It is telling, for example, that the Ithacan singer Phemius ('The Famous One'/'The One Who Gives Men Fame') has a father whose name is Terpis (or Terpius, see *Odyssey* 22.330), 'The One Giving Pleasure'. However, far more ambitiously, song in Homer is portrayed as a response to the precariousness of mortal life, as an act of seeing and telling of the mortal condition from within the mortal condition itself, an immanent act that stresses mortality even as it claims to transcend it and preserve fame beyond the lives of its heroes. It is a seemingly impossible act of remaining inside of one's existence yet looking at one's self from the outside.

Such poetry, if it is to make good on its claims as a tradition of 'un-dying' speech or fame, must on the one hand project an image of permanence. Yet, on the other hand, it must portray itself not simply as an inert, inanimate sign or a monument in stone, but as a living portent, a sign of the past that points to the future. Not surprisingly, one of the most common words for a sign in the *Iliad* and *Odyssey* is *sêma*, which is also the word used to denote a 'funerary monument', a 'tomb', and, significantly, also a 'sign of recognition', and a 'divine portent'. A *sêma* is not only the burial place of a hero (*Iliad* 21.322, etc.), a sign of the dead and of the past, but also, most prominently in the *Odyssey*, a word denoting a personal identification mark, such as the scar of Odysseus that allows the hero to be recognized and enables him to reclaim his identity, to come back from the dead and resume life at the head of his household, beside his wife, son and father (e.g. *Odyssey* 23.73 and discussions further below).

A different, more complicated example of how Homer keeps fame 'imperishable' is his dynamic approach to time and the way the poems narrate their story. On the one hand, the *Iliad* and *Odyssey* rely on the clearly demarcated movement of linear, and thus finite, mortal time. Yet, as they tell their stories, the poems also cut, rearrange and extract time from its chronological order. Of course, every narrative rearranges time by the very act of telling, which is a kind of 'going back in time'. But in Homer, narrative is used, for the first time in Western literature and, what's more, expressly as a response to mortality. This, we might say again, is the 'project of Homeric poetry'.

The war in Troy lasts for 10 years and concerns events well before and after this period of time, from the Judgement of Paris to the fall of Troy. But the *Iliad*, in fact, describes directly only a short period – 51 days of events that occur 'in the middle of things'. Furthermore, most of the poem's action occurs over the course of just 4 days. The *Odyssey*'s time frame comprises Odysseus' 10 years of wandering as well as the 10 years of the war and reaches as far back as his birth and childhood and as far forward as his death. Yet the poem describes in 'live-action' only 41 days, and it chops and changes the sequence of its time, for example, in Odysseus' famous 'flashback' stories in Phaiacia. Given the project of Homeric epic and its goals, such narrative mastery over time takes on its special meaning. If the poet can translate events into song, if he can stretch them and compress them in words which, unlike lives and events, can be 'handed over' (in Latin, *trado*, hence our word 'tradition') to others, if he can change and rearrange the natural order of mortal time, he will have found, within the conventions of epic poetry, a stable form of flexibility (the 'stretching' and 'compressing') and a route to confronting finitude from within the mortal world. Song thus offers a response – not a solution, of course – to the condition of mortality.

Following Homer, permutations of this idea become common literary convention. Horace famously says 'I have built a monument [in words] more durable than bronze' (*Odes* 3, 30). However, as we shall see in our later discussions, Homer's mechanisms for achieving transcendence are unique. The principles of flexibility and transferability are important if the poems are to be what they clearly have succeeded in becoming: narratives that can be told again and again.

The materiality of Homer

Giambattista Vico (1668–1744), one of the fathers of the modern study of Homer, had argued that Homer was 'an idea', that he was not a real person, not a single figure but 'the whole of Greece'. As we shall see, Homer the poet, singer or author is indeed in many ways an idea, or at least (as a cultural critic like Michel Foucault might have put it) a name that we use and around which we organize and characterize the existence, circulation and operation of certain texts in society (see Foucault 1977: 123–4). The 'idea of Homer' can be expressed differently in different historical periods by readers, in the work of poets, dramatists, and film-makers, and in the work of philosophers and scholars. But Homer is not just an idea. In antiquity, for example, he always had a face. Homer was depicted in busts or otherwise conventionally portrayed as a blind, bearded old man. There were many busts of the poet. The faces in those that survive today, if compared, are clearly not of the one same person. We can assume that the ancients realized this, too. Yet, despite this multiplicity of portrayal, Homer was always thought of, paradoxically, as a single person. What we call Homer, of course, is also a text, a body of poetic work. This text conventionally contains an fixed number of lines, 27,803, as we noted. Many of the lines in the *Iliad* and *Odyssey* contain elements repeated elsewhere ('formulae', see further below). This repetition creates what John Foley (1991) once described as 'vastly echoic' language, which is capable of resonating with many voices, representing a tradition of song that is much larger than the poems as we have them. Ancient audiences and ancient readers too, will have been closely familiar with Homer. When the poet spoke, for example, of 'winged words' (*epea pteroenta*), a whole world, a myriad of different yet familiar repetitions and echoes will have fluttered, as it were, in their ears. At the same time, as we have already noted, the text of the *Iliad* and *Odyssey* that has come down to us from antiquity contains fewer and less significant variations than almost any other ancient text – far less than those found not only in the traditions of the *Epic Cycle* and the *Homeric Hymns*, but also in most other ancient canonical traditions. The texts of Greek tragedy, for example, have been precariously preserved. Most of the known tragedies of Aeschylus, Sophocles and Euripides are lost, and there are significant textual difficulties in the manuscripts of many of the extant plays. The poems of Homer, we must stress, comprise a fixed and stable object. Putting specialist discussions aside, the text as we read it today is more-or-less the same as it was read when Homeric scholarship began, in Alexandria in the third century BCE. Likewise, although the language of Homer's poetry is often flowing and elusive, it conforms to strict metrical and formulaic rules and it is closely embedded in the rigid musical and rhythmic patterns of the hexameter. It is a language that invites formal and even statistical analysis. In this sense, Homer's hexameter is not a free-flowing stream of words. Similarly, we must stress that Homer's representation of time is clear and precise. The passage of time is marked, day by day, using some of Homer's the most memorable and frequently repeated verses, like the ones describing the rising of Dawn: 'When early-rising rosy-fingered Dawn appeared' (*êmos d' êrigeneia phanê rhododaktylos Eôs*. See *Iliad* 1.477; 6.175; 9.707; *Odyssey* 2.1; 3.404; 3.491, etc.; the verse was often imitated in antiquity, for example, in the lyric poetry of Sappho, 96.8). Epic time may stretch widely, perhaps even to infinity, but audiences and readers know exactly when events in the direct narrative occur.

The point is crucial: The *Iliad* and *Odyssey* are vast, monumental texts. They have come to us from the distant past of archaic Greece. They are fluid and elusive works of art. Yet the poems are also with us here today, in stable material form, in their canonical completeness. They comprise a flexible infinity that we can, as it were, hold in our hands, something we have received from our predecessors and can pass on to those who will come after us.

CHAPTER TWO

Homeric histories

The necessity of history

Poetry is never detached from its historical surroundings, and Homer's poetry, which tells the story of heroes and war, standard topics of historical writing, must also be seen against the background of historical, social and material contexts. Indeed, questions about the historicity of the events described in the poems characterize Homeric tradition from its first moments. As one recent scholar puts it, 'throughout Greek History, the Trojan war figured as a prominent point of reference' (Grethlein 2010). Homer was the ancients' prime source of information for the war. They placed Homer historically and often followed his lead as a model for recounting the past, but they also argued with the historical accuracy of many of the details in the *Iliad* and *Odyssey*. Already in the fifth century BCE, Herodotus, 'The Father of History', commented on the date of Homer (about 400 years before his time, *Histories* 2.53.4–5) and debated Homer's account of the Trojan War (2.116–20). Other ancient historians like Thucydides (*The Peloponnesian War* 1.1–20) and Polybius (34.2.1–3, etc.) followed suit in discussing Homer's accuracy. Ancient geographers, like Strabo, and generals, like Alexander the Great, visited the site of Troy.

In the modern age, historical interest in Homer is attested even more intensively. It was for a long time assumed, on account of many details, that the events narrated in the poems, and especially in the *Iliad*, were to be situated, historically, in the Bronze Age. Scholars and archaeologists have been searching for the material remains of Troy and for evidence of the events of the Trojan War and Homeric cultures, digging in a variety of Bronze Age sites in Mycenae, Pylos, Crete and most notably at what is generally accepted as the site of a historical city of Troy at Hisarlik, a few miles from the coast of the Dardanelles in Anatolia in the north-west of today's Turkey. Extensive remains have been uncovered in many of these sites: palaces, fortifications, domestic compounds, arms, luxury goods and precious objects. They attest to highly structured human habitation and often also to intense conflict. The site at Hisarlik comprises nine basic archaeological strata and numerous phases within each level. It was inhabited from around 3000 BCE to 950 BCE (broadly, the Bronze Age) and prior to these dates and in later periods (see Rose 1997). Some of the layers on the site clearly attest to catastrophic destruction, notably the level known to archaeologists as Troy VII, which dates back to the eleventh century BCE. Some of the artefacts discovered at this level in Hisarlik and in similarly dated levels in other sites have been compared to objects described in the Homeric poems. This body of evidence is too large and too detailed to ignore, even though some of the associations are clearly mistaken and many have been challenged. Hisarlik is one of the most spectacular Bronze Age sites known, but its direct link to Homer is now considered highly problematic. Instead, many historical elements found in Homer are today often associated with a later period, perhaps in the Iron Age (although greater degrees of overlap and mixing of 'ages' is now generally allowed). There is today much greater emphasis on the patterns, structures and values of social and cultural history reflected in the Homeric poems rather than on their account of events. Homer's historicity is now seen by many as a complex mix of eras, contexts, perceptions and imaginations. The debate is still open, and it is almost as much about history and archaeology themselves as it is about the historicity of Homer, Troy and the Trojan War.

Before we can look at some of these controversies, we need to ask a basic question about Homer and his relation to historical reality. As historian Kurt Raaflaub puts it,

> Why is it important to believe that at the base of Homer lies a tradition about 'an actual and real Trojan War' and

that Homer describes the world of this Trojan War? Why is this question so fascinating to scholars and amateurs alike? (Raaflaub 1997: 77)

The answer, he suggests, has to do, partly with the appeal of great archaeological discoveries and mysteries, and partly with the appeal of the Homeric poems. What we need to stress is the interlinked character of such attractions. One can study Bronze Age armour, Iron Age artefacts and the remains of buildings, fortifications and other historical and archaeological materials on their own. But as one of the cornerstones of the West's culture, Homer's poetry provides, on the one hand, an enticing frame of reference for interpreting certain sites' artefacts and, on the other hand, it calls out for a historical frame to its own interpretation. The *Iliad* and *Odyssey* are great stories 'in need' of a historical site, just as great archaeological sites are in need of a good story. We want to touch the stones of the past and we want to hear them speak. This does not mean that words, history and material objects connect without difficulty or that stones and material objects speak for themselves. It is one thing to unearth an ancient burial mask, as Heinrich Schliemann did when digging at the Bronze Age site in Mycenae in 1876, and another to declare, as Schliemann had, that he found 'the mask of Agamemnon'. The mask in question is a spectacular find, elaborately worked in gold and not unworthy of the *Iliad*'s 'lord of men'. Yet there is an almost general consensus today that it belongs in an earlier period in the sixteenth century BCE, a date far too early for Homeric poetry. Furthermore, even if we could associate the chronologies, there is nothing to link the eerie golden face on the mask to the Greek overlord in the *Iliad*. Some historical claims, then, have been unfounded or require great leaps of faith. Yet a basic fact remains: Homer's monumental opus could only have been created in history.

Homeric poetry itself invites a 'historical' reading. The past and its fame are central concerns in the poems. Whatever is our view of the historicity of the *Iliad* and *Odyssey*, the poems inaugurate a tradition of speaking about the past and, in this sense, a tradition of historical reflection and enquiry. It is no accident that the ancient historians, starting with Herodotus and Thucydides, modelled their own narratives or parts of their narratives on Homer's poems. Thucydides' famous description of the Sicilian expedition, for example (*The Peloponnesian War*, Books 6–7), contains many Homeric references.

The 'historical' impulse in Homer is easy to spot. In Book 2 of the *Iliad*, for instance, the narrator, appealing to the Muses for precise information, says (2.484–7), 'Tell me now . . . who were the leaders of the Danaans [a name sometimes used in Homer to denote the Greeks] and their lords?' A few lines later, as if proving that the Muses have given him what he has asked for, the narrator says, 'I will [now] name the lords of the ships, and the ships' numbers' (2.493). There follows a long list, in verse, of course, known as the Catalogue of Ships (2.441–887 – Dickinson 2007, Sammons 2010). Here is the first item to be mentioned (2.494–510):

Of the Boiotians Peneleos and Leïtos were leaders,
and Arkesilaos and Prothoenor and Klonios;
those who lived in Hyria and in craggy Aulis,
in Schoinos and Skolos, and mountainous Eteonos.
Thespeia and Graia, and wide Mykalessos;
and those who dwelt about Harma and Eilesion and Erythrai,
they ruled Eleon and Hyle and Peteon,
with Okalea and Medeon, the well-built citadel,
Kopai, and Eutresis, and Thisbe of the many doves;
and they held Koroneia, and the meadows of Haliartos,
and held Plataia, and they who lived about Glisa
and were masters of the lower Thebes, the well-built citadel,
and holy Onchestos, the shining grove of Poseidon;
and they held Arne of the many vineyards, and Mideia,
with sacred Nisa and distant Anthedon.
Of these there were fifty ships in all, and in each
there were a hundred and twenty sons of the Boiotians.

The Catalogue is densely packed with precise numbers of ships and men and with the names of leaders and geographic places. Its character and function as poetry have been the subject of long debates (see Edwards 1980, Minchin 2001), but it is an obvious *tour de force* of memory and performance. As a list, it also provides a framework of apparent facts for the whole of the *Iliad*. Many place names in the Catalogue (there are 29 named Greek contingents) are indeed historically attested, for example, Athens, Salamis, Argos, Crete and Rhodes. The abundance of geographic and personal details and precise numbers of ships and men invite us to read Homer historically. In truth, modern scholars have shown that there are difficulties in matching some of the details in the Catalogue to material and historical record. For example, several of the place names seem to refer to landlocked sites. The consensus today is that the materials of the Catalogue are likely to have been gleaned from different periods and origins. Yet it is impossible to read this part of the poem without constantly invoking the historical imagination and the idea of history.

In the *Odyssey*, too, geography and history are prominent, although precise identification is sometimes inherently more difficult. Homeric Pylos, the hero Nestor's city (*Odyssey* Book 3), has been associated with various locations in the west of the Peloponnese. Homeric Ithaca, Odysseus' homeland, lies off the western coast of Greece. Its precise identification and whether it is identical with the modern Greek island of Thiaki/Ithake is the topic of debate, although a general geographic resonance is not in doubt. Trying to identify some of the other places in the *Odyssey*, such as the Phaeacian Never-Never-Land (Books 6–12), the nymph Calypso's island of Ogygia (Book 5), the witch Circe's island Aiaia where Odysseus' men were magically turned into beasts (Book 10), the Underworld (Book 11) or the cave of the cannibal Cyclops (Book 9), can be a little more tricky, although not all scholars have been daunted by the task. But even putting aside the *Odyssey*'s fantastic places, especially those which are contained in speeches by Odysseus – who is a self-confessed trickster, the teller of typical sailors' tales, and sometimes an outright liar – it is clear that Homer's world and his geography bear at least some relation to the named geographic world of historical Greece. Does this mean that the poem preserves a cartographic image? Clearly not. Is the *Odyssey* an amalgam of fantasy and fact, of contemporary and anachronistic or archaizing features? If so, can these features be properly disambiguated? Whichever way we choose to answer these difficult questions, Homeric poetry could not have played its prominent role in history without in some way itself being closely associated with historical events.

We need to stress one more general point about Homer's historical principle: The *Iliad* and *Odyssey* claim to preserve 'imperishable fame', to provide a record of mortal heroes and pasts that would otherwise be lost. The poems underscore their claim, as Jonas Grethlein, for example, puts it, by 'juxtaposing' themselves with 'the material media of memory' (2010: 133). Yet for the poems to have kept a full and accurate record of ancient historical Troy would have worked against their own purpose. In today's world, we often suspect the authenticity of signposted, perfectly reconstructed and preserved sites and 'visitor centres': We can always catch sight of the gift-shop from the corner of our eye. In other words, partial erasure, ruin and loss are necessary in order to create the distancing effect of any past, and of Homer's past, too. Without the idea of something that has been and gone, history itself is not possible. Homer depends on invoking a sense of history, but, since this history is distant, it cannot be seen as clearly as the present.

This principle is at work not only in the contents of Homer's poems but also in very substance of the poems and, for example, in the idea of Homer's oral provenance (which we shall explore in greater detail in the next chapter). The living voice of song is more fragile than the written word. Once uttered, voice as such remains in memory only. It has to be reconstituted afresh every time a song is performed. Such re-performance opens up a 'historical' gap: the poet is forever creating a 'new' version of something 'lost', preserving it on the one hand, but in the process also affirming the essential idea of mortality and loss. The historical past thus lives in the poems, but the poems must live in the present, not in the historical past.

The Trojan War and the ancients

The most prominent event referred to in Homer's poetry is the Trojan War. It is not surprising, then, that this war and the city of Troy around which it was fought have been the focus of debates about historicity.

In antiquity, Herodotus (*Histories* 2.116–20, 2.145) and Thucydides (*The Peloponnesian War* 1.9–12; 3.104.4–6) speak of the Trojan War and of Homer in historical terms, even when they doubt his account. 'I asked the priests [in Egypt] if the Greek story of what happened at Troy had any truth in it', says Herodotus, 'and they gave me in reply some information which they claimed to have had from Menelaus himself. This was that after the abduction of Helen . . .' (2.118). Herodotus proceeds to tell a tale in which Troy is sacked, yet, in direct contradiction to Homer's version, Helen has been kept away from Troy and unharmed in Egypt. The details, thus, are a matter for debate among historians, even those, who like Homer, may have got their facts wrong . . .

Time and precise dating are always important in historical accounts, and for the ancients, they certainly were with regard to the Trojan War. In the fourth century BCE, the historian Ephorus, for example, provided a precise date, the equivalent of July 6/7, 1135 BCE. In the Hellenistic age, the scholar Eratosthenes calculated the date of the War to be 1183 BCE. The chronological list known as the Parian Marble gives a date of 1208/9 BCE. Other ancient historians and scholars set the date as late as 910 BCE. They present their conclusions not as poetic musings or as literary play, but, essentially, as historical fact. The ancient calculations are sometimes close to modern chronologies dating the destruction of Troy to the late Bronze Age. Yet scholars generally agree that all of the ancient arguments are based on speculation. What, then, are we to make of such historicity? The words of the geographer Strabo (63 BCE to AD 24), a man deeply versed in Homer, are telling. Strabo's Troy is a precise point on the map, a real place. Yet, as he openly says, there is nothing to see on the site, not even ruined stones (*Geography* 13.1.38.1–5, cf. Alcock 1993: 207):

> No trace of the ancient city [of Troy] has survived. This might be expected, for the cities around were devastated, but not entirely destroyed, whereas when Troy was overthrown from its foundation all the stones were removed for the reparation of the other cities.

Strabo's Troy is a Troy of words and narrative which is superimposed or projected onto the empty but absolutely concrete material reality of the site. He is looking at stones that are no longer there. Strabo, in what we could take to be an emblem of Homeric tradition and the relationship between Homer and history in antiquity, is looking at a historical city that cannot be seen. As, in our era, archaeologist Brian Rose says: 'It should be clear by now that Troy was not just an ancient city but rather a concept that could be moulded to fit a variety of times and places' (Rose 1997: 109).

Troy, the Bronze Age and modern studies

Whatever allowances we make for ancient arguments about the historicity of Troy and Homer's relation to history, the debate has only intensified in modernity. It is perhaps most dramatically illustrated in the work and in the person of Heinrich Schliemann (1822–90), the man who is widely credited with the rediscovery of Troy (1870) in the modern era, at the site of Hisarlik.

Schliemann was not the first modern scholar to point to Hisarlik as the site of Homeric Troy. The idea was suggested earlier in 1820 by Charles Maclaren. Nor was Schliemann the first to dig on the spot. Frank Calvert did so in 1863. Schliemann was, however, the first to set up systematic excavations and to bring to light important Bronze Age remains. He associated these directly with Homer's poetry and with the actual existence of a Bronze Age Trojan War. There were signs of ash from a fire, fortifications, a two-handled cup (see *Iliad* 1.584, *Odyssey* 3.63, etc., in Homeric Greek a *depas amphikupellon*) and various other artefacts. Most of these were found by Schliemann in the archaeological level known as Troy II. However, this level, now dated to 2600–2250 BCE, is considered by almost all scholars to be too early for Homer's city.

Schliemann was no ordinary scholar. He is a figure of myth and controversy. He has been described, alternatively, as the 'father of scientific archaeology' and as a fraud. His method of systematically marking historical levels in excavated trenches has been praised by some as ahead of its time. But he was also severely criticized for destroying valuable evidence in his single-minded quest. Some critics have not minced their words and described him as a man 'ill, like an alcoholic, a child-molester or a dope-fiend' (see Calder 1986: 37). He opened up the field in a manner that has led to important later views, but his own arguments and conclusions were reached more on the basis of faith than of fact (see overviews in Allen 1999 and Easton 2002). It has been convincingly argued that he falsified some information in his notes.

Did Schliemann discover Troy, then, and establish its historicity? The answer – here the perplexing nature of Homeric questions becomes evident again – is 'no', 'yes' and 'maybe'. There is almost universal agreement that Schliemann's Bronze Age Troy II at the site of Hisarlik cannot be Homer's Troy. There is, as we said earlier, wide agreement that the site itself is the site of a city of Troy and that this site attests to some catastrophic destruction. Hisarlik contains other historical strata, earlier than Troy II and, more importantly, levels dating to later periods which some scholars do associate with the poetry of Homer. But many other critics suggest that no literal connection between Hisarlik and Homer's descriptions of the Trojan War is possible. There were doubtless wars on the site, but who exactly fought them and why, remains, as many insist, unknown. Amidst such diversity of opinion, it is, nevertheless, certain that Schliemann inaugurated the modern debate about the historicity of the War and its relation to events described in Homer.

Schliemann was in many ways an outsider to the world of professional scholarship and a romantic. He started out as an entrepreneur and shady businessman. He owned a bank in California during the gold rush and made a fortune profiteering in the Crimean War. His figure is therefore a magnet to controversy. Yet, well after Schliemann, elements of sharp disagreement continued to characterize the debate even within professional scholarship.

German archaeologist Wilhelm Dörpfeld, working first with Schliemann and later independently, continued the excavations at Hisarlik and other Bronze Age sites. Dörpfeld expanded the idea of archaeological stratification and essentially espoused Schliemann's belief in the identity between the remains at Hisarlik and Homer's Troy. After Dörpfeld, Carl Blegen from the University of Cincinnati directed excavations on the site (1932–38). He argued that Homer's Ilium was not to be located in level II, but in a later Bronze Age level known as Troy VIIa and dating back to 1300–1180 BCE. Summing up his work and his views, Blegen wrote (Blegen 1963: 20, cited in Raaflaub 1997: 75):

> It can no longer be doubted, when one surveys the state of our knowledge today, that there really was an actual historical Trojan War, in which a coalition of Achaeans, or Mycenaeans, under a king whose overlordship was recognized, fought against the people of Troy and their allies.

Indeed, looking to the poems, Blegen extended his argument well beyond archaeology, claiming that:

. . . a good many of the individual heroes [in the *Iliad* and *Odyssey*] . . . were drawn from real personalities as they were observed by accompanying minstrels at the time of the events.

If we are to believe Blegen, we have, on the site of Troy, found the literal place of the Homeric poems, although it is not evident exactly how one leaps from stones to 'individual heroes', 'real personalities' and observations by accompanying minstrels, given that absolutely no evidence for these personalities is available.

In the 1930s, when Blegen was conducting his excavations, relatively little was known about the Bronze Age, its material remains, culture and societies. Yet as more information became available through the work of archaeologists and historians, the difficulties of associating Homer directly with the Bronze Age and its material and social contexts at Hisarlik and elsewhere became clear. In 1950, H. L. Lorimer surveyed cremation methods, burials and grave goods, shields, helmets, spears, swords, chariots, clothes and personal apparel and houses. As she, and many others since (see, e.g. Van Wees 1992) have argued, the material evidence suggested a great deal less contact between Homer and the Bronze Age than was previously assumed. Alongside work on the material remains, studies of the unique language of Homer's hexameter poetry and especially that by Milman Parry and his student and successor Albert Lord had since the 1930s argued persuasively that Homer's poetry was the result of a long tradition of oral discourse, despite the poems' eventual written form. One of the conclusions emerging from these researches (see further in the next chapter) was that the formation of this tradition could not be located in the Bronze Age and that it was far more suitable to situate the poems at a much later date, perhaps as late as the eighth or even seventh century BCE.

Equally important to the historical placement of Homer and Troy were thousands of documents composed in Bronze Age scripts and preserved on seals, stone tablets, items made of precious metal and above all on clay tablets, that were discovered in excavations in Minoan Bronze Age sites in Greece, such as Knossos (by Sir Arthur Evans), Phaistos, Pylos (by Blegen himself and others) and at Mycenae since the beginning of the twentieth century. Many of the clay tablets were burned in fires that accompanied the violent destruction of their surroundings. The tablets were thus, paradoxically, hardened and preserved by catastrophe.

For many years, the scripts in the tablets were undeciphered, and some scripts (e.g. the one known as Linear A) remain so to this day. Thus, initially, the texts had little effect on question of the relation between Homer and the Bronze Age and the debate over historicity. However, in 1952, a British codebreaker by the name of Michael Ventris working with classicist John Chadwick did decipher the script known as Linear B, which proved to be an early dialect of the Greek language. The texts revealed striking verbal links to Homer's poetry. For example, in the tablets, we find the word *wa-na-ka*, denoting a distinct position of leadership. The word is undoubtedly cognate with the word *wanax*, or, as it is written in Homeric Greek, *anax*, meaning 'leader'. The latter is a very common Homeric word, often used, for example, in the expression *anax andrôn Agamemnon*, 'Agamemnon, leader of men' (*Iliad* 1.7, etc.). Many other echoes of Linear B texts can be found in Homeric Greek. The *wanax* was apportioned a plot of land called a *te-me-no*, a word we find in Homer in the form *temenos* (e.g. *Iliad* 6.194); the term *qa-si-re-u* in the tablets is, most linguists agree, *basileus*, the standard word for 'king' in Homer; the word *po-ti-ni-ja* is cognate with Homeric Greek *potnia*, 'lady' or 'powerful mistress', as in 'the lady Hera' (*Iliad* 1.551, etc.); we find the word *ti-ri-po-da*, a 'tripod' or three-legged cauldron which in Homer has become *tripos* or, rather, more commonly (in its inflected form) *tripoda* (e.g. *Odyssey* 8.434), and many more analogies.

And yet, crucially, close verbal links between Linear B vocabulary and Homer also exposed the true differences between the image of Bronze Age society that emerged from the clay tablets and the society depicted in Homer. The tablets attested neither to the loose association of local overlords described in the *Iliad*, nor to an Odyssean aristocratic household, but to a highly bureaucratized society that kept strict records, contracts and accounts, which defined formal officialdom, social roles, institutions and elites; levied taxes and calculated values; regulated labour; stored allocated goods centrally and kept track of them (see overview in Bennet 1998).

In later years, some linguistic arguments linking Linear B texts to traditions of epic hexameter and, for example, to iconographic evidence for poetic performance in Minoan and Mycenaean culture were put forward (see Ruijgh 1985, Younger 1998). There remains, however, a fundamental difference between the matter-of-fact lists, inventory records and all other materials in Linear B texts and the reflective poetic narrative and character speeches of the *Iliad* and *Odyssey*. The tablets attest to interesting and important historical linguistic developments and to undisputed verbal links with the language of the *Iliad* and *Odyssey*, but they no less prove that historically speaking, Homer's world and the world of Mycenaean Bronze Age cultures are not the same.

Decisive in declaring the split between these worlds was the work of Moses Finley, who collected and reassembled the evidence and eventually created a very different picture of Homer's historicity. Commenting directly on Carl Blegen's convictions, Finley writes (1964):

> Whatever 'the state of our knowledge today' may be . . . one must insist that there is nothing in the archaeology of Troy which gives the slightest warrant for any assertion of that kind [made by Blegen], let alone for writing 'it can no longer be doubted'. Blegen and his colleagues may have settled that Troy VIIa was destroyed by human violence. However, they have found nothing, not a scrap, which points to an Achaean coalition, or to a 'king whose overlordship was recognized' or to Trojan allies; nothing which hints at who destroyed Troy . . . It needs to be reasserted . . . that statements of the order of Professor Blegen's 'the tradition of the expedition against Troy must have a basis of historical fact' are acts of faith not binding on the historian.

Finley's unequivocal verdict is that 'Homer's Trojan War . . . must be evicted from the History of the Greek Bronze Age' (see Raaflaub 1997 and 1998 for discussion).

Finley had persuaded many scholars to abandon the association between Homer and the Bronze Age, although his own suggestion of a link to the ninth or tenth century BCE was not equally well received. Archaeologists and historians studying Homer have since become increasingly aware of the disparities between the depictions in the poems and Bronze Age Greece, and have begun to explore links – independent of any one event which we could call the Trojan War – between Homeric poetry and Greek Iron Age and periods closer to the eighth century BCE in particular (see further below).

While changing many of the terms of the debate, arguments by Finley and his followers certainly did not end it. In the late 1980s and in the 1990s, Manfred Korfmann from the University of Tübingen led excavations at Hisarlik. On the site, in the lower city, beneath and around the old citadel of Troy VII, he discovered a defensive ditch, the remains of what might once have been a wide gate, and traces of other fortifications, all dating to the second millennium BCE. This newly discovered lower city was about ten times the size of the original citadel. It covered an area of about 200,000 square meters, and, by Korfmann's estimate, could support a population of between 5,000 and 10,000 inhabitants (Korfmann 1997). Here, in other words, was evidence for a city substantially bigger and more prominent than any discovered before on the site. Relying on known, but not uncontroversial arguments, Korfmann identified the name of the place, *Ilios*, with the name *Wilusa*, a city mentioned in documents of the Hittites, a late Bronze Age eastern people who occupied north-central Anatolia. These documents also mention a place named *Ahhiyawa*, sometimes assumed to refer to Achaea, the land of the Achaeans, Homer's collective term for the Greeks. Korfmann pointed to the evidence of a hieroglyphic seal in Luwian, a Bronze Age Anatolian language related to Hittite, and to ceremonial stelai, or columns, found in Troy as proof of Hittite links. Similar stelai were discovered in the Hittite capital of Hattusa. His conclusion was that Ilium/Troy was a large Anatolian trading centre surrounded by allies and part of a Luwian-language territory. Korfmann located these finding at the level of Troy VII or VIIa, destroyed in about 1180 BCE. So impressive was this large site, Korfmann argued, that the fame of its destruction could have reached the poet Homer, who, composing many centuries later in the eighth century BCE, immortalized the event. The eighth century is a date which, by general accord, is too late for the historical fall of Troy. Korfmann's argument is thus a remarkable attempt to reconnect the Bronze Age remains of Troy and the events of a Trojan War to Homer's Iron Age poetry while keeping them chronologically apart.

Korfmann's trail was picked up in 2004 by another scholar, Joachim Latacz, who, in a book titled *Troy and Homer: Towards the Solution of an Old Mystery*, re-evaluated much of the literary evidence and argued that indeed, in the eighth century BCE, Homer recorded the destruction of a Bronze Age Troy, 450 years after the event. The attractions of finally solving 'old mysteries' are obvious.

But the risks of erecting a new house from stones that are no longer there (if we think of Strabo's description) are considerable too. The argument rests on the suggestion that Troy VIIa was a large and thus memorable city. Yet even the expanded 'Anatolian' Troy was not large in comparison to the major cities of its day. How big, then, does a city need to be to be immortalized as the most important literary city of antiquity? Would the poetry have 'expanded' it beyond its material size, and if so, what else could have been created by the poet? As Kurt Raaflaub and others note, although the remains identified by Korfmann attest to the destruction of a city, 'neither the archaeological evidence nor the contemporary documents tell us who destroyed Troy and why' (Raaflaub 1997, see also Grethlein 2010).

Korfmann and Latacz believe that historical events that occurred in the Bronze Age have been preserved in discourse which belongs in the eighth century BCE. This brings us to the all important question of transmission. We would have to assume that the account of Troy's destruction remained essentially unchanged for almost half a millennium – a difficult, though perhaps not impossible assumption. More significantly, since writing is almost unattested in the so-called dark ages intervening between the end of the Bronze Age and the Archaic Age in Greece, the widely accepted idea is that transmission of the account relied, fundamentally, on oral traditions of song. Latacz' argument claims that rigid formulaic patterns of oral discourse allowed for the precise preservation and repetition of contents and thus for the carrying over of Bronze Age narratives into the eighth century. But, in fact, increasingly since Parry's and Lord's initial researches, studies have shown the opposite. Oral traditions do contain archaic and archaizing phrases and many repeated expressions, and they are based around the *idea* of permanence and the preservation of 'imperishable fame'. Yet, in practice, the structure of Homer's hexameter and its formulaic diction provide the technical apparatus for affecting what oral-poetry scholar Paul Zumthor (1990) calls *mouvánce*, an essential capacity to recompose and transform words and ideas (see later in Chapter 4). Just as over centuries and millennia the later reception of Homer's poetry changes and reinvents its heritage with every new historical phase, so, even technically, within the language of the poems and the process of their early transmission, change is an essential part of the process.

The representation of culture and society

'Homer is not much use as a guide to the history of events [such as the Trojan War]', said one commentator recently. The same scholar nevertheless rightly points out that this in no way isolates Homer in a timeless bubble. 'He presents important evidence for social history . . . social structures of the time when the epics were composed are inscribed in the text, albeit in poetic transformation' (Grethlein 2010: 129).

The move away from reading Homer as a direct account of what happened in history to reading the *Iliad* and *Odyssey* as reflections of the values and practices of historical societies is partly driven by the specific difficulties of interpretations that focus on the Bronze Age. The move is also influenced by more general changes to critical perspectives in cultural, political, social and economic history, sociology and social anthropology, by reception theory and reader response criticism, by New Historicism (an approach to history that stresses the relationship between verbal representation and the social and historical contexts of ideas) and by materialist historical theory and hermeneutics. I mention this background here not in order to introduce theoretical dimensions into the discussion (theory is important, but belongs elsewhere), but rather to indicate that, just as poets like Virgil or Walcott, or film-makers like the Coen brothers or Wolfgang Petersen, have created their images of Homer within the context of their times, so do historians and archaeologists interpret Homer and his relation to history and material remains within the context of *their* historical times, critical frameworks and sensibilities. Homer is not a pickled relic from the past, but the focus of a dynamic tradition of creative responses and critical analyses that reflect their contemporary conditions and contexts.

What aspects of social and political structure can we see in Homer, then? We see, for example, reflections of a commonwealth, of urbanization, hints of colonization and the components of incipient city states, or *poleis*. In the *Iliad*, we find the city of Troy and on the Greek side, an association of kings and contingents under Agamemnon's strategic command from which individuals (like Achilles) can nevertheless withdraw at will. In some ways, this latter association, the Greeks assembled by their ships, is an abnormal commonwealth, but it can also be seen as a reverse-image of society. Part of the significance of the Greek camp in the *Iliad* is that it lacks many of the 'normal' trappings of the city, the *polis*, for example, permanent living structures and permanent social and economic institutions. The Greek camp also lacks many of the trappings of the household, the *oikos*, of course, notably children and family life.

In the *Iliad*, there are two more important cities, briefly portrayed in relief on the shield Hephaestus makes for Achilles when the latter decides to return to battle (*Iliad* 18.483–608). One city is at peace – we observe a marriage ceremony, the workings of a lawsuit which concerns the payment of compensation for homicide (scholars have debated the laws and practices represented in this scene at length) and surrounding farming scenes. The other is a walled city at war. The conflict, like the Trojan War itself, is between two organized armies (cf. 18.509). On the face of it, these cities are doubly fictional, poetic imitations within the imitation of the poem, and thus twice removed from the real world. This would suggest that Homer's portrayal of the cities on the shield is less reliable as a representation of historical practice. Yet if we allow that Homer's poetry is, to begin with, not a direct representation of any single historical event, but words that describe and reconfigure perceptions, ideas and reactions to historical surroundings, we have something closer to evidence in these depictions: They show us how Homer describes a city and its social context. Unlike the Greek Camp by the shores of Troy, the cities depicted on the shield of Achilles are permanent habitations. Some scholars associate this portrayal with the emerging *poleis* of Archaic Greece.

In the *Odyssey*, we find two main cities: the one in Ithaca (Books 1–2, 13–24), the other in Scheria, the land of the Phaeacians (Books 6–12). Homer offers us further images of organized commonwealth structures when he describes Pylos, home to Nestor, and Sparta, home to Menelaus and Helen (*Odyssey*, Books 3–4), in descriptions in similes (e.g. *Iliad* 18.207–214) and also, in highly compressed form, at the very beginning of the *Odyssey*, where we are told that Odysseus had 'seen many cities' (*Odyssey* 1.3). This verse offers no details, but marks, at a crucial moment of 'global perspective', a world full of organized communities. In a violent but important antithesis to social life in the *Odyssey*, we also find a portrayal of the monadic existence of the Cyclopes (9.105–15),

who have 'neither advisory councils nor established laws' and live
in mountaintop wildernesses and hollow caves, 'each one . . . a
judge of his wives and his children' (9.114–15). The abnormal,
asocial nature of these solitary beings is epitomized by the Cyclops
Polyphemus' cannibalism and his total disregard for even the basic
laws of hospitality when he meets Odysseus and his companions.

Not all Homeric commonwealths are the same. The Phaeacians'
Never-Never-Land, for example, has been associated with Near-
Eastern cities. Odysseus' palace is an aristocratic estate of sorts.
But most communities in Homer are nevertheless characterized by,
for example, public gatherings, assemblies (*agorai*) and councils
(*boulai*), institutionalized political spaces for the people (*demos* –
the word also describes a demarcated territory), who can be
summoned by officials (*kêrukes*, or 'heralds') to public events and
to meetings. There are fortification walls and temples (in Scheria,
around Troy, around the city depicted on Achilles' shield) shared
by the city's inhabitants. There are streets (implying organized
dwelling in close proximity rather than, e.g. isolated farmsteads)
and great halls (*megara*) for gatherings and for holding banquets
where male and female servants provide centrally prepared food
for guests and where singers provide public entertainment. Public
action often involves office holders (*basileis*, 'kings'; *protoi, archoi,
hêgêtores*, 'leaders') and at least some formalized procedures, for
example, for speaking and deliberation in public. There are, in
both poems, frameworks for exchange, for example, sea-trade (see
the Lemnians in *Iliad* 7.467–75), and more prominently for the
exchange of gifts. The latter is commonly seen as representing
an elite code among aristocracies possessing power and wealth.
There are procedures for regulating labour, both indentured (see
Achilles' speech in the underworld, *Odyssey* 11.489–91) and
that of craftsmen. There are conventions for the distribution,
redistribution and management of wealth (most prominently, of the
hero's prize, or *geras*, in the *Iliad*) and land ownership, which, it has
been argued, echo real-life *polis* scenarios and perhaps even reflect
institutionalized features of citizenship. There are social divisions
between persons of higher status (*esthloi* – the 'noble'/'good') and
lower status (*kakoi*, 'bad'), formalized relations between men
and women, servants and slaves and elaborate networks of guest-
friend relationships (*xenoi*) between individuals and households.
In the Greek camp in the *Iliad*, the overlord is not a sovereign
monarch, but a leader whose position is more heavily dependent

on other leaders or members of an aristocracy and on consensus. The leaders command their own men and have their allocated share in the takings. We must stress, of course, that Homer is not a documentary amanuensis or a social scientist. His reflections on and of social life have passed through a poetic prism. Yet Homer's portrayal can be usefully considered alongside eighth century BCE social–political developments.

Warfare is another important area of historically resonant descriptions in Homer. There is much variety and a great deal of dispute in interpreting the historicity of fighting scenes. These, especially in the *Iliad*, not only involve single combat and duels, but also raids and mass fighting in general melees, as well as chariot warfare. Some descriptions have been compared to organized Iron Age and Archaic Age fighting. Homeric heroes are often described, for example, as bearing two spears (e.g. *Iliad* 10.76), which is a late element not attested in Bronze Age cultures. There are social distinctions between high status warriors, lower status masses and the common soldier (for the latter, see, e.g. Thersites in Book 2 and Dolon in Book 10 of the *Iliad*). The Trojan War, regardless of whether it happened or not, is a conflict which begins with a personal dispute, and with a myth that concerns individuals – Helen, Menelaus and Paris. But in Homer, this myth has seamlessly transformed into a war between two organized commonwealths, in which aspects of the *polis* may be recognizable. Some descriptions of warfare in Homer are echoed in other early Greek poetry of the Archaic Age, but such poetry may itself be imitating or reflecting epic discourse. Heroes do not, of course, fight in phalanx formations, that is formations of heavily armoured hoplite warriors that characterize later warfare in Greece. But some scholars have suggested that the depictions in Homer represent proto-hoplite warfare. Weapons in Homer are made primarily of bronze, but iron is also used in the poems, especially in tools. Some important items of armament, such as shields made of oxhide layers (sometimes interlaced with bronze, cf. *Iliad* 7.219–23), or a boar's tusk helmet (cf. *Odyssey* 10.261–5), are closer to Bronze Age artefacts, but scholars have argued that the descriptions in Homer contain significant poetic licence or may be introduced, sometimes as deliberate archaisms. The archaizing practice, with specific relation to Homer is attested in real-life evidence from the Iron Age in Greece. An Iron Age hero-burial at Lefkandi, for example (dated 1000–950 BCE), contained much older pieces of jewellery.

When we look at the historical evidence and its interpretations, then, we find a complicated picture. It seems difficult to locate the *Iliad* and the *Odyssey* in the Bronze Age. It seems more plausible to view aspects of the *Iliad* and *Odyssey* as reflections of society and social practice in times closer to the Archaic Age, and perhaps to the late eighth century BCE. Yet it also seems that the poems are not simply amalgams of different features and characterizations nor interpenetrating 'bundles' of historical reflections, retrojections of more recent surroundings into a distant past and thus also projections of past surroundings into a more recent setting of relevance. There is, as we have noted, an overwhelming sense of that past in the *Iliad* and *Odyssey*. The immediate present of the Homeric narrator is only minimally and generally attested in the poems, as Wolfgang Kullmann and others have noted. When this present is mentioned, the temporal reference is brief and non-specific. In several verses, for example, a hero in combat picks up and easily hurls a great boulder which not even two men 'of today' can lift (*Iliad* 5.305; 12.383, 449; 20.287). Such references are powerful indexical markers that separate the present from the past and mark their contrast. Indeed, there is an almost 'numerical' ratio between the past and the present expressed when a hero hurls a large rock. The contrast defines the idea of a past as a time of greater beings and in this sense as a model for action for the present. A different type of non-specific but crucial present is attested in the 'Pan-Hellenic' characterization of the poems and the absence of reference to specific local cults, as Anthony Snodgrass, Gregory Nagy and others have argued (Snodgrass 1971, Nagy 1979). This Pan-Hellenic image fits emergent strands of social practice in the eighth century, yet is not tied down to any particular *polis*. It thus allows the poems to resonate widely throughout the worlds of early Greece. 'Epic', as archaeologist and historian Ian Morris says, 'was not some kind of bad history. It was a poetic creation that *some* eighth-century Greeks thought the heroic world *ought* to have been like' (Morris and Powell 1997: 558).

Homer's historical voices

Reading Homer's poetry in relation to his historical pasts is always a difficult process, first, on account of the scarcity of early evidence and the difficulty in interpreting such distant material and, second, on account of the verbal and poetic prisms through which every description in Homer must pass. But illustrations of the archaizing mechanism of projection and the relation between history and poetry which is essential to our view of Homer can also be observed in other texts whose dating is more easily confirmed, and in the relation between the presents of such texts and their Homeric pasts.

Among the earliest Greek inscriptions we possess is a short but famous text that appears on the so-called Nestor's Cup. The cup itself is a humble two-handled clay drinking vessel from the island of Pithecusae near the bay of Naples, dated to the late eighth century BCE. The text, written mostly in Homer's metre, the hexameter, reads as follows:

I am the cup of Nestor, good for drinking.
Whoever drinks from this cup, desire for beautifully
crowned Aphrodite [i.e., for sex] will seize him instantly.

Although there are disputes about the precise meaning and function of this cup and its text, they are often thought to refer, perhaps humorously, to the great golden 'cup of Nestor' described in the *Iliad* (11.632–7). The real-life historical object is a small clay cup. The poetic version in Homer is a monumental drinking vessel which, when full, another man could barely lift, but which the old hero Nestor could lift with ease, somewhat like those great boulders hurled with ease by other heroes in the *Iliad*. (There is also a real-life golden cup, found by Heinrich Schliemann, which he fancifully named, 'The Cup of Nestor'; but its dating circa 1600 BCE makes it much too early for any historical match with Homer.) The distance that separates the poetic cup and the real-life object is clear. But likewise is the link between them. Whoever raised the clay cup to his lips and read its text was almost certainly channelling his perceptions of reality through the mirror of Homer, as if he the drinker – the ordinary man 'of today' as Homer would say – and Nestor, the oldest of the mighty heroes of the past, were sitting side by side at the moment of the toast, as if the present and the past were united in the act of raising the cup. Here, then, the historical reality of the present is lived through the imagination of the past.

Less well known, but also useful for our purposes is another early Greek inscription, a funerary text from the island of Kamyros:

I, Idameneus, made this tomb [*sêma*], so that I might have fame [*kleos*]
Whoever harms <it>, may Zeus make him totally accursed.

The inscription has been dated on the basis of language, the stone on which it was carved, its context and the lettering to the sixth century BCE, in other words, well after the assumed formative period of Homeric poetry let alone any possible events surrounding Troy and the Trojan War. As with the 'Cup of Nestor', this text appears on a real-life object – a simple stone marker which has no ornate carvings or other decorations. The expression 'this tomb' in the first line points to the stone on which this text is inscribed. The protective spell (an 'apotropaic' formula) in the second verse, 'Whoever harms <it>', resembles expressions found in other early funerary inscriptions and is also very similar to the words used in the second line of the clay 'Nestor's cup', which were themselves likely to have been used as a kind of spell. And yet the tenor of the verse is unmistakably Homeric. The first line is written in hexameter (technically flawed, but hexameter nonetheless). Idameneus is a variation of Idomeneus, a good Homeric name (*Iliad* 1.145; 5.43; *Odyssey* 19.190, etc.). The idea of a 'tomb' or sign (*sêma*), in the inscription is, as we have noted, common in the *Iliad* and *Odyssey*, as is the idea of the preservation of 'fame' or *kleos*. What does Idameneus' funerary epigram tell us? It is a real-life historical document that superimposes an idealized image of the past onto its contemporary settings. Our sixth-century dead man clearly wished the memory of his real-life existence to be preserved using the terms of Homer's heroic poetry of the past – be it the eighth or even seventh century BCE or the more distant Bronze Age. If we keep Idameneus' practice of historical projection in mind, it becomes easier to understand how Homeric poetry itself, although a vastly more complex undertaking, might superimpose images of its own pasts on its presents and on its contemporary composition settings.

It seems, then, that we should not read Homer as a straightforward record of history. A Bronze Age Trojan War, if it ever occurred, is not quite the one described by Homer, just as the Bronze Age Mycenaean official referred to in the Linear B tablets as *wa-na-ka* is not Homer's *anax* or 'ruler' of men. Yet, paradoxically, despite Moses Finley's call to 'evict the Bronze Age' from Homer, the Bronze Age continues to live in the poems.

The first letter of *wa-na-ka*, representing the sound '*w*' is written ϝ in the original Linear B tablets. This letter is called a 'digamma'. It is often found in other early inscriptions, where it marks the same '*w*' sound, also found in *Wilusa*, the Hittite name for *Ilios* or [*W*]*ilios*. However, this '*w*' sound was probably not pronounced in performances of Homeric poetry later on in time, and the digamma is not found in any of our written texts of the *Iliad* and *Odyssey* or in any of the sources mentioning or citing Homer. Nor is the digamma attested in the scripts of the later classical Greek dialects. Yet critics have proved that traces of this 'letter from the past' are unquestionably present in Homer as ghostly apparitions. In the eighteenth century, the Cambridge philologist Richard Bentley showed that several metrical and linguistic phenomena in Homer (these are too technical to be discussed here. On the metre see, however, Chapter 4) cannot be explained unless we assume the hidden presence of the digamma in Homeric Greek. Without the effects of the digamma, it is almost impossible to understand how some important features of Homer's hexameter language work. When we do assume the effect of a digamma, things seem to fall into place. Thus, for example, it can be shown that the Homeric word *anax* preserves within it the presence of *(w)anax*; the word *oikos* 'house' preserves an earlier *(w)oikos* and indeed the word *epos*, which means 'word', 'something said', 'speech' and later 'epic' itself, preserves (like Strabo's stones which are no longer on site) the invisible and silent trace of *(w)epos*. Following the lesson of the digamma, we realize that Homer's historical past is lost, yet the echoes of its voice remain.

CHAPTER THREE

The poet and the making of the poem

The biographical figure in antiquity and in the poems

The relationship between history and the Homeric poems is closely linked to questions about who composed them, when and how. Authorial biographies, the attribution of works to an author, their dating and contextualization are important and often problematic topics. Yet the status of many ancient authors and texts is in principle straightforward. The figures of Aeschylus or Virgil, to take two examples of canonical poets in Greco-Roman antiquity, are both deeply embedded in their historical contexts. Although there are specific difficulties concerning the authenticity of some of Aeschylus' extant plays (e.g. the *Prometheus Bound*), dates and production, the tragedian's historical persona, his authorship of most of the plays, his dating, 525/524 BCE to c. 455/456 BCE, and indeed his historical existence in classical Athens are not in doubt. Likewise, there are important disputes surrounding Virgil's biography and work, but the basic data are widely accepted. He was born on October 15, 70 BCE and died on September 21, 19 BCE. He wrote the *Bucolics*, the *Georgics* and the *Aeneid*. We possess detailed knowledge about his historical surroundings in Augustan Rome. The question of his historical identity and the composition of his verse is, relatively speaking, straightforward. There is no general 'Virgilian problem'.

Homer is different. Questions about his historical identity and the formation of the poems have generated wide debates and polarized arguments. Information outside of the poems is scarce. Inside the poems, the difficulties of identifying the Homeric narrator and defining his relation to 'Homer' and the poems emerge already in the first lines and the proems of the *Iliad* and *Odyssey*, when, in each poem, an unnamed narrator calls upon the Muse for inspiration. Who are these unnamed speakers? 'Homer', of course. And who is Homer? The unnamed narrator at the beginning of each poem! The absence of external evidence creates many opportunities for interpretation, which we will explore in detail in Chapter 5.

In addition to the narrators of the poems, many singers (*aoidoi*) are depicted inside the world of the heroes in the *Iliad* and especially the *Odyssey*. Foremost among the *Odyssey*'s singers are Phemius, the singer at the Ithacan court, and Demodocus, the singer in the Phaeacians' fabled land. Both are professionals who earn their keep by their song. Demodocus is blind (like Homer, traditionally). Phemius is 'self taught' (*autodidaktos*), although he tells us that a god has planted the lays in his thoughts (*Odyssey* 22.347–8). Odysseus praises Demodocus for having learned his craft from 'the Muses or Apollo' (*Odyssey* 8.488). Phemius and Demodocus usually sing to an assembled audience after a feast in the hall. They accompany themselves by a lyre, and get rewards, often food, for their singing. There are several other singers in the poems, including a bard left to guard Clytemnestra when Agamemnon sets off for Troy (*Odyssey* 3.267; Aegisthus exiles him to a desert island), a singer at the wedding celebrations in Menelaus' court (*Odyssey* 4.17), singers accompanying a choral dance on the shield of Achilles (*Iliad* 18.604) and the singer Thamyris (*Iliad* 595–600) who vies with the Muses and in punishment is made to forget his 'wondrous song' (*aoidên thespesiên*) and the 'art of his lyre' (*kitharistyn*). The Muses and Apollo too know song, and the Sirens' song in the *Odyssey* (12.39–54) is so enchanting that it draws passing sailors to their death. There are professional singers of dirges at Hector's funeral (*Iliad* 24.720–72), and wives, mothers and friends, including Helen herself, also mourn those dear to them – although there are distinct differences between personal mourning (*goös* – pronounced *go-os*) and professional dirge-singing (*threnos*). Achilles, having withdrawn from battle, sits in his hut, entertaining himself by singing *klea andrôn*, 'the fame of men' (*Iliad* 9.89). Odysseus' long narrative of his past adventures is compared by the Phaeacian king Alcinoos to poet's words (*Odyssey* 9.189). Yet, as Andrew Ford (1992) rightly notes,

> . . . the picture [of singers and singing] in Homer cannot be supposed to reflect directly the practices and circumstances of early epic poets. His representations of singers are infused with a mixture of traditional and fictional elements that is not easily removed. Drawing on internal evidence . . . we have to choose between clearly depicted poetic constructs inside the narrative and ambiguous depictions at its edges.

The ancients, we should note, did not see it in quite this way. They viewed both options, the clear and the ambiguous, as historical. Just as they upheld the historicity of Troy and the Trojan War, so did they believe in the existence of Homer the individual, inside and outside of the poems. Both Aristotle (fourth century BCE) in the *Poetics* and the treatise *On the Sublime* (whose date is uncertain, but much later, perhaps the first century AD) attributed to Longinus, we find unhesitating reference to 'Homer' as the poet of both the *Iliad* and the *Odyssey*. Aristotle and Longinus offer many insights into the poems, but neither is deeply concerned with historical problems surrounding Homer's authorship. *On the Sublime* does distinguish between the *Iliad* as a product of Homer's 'maturity' and the *Odyssey* as the product of his 'old age'. However, this is merely a way of expressing literary judgements in terms of a personal biography. There is no external support for Longinus' assertion.

The practice of extrapolating biographical data from the poems is frequently attested in antiquity. The so-called *Herodotean Life of Homer* (dated to the first or second century CE and certainly not composed by Herodotus) names the poet's adoptive father as Phemius. No external evidence exists to support this suggestion, but Phemius is, of course, the name of the singer in Odysseus' house in Ithaca. The *Life* is creating an historical image which is free of historical anchors.

The Herodotean *Life* provides a relatively consistent view of Homer and his history. Other ancient biographies (whose dating is uncertain) provide a more typical image comprised of several alternatives, for example, with regard to Homer's place of birth. Similar variety, we noted, is attested among the ancient busts of Homer that portray the face of a real person with distinct features, yet each portraying a different face. Such paradoxical 'multiple unity' is, in fact, less exotic than it seems, and is often matched in depictions of Christ and other religious or revered figures in Western iconography and art and in many other traditions too.

Herodotus dated Homer's life to about 400 years before his own time (*Histories* 2.53), but left the figure of the poet otherwise unspecified. The *Homeric Hymn to Apollo* (172, cited by Thucydides, *The Peloponnesian War* 3.104) speaks of a 'blind man from Chios' without providing any further historical information. No name is actually given, but it is universally accepted that the reference in the hymn is to Homer. A Greek epic poem from the second century CE entitled *The Contest of Homer and Hesiod* describes a dispute over poetic supremacy between these two early poets and portrays certain features of Homer's life. The poem, which probably goes back to a fourth century BCE work by the critic and philosopher Alcidamas, contains the usual ambiguous biographical detail, for example, concerning Homer's provenance. Several anonymous but famous epigrams from the ancient collection of poems known as *The Greek Anthology* make the problem of provenance particularly clear. One of the epigrams comprises a list of the cities vying for the privilege of being known as Homer's place of birth. The poem, however, makes no effort to adjudicate these competing claims. A man can only be born in one place, but Homer is no ordinary man and the poem betrays no anxiety over the open-ended character of the problem (16.297):

> Seven cities vied to be the place of Homer's birth,
> Cyme, Smyrna, Chios, Colophon, Pylos, Argos, Athens.

A second epigram (16.295) turns the absence of a single answer into a positive argument:

> It was not the field of Smyrna that gave birth to divine Homer,
> not Colophon, the star of luxurious Ionia,
> not Chios, not rich Egypt, not holy Cyprus,
> not the rocky island homeland of the Son of Laertes
>   [Odysseus],

not the Argos of Danaus or Cyclopian Mycene,
nor the city of the ancient sons of Cecrops [the Athenians].
For he was not born the work of the earth: the Muses sent him
    from the heavens,
so that he might bring desired gifts to men who live only a day.

Despite such 'immortal' provenance, antiquity generally upheld
the idea of a single Homer. Only a few scholars, known as the
chorizontes, 'the separators', advocated separate authorship for
each of the poems. We know the names of some of these ancient
scholars, such as Xenon and Hellanicus, but in fact, only arguments
opposing their views remain. The possibility that some, or all, of
Homer's poetry was composed not by an individual, but through
the process of a long tradition of singers is not explicitly mentioned
in antiquity, although we do perhaps find reflections of this idea in
the ancient biographies' multiplicity of detail. There is an ancient
tradition, best attested later in the work of the Roman author and
politician Cicero's *On the Orator* (written 55 BCE), of a recension
of the text of the *Iliad* and *Odyssey* at Athens in the sixth century
BCE by the tyrant Pisistratus or by his son Hipparchus. According
to Cicero, Pisistratus 'is said to have been the first to arrange the
books of Homer, which were previously in a state of confusion,
into the order in which we have them today' (3.137). Implicitly,
the recension points to a wider process of compilation. Another
ancient tradition, found in ancient comments on the poet Pindar
(sixth/fifth centuries BCE. The comments are on Pindar's *Nemeans*
2.1) and in later sources, for example, in Plato's famous depiction
of the Homeric rhapsode Ion (*Ion* 530d), suggest the existence of a
body of singers called the Homeridae, or 'descendents of Homer',
on the island of Chios, one of Homer's alleged birthplaces. The
Homeridae were supposed to have picked up the tradition of
Homeric song and were performers and interpreters of his poetry.
There is disagreement about the historicity of the Pisistratean
recension and the characteristics of the Homeridae. These traditions
firmly uphold the authority of an original poet 'Homer', but they
also suggest the possibility of wider creative processes. Also worth
mentioning but more abstract are ancient 'allegorical' approaches
to Homer in antiquity. Such approaches are already associated
with Theagenes of Rhegium, a critic who lived in the sixth century
BCE, but they are more prominent later, in Middle-Platonist and

Neoplatonist philosophical traditions (especially from the third century CE and on). Allegorical readings remain, for the most part, committed to the idea of single authorship, but they allow for a certain plurality of interpretation.

The argument in favour of a tradition that comprised not one but many singers and spanned several generations was not found in antiquity, although it did take centre stage in the modern study of Homer (see further below). Likewise, the modern association of Homeric tradition with oral composition is not attested by ancient discussions, except in a few occasional comments, most prominently in the work of the Jewish author Josephus (first century AD. See *Against Apion* 1.2.12). Josephus' view, however, seems to have been guided by motives that did not concern Homer directly. He wanted to prove the superiority of the written Jewish Bible and its laws over the early unwritten and thus 'oral' codes of the Greeks. There are one or two other ancient sources that may hint at Homer's oral provenance (e.g. a brief statement by the second/third-century author Julius Africanus in an anecdotal work called *The Magic Girdles*), but no discussion of any implication this may have for our understanding of the historical figure of Homer.

Particularly important views of Homer in antiquity were developed in the Hellenistic era (third to first century BCE), with the emergence of highly institutionalized scholarship. The centres of learned activity were the great Library and Museum (not a modern museum, but a 'house of the Muses' – a place for knowledge and learning) in Alexandria in the Ptolemaic kingdom in Egypt and in the Library in Pergamum, the capital of the Attalid kingdom in Asia Minor. Some of the prominent intellectual figures of the period, most of them Librarians in Alexandria or Pergamum, were also among the greatest Homer scholars: Zenodotus of Ephesus (born c. 325 BCE), Aristophanes of Byzantium (c. 257–180 BCE), Aristarchus of Samothrace (c. 216–144 BCE) and Crates of Mallus (a contemporary of Aristarchus). Many of their comments are preserved in the scholia, the ancient commentaries in the margins of manuscripts. Nevertheless, the focus of Alexandrian and Pergamene scholarship was not the person Homer, but the text. The text was a material object which the Hellenistic successors of Alexander the Great could physically import from Greece to their own libraries in Egypt and Syria. It could thus embody the

Hellenistic kings' claims as heirs to the tradition and authority of their Greek pasts and was an important part of their symbolic 'cultural capital'. Hellenistic scholars introduced new ways of studying the text, and in this sense of claiming a stake in Homer and appropriating him for themselves. It is generally accepted that our current division of the *Iliad* and *Odyssey* into 24 books each (from Alpha to Omega, the letters of the Greek alphabet) originates in this period. The division allowed for analysis and easy reference to the otherwise large and unwieldy poems. Hellenistic scholars also separated the poems into individual lays, which could be discussed in detail and compared. They considered alternative versions ('variants') of particular verses and passages in the text, thus de facto acknowledging multiplicity while always striving to determine which, in their view, was the single best reading.

What we find, then, in antiquity in different forms, are images of Homer and the Homeric poems that, although never openly challenging a personalized figure of the poet Homer and the idea of single-authored texts, hint at a wider and more complex conception of the process of composition and the nature of the poems. This conception was developed and expanded in modern discussions to create a new view of Homer, his poetry and the process by which archaic heroic epic came to be.

Homer and the moderns: The first steps

For a long time in the history of Western literature, it was Latin and Virgil, the epic poet at the centre of the Roman literary canon, that were the focus of poetic traditions and the backward gaze towards antiquity. But from the early Renaissance, with the gradual reacquisition of the knowledge of ancient Greek in Europe, Homer's place as a central text in the West's literary canon was greatly strengthened. Modernity's evolving narratives of self-definition in relation to antiquity (the idea of 'ancients' and 'moderns') and later the development of professional scholarship produced important revisions of the image of Homer and reformulated the arguments about his historical existence. In the seventeenth century, the Abbé d'Aubignac in France, and after him in the eighteenth century, Richard Bentley in England, Jean-Jacques Rousseau and others in France and elsewhere had been forming their views of the poems, either as the work of an early bard who possessed raw, powerful poetic ability, or as a collection of rhapsodies. In Italy, Giambattista Vico in his *New Science* (1744) read many of Homer's fantastic details with reference to some historical reality. The *Odyssey*'s Lotus Eaters were a people 'who ate the bark of a plant called lotus' and they were situated geographically only 'nine days journey' from Maleia, as the *Odyssey* says. The *Odyssey*'s Cimmerians, Vico thought, must have been situated 'in the most northerly part' of Greece, since they had the longest nights (sections 756–7). Yet Vico also noted the incongruent diversity of detail in relation to Homer. The contest among the Greek cities for claiming Homer to themselves came about, he says 'because almost all of them observed in his poems words and phrases and dialectical locutions that belonged to their own vernacular'. Vico assumes – this is simply a more extreme version of what is already implied in the Hellenistic efforts to correct the text – that 'the two poems were composed and compiled by various hands through successive ages' (sections 790; 804). Vico rejected the historicity of the Trojan War. Fables created at the time of the heroic age, he thought, reached Homer in corrupted state. In his view, the materials originated in 'vulgar rhapsodes, each preserving a memory of part of the Homeric poems' (section 849). Significantly, on the sparse evidence of Josephus (*Against Apion*, 1.2.12), Vico thought of Homer as a sublime poet who knew no writing, who possessed imaginative and turbulent vigour but lacked the force of philosophical reflection. Equally important, despite assuming the existence of the bard, Vico concluded that Homer was, in the wider historical perspective, 'an idea or a heroic character of Greek men insofar as they told their history in song', in other words, Homer was a reflection of the Greeks as a whole over an extended period of time in their early history. The Greeks vied with each other, each city claiming Homer for itself because, Vico says, 'the Greek peoples were themselves Homer' (sections 873–5).

Vico's argument was an important first step in the formation of a modern view of Homer and of Homer's traditionality and its paradoxes. His line of thought was followed by professional scholars, especially in Germany, who shifted the discussion onto more technical 'scientific' grounds, retaining and developing ideas about the cumulative character of monumental epic poems. These discussions eventually formed the debate over what in the nineteenth century became known as the 'Homeric Question'.

In 1795, Friedrich August Wolf published his *Prolegomena to Homer*. This was a path-breaking work. Wolf accepted that the poems were composed of many parts, but he could see no reliable way of clearly separating these. He was, as he put it, less concerned with 'elegance', and more with the 'historical facts' surrounding the making of the *Iliad* and *Odyssey* (1985: 69–70). His most important arguments explore the relation between spoken words and written texts – a relation that defines much of the modern view of Homer. Wolf argued that the long poems as we have them could not have been composed without the use of writing and its equipment, but, that, at the time of the early composition of the poems, writing could not have been available to the poet. Thus (1985: 16),

> If as the only man of his time to have such equipment, he [Homer] had completed the *Iliad* and the *Odyssey* in their uninterrupted sequence, they would in their want of all other suitable contrivances have resembled an enormous ship, constructed somewhere inland in the first beginnings of navigation: its maker would have had no access to winches and wooden rollers to push it forward, and thereof no access to the sea itself in which he could make some trial of his skill.

The poems could not, therefore, have 'burst forth suddenly from the darkness in all their brilliance, with both the splendour of their parts and the many great virtues of the connected whole' (1985: 148). According to Wolf, what we know as 'Homer' is only a tradition of poetry that begins without the use of writing, and which was slowly transferred into written form and transformed by writing in a long editorial process. Only with the Alexandrians and through the energies of several generations did the great epics that we know as Homer's poetry come about.

Analysts and Unitarians

In typical Homeric diversity, Wolf's work provided the impetus for two opposing later views. He was, as one scholar put it, the 'ambivalent patron saint' of both Analyst and Unitarian critics

(Porter 2010: 939). Both groups attempted to characterize the structure of Homeric narrative. Each, however, tried to do so in a different way (see Turner 1997).

The Analysts set out to identify the separate components or lays woven into the text of Homer, for instance, the *aristeiai* or 'narratives of excellence' describing individual heroes' martial exploits. Another example which has generated Analyst arguments and long debates is the scene describing the Greek embassy to Achilles in Book 9 of the *Iliad*. In the *Embassy*, Nestor proposes to Agamemnon to send the heroes Phoenix (*Iliad* 9.168), Ajax and Odysseus (9.169) on a mission to plead with Achilles, who has withdrawn from battle, to come back and help the Greek armies. It makes sense for wise Odysseus and mighty Ajax to undertake this task. They are well-known heroes. But readers have always felt that the figure of Phoenix, Achilles' old tutor, presents some difficulties. Part of the problem here is also that three heroes set out on their mission, yet strangely Homer says: 'So *these two* walked along the strand of the far-resounding sea' (*Iliad* 9.182). The text continues to refer to two emissaries (using a special Greek linguistic form known as a 'dual', referring to two persons). Not all translations preserve this discrepancy, but classical scholars have over puzzled how three could have turned into two. Some Analyst critics of Homer argue that in this scene we can observe the open stitches of composition, whereby the original tradition of a two-man embassy by Odysseus and Ajax suffered the imperfect addition of Phoenix, a third member of the team.

Among the best known early Analysts was a German scholar by the name of Karl Lachmann, who is also often regarded as the father of the scientific analysis of manuscript traditions and especially modern textual criticism. Through minute comparative analysis of textual variants among different sources, Lachmann tried to trace a genealogy or family tree (a 'stemma') of manuscripts and manuscript traditions and, stepping backwards up this genealogy, to reconstruct an 'archetype' or original manuscript. A similar method was applied in an attempt to trace different narrative strands in the poems of Homer. In 1847, Lachmann, comparing the composition of the *Iliad* to the composition of the early German *Nibelungenlied* saga, identified 18 individual original lays in the poem, the weaving together of which he attributed to Pisistratus (Lachmann 1847, in German).

Many Analysts, among them some great scholars of the nineteenth and twentieth centuries (Gottfried Hermann, George Grote, Maurice Croiset, Richard Jebb and especially Ulrich von Wilamowiz-Moellendorff), relying in part on what they felt the story of the poems *should be like*, attempted to identify the core material and later additions or interpolations. In the *Iliad*, they questioned, for example, how a back-handed nightly ambush scene describing the capture of the Trojan Dolon by Diomedes and Odysseus in Book 10 could fit into the heroic fighting ethos of the poem. In the *Odyssey*, picking up on a brief comment in the scholia, Analysts sometimes argued that the last book of the poem was an extraneous addition to the 'natural' ending, once Odysseus and Penelope are united.

Although the Analyst's approach had forceful supporters in the past (and more recently, for example, Denys Page and Helmut Van Thiel), it is less widely practised today. One of the important causes for this was the rising influence, since the first half of the twentieth century, of Milman Parry's arguments about traditional oral poetry, which reformulated the relationship between the text as a whole and its parts (see our discussion further below). And yet, both Analyst and Parryan approaches, each in its different way, resonated well with idea of multiplicity within the single object that we call Homer. In antiquity, multiplicity was characterized by means of biographical narratives and through the competing claims of different cities to have been the birthplace of Homer. Among Analysts, this is reflected by means of nineteenth-century humanist and scientific practice and by marking out separately composed lays and thematic traditions. In Parryan criticism, this image of Homer is achieved using statistical, ethnographic and anthropological approaches that made it possible to divide and unite elements of the text in new ways.

August Wolf focused his enquiry on historical questions. It was arguably his views of the *process of the making* of Homeric verse and the manner by which the poems were put together over generations that influenced Analyst arguments. In contrast, it was Wolf's views about the poems in their *final form* that helped develop Unitarian positions. These latter positions, like Analysis, concern the question of authorship and of composition by one, two or more authors or by groups of singers and editors over time, as well as the literary – aesthetic question of poetic and thematic coherence in the poems. As the name suggests, Unitarians tend to acknowledge elements of unity. The poet Goethe, for example, despite his espousal of ideas of personalized genius that prevailed in German Romanticism of the period, accepted Wolf's arguments against the existence of a Homer as an individual who was accountable for the poems as a whole. This helped characterize Homer as an 'early', rather than as a 'modern' phenomenon. Goethe did, however, strongly believe in the unity and genius of the *Iliad* and *Odyssey* as poems. Other critics, especially in Germany and England, for example, G. W. Nitzsch, Andrew Lang, J. A. Scott, E. Drerup, Wolfgang Schadewaldt and Karl Reinhardt, argued for unity of both poem and poet and provided overall readings of the poems and integrative explanations of their parts. Archaeology and material arguments were also invoked by those who believed in single Homer (or at least in a single poet for each poem), although, as we have seen, Homer's representation of material culture cannot be located exclusively in any single historical period. In the twentieth century, beginning with the works of Johannes Kakridis (Kakridis 1949), Wolfgang Schadewaldt (Schadewaldt 1965) and his student Wolfgang Kullmann (Kulmann 1984), some scholars developed an approach known as Neoanalysis that stands midway between Analysis and Unitarianism. Neoanalysis regards the poems as wholes which were nevertheless created through the adaptation and incorporation of diverse but specific strands, themes and poetic traditions.

No final consensus about Homer exists, of course. But as a historical phenomenon of nineteenth- and twentieth-century scholarship, the Homeric Question has today lost much of its intensity. The substantive question reaches much further back in time and the underlying historical, cultural and poetic problems remain. These problems, in their openness and persistence, are, one might say, also answers of sorts inasmuch as they characterize the poetry and the tradition we associate with Homer as a dynamic concern. What marked the decline of the specific historical Homeric Question and carried the substantive questions forward to their next phase was, again, research which began with the work of the American scholar Milman Parry (1902–35) concerning the unique nature of Homer's language. In the absence of clear external information about Homer and his times, this language is the most important evidence available to us.

Milman Parry and oral-formulaic theory

What, then, did Parryan scholarship achieve that others before it had not? How did he change our understanding of Homeric language? And how did his new perspective on language change our wider understanding of Homer? Parry (who died aged 33 years from an accidental, self-inflicted gunshot wound[1]) is a singular figure in the history of Homer studies and a scholar whose influence on contemporary views of Homer is decisive, although we need to stress that (like Homer . . .) he was not working alone, but within a tradition and along established lines of critical thought.

Parry placed orality, the idea of composition without the use of writing, firmly at the centre of our understanding of Homer. Yet the idea of orality was hinted at even in antiquity, and it certainly played an important role in modern studies by the Abbé d'Aubignac in 1715, by Vico and Wolf, as well as in the work of Analysts and Unitarians too sometimes. Parry stressed the idea of poetic traditions and traditional language. But this too, was not new. Already the ancient Pisistratean recension and the Homeridae embodied the idea of a long tradition. Parry drew attention to the repetitive nature of Homer's language more prominently than ever before. But in itself, Homeric repetition was not a new discovery. Anyone hearing or reading Homer in its original Greek hexameters will immediately notice its repetitive qualities. The ancients too were aware of this. When a character speaks, for instance, the most common introductory line in Homer is 'Then in response said . . .' followed by the name of the hero or speaker (*ton d'apameibomenos prosephpê* . . .). This line appears (with minor variations) over 100 times in the *Iliad* and *Odyssey*.

What, then, was Parry's achievement? In the early twentieth century, against the background of rapid development in the sciences, Homer's repetitive qualities readily attracted scholarly attention and invited new explanations. Parry's focus was on the process of the composition of the poems. Using formal analysis and often quantitative methods, he argued for the unique, interconnected

---

[1] I owe this detail to Mary Sale, in a personal communication, reporting on a conversation with Adam Parry.

structure of Homeric repetition and, especially for its *systematic* nature as a tool for traditional oral composition and a consequence of this process. Parry claimed he could prove, from the language itself, that Homeric poetry was traditional and oral in character. At the core of Parry's argument was the idea of the 'formula'. This idea bound together orality, the traditional nature of Homeric poetry and its repetitive qualities as never before in what is commonly known as oral-formulaic theory.

The fine-points of the theory and the debates around it are highly technical and their discussion belongs in specialist work (see, e.g. Finkelberg 2004). The basics, however, are not hard to describe. Yet, in order to do so, we must first note what is perhaps the most immediate quality of Homeric poetry: It is composed in verse and follows a strict rhythmical pattern. This is the metrical structure called the hexameter. It comprises a sequence of syllables (e.g. the syllables 'Ho' and 'mer' in the word 'Homer'), some of which have a longer duration and are thus 'long', while others are 'short'. The abstract pattern of the hexameter comprises six sections or units (each called a *mêtron* or 'foot'), each made up of a combination of long and short syllables having the rhythm *dum-da-da* (i.e. long–short–short). Each of these units is called a 'dactyl'. Combined, six-dactyl units create the sequence *dum-da-da-dum-da-da-dum-da-da-dum-da-da-dum-da-da-dum-dah* as follows (where the symbol '-' = long, the symbol '˘' = short and the symbol 'x'= either long or short):

$$- \smile \smile - \smile \smile - \smile \smile - \smile \smile - \smile \smile - \mathrm{x}$$

Although some variations are allowed (e.g. a single long syllable can replace two short ones), each line of epic is metrically the same as every other. The first line of the *Odyssey* provides a good example:

An-*dra moi* **en**-*ne-pe* **Mou**-*sa po-***ly***-tro-pon, ***hos*** ma-la* **pol**-*la,*

(The man, to me tell, Muse, of many ways, who very much,)
Tell me, Muse, of the man of many ways who wandered very far,

The top line above is a transliteration of the original Greek. Long syllables are marked in bold, the others are short. The line below it describes the abstract pattern. The third line, in brackets, is a word-for-word translation that preserves the exact original order of words. The fourth line is a conventional translation. Parry's theory, as we shall see, depends heavily on metrical arguments.

The second thing we must stress before we describe Parry's theory is Homer's repetitive character. Such repetition involves many ordinary expressions and not just prominent speech introductions and poetic phrases like the rise of 'rosy fingered dawn' or 'winged words' (see above). Almost every Homeric line contains repeated expressions, word groups and other kinds of patterns. Indeed, repetition is more frequent and far-reaching in Homer than in almost any other text we know. It is important to make this point, since the full extent of Homeric repetition is almost impossible to preserve in translation. Thus, when heroes are named in the poems, they are usually described by means of fixed, recognizable phrases, each of which is repeated, dozens, in some cases hundreds, of times. Achilles, for instance, is *dios Achilleus*, 'divine/bright Achilles', or *podas ôkus Achilleus*, 'swift-footed Achilles'. Odysseus is *dios Odysseus*, 'divine/bright Odysseus', or *polymêtis Odysseus*, 'many-minded Odysseus'. Athena is *glaukôpis Athênê*, 'grey-eyed/owl-eyed Athena', or *thea glaukôpis Athênê*, 'the grey-eyed goddess Athena', and more. Similarly, many important words like 'ship' and 'spear' often appear in preset combinations such as *nea thoên*, 'swift ship' or *dolichoskion enchos*, 'long-shadowed spear'. These combinations of the name of a person or a thing to which a particular adjective or 'epithet' is added are very common indeed. Verbs like 'to throw' or 'to fall' are often used with preset added descriptions, as are expressions describing the casting of spears, eating, running, sitting, falling, dying, bathing and more.

And now to the argument. What Parry pointed out (see Parry 1971) was that this vast collection of repeated expressions was almost invariably arranged in larger systematic, recognizable patterns. For example, the words *dios Odysseus*, 'divine/bright Odysseus', are not simply repeated at random. They appear in exactly the same place in the line, at the very end (other, more technical conditions apply) in each and every one of the 102 repeated instances in the *Iliad* and *Odyssey*, albeit preceded by many different words and expressions, as required by the context. We find, for example, the line *hê Aias hê Idomeneus hê dios*

Odysseus // (where '//' indicates the end of the line), 'Ajax, or Idomeneus, or **bright Odysseus**' (*Iliad* 1.145); *ou gar pô tethnêken epi chthoni dios Odysseus* //, 'not yet has he died upon the earth, **bright Odysseus**' (*Odyssey* 1.195); or *ton d' êmeibet epeita polytlas dios Odysseus* //, 'to him replied much suffering **bright Odysseus**' (*Odyssey* 17.280), and more. Parry called the element of recurrent words (in our case 'bright Odysseus') 'formulas'. He famously defined the formula as 'a group of words regularly employed under the same metrical conditions to express an essential idea' (Parry 1971: 11).

Having defined the formula, Parry also described some more general features of groups of formulas, or 'formula types' and 'formula systems'. He noted, for example, that there were sets of expressions that described different heroes and gods, yet which could all fit conveniently into the same part of the line (what he called 'metrical conditions'). Thus, a poet could, for example, begin the line by saying 'to him replied . . .' (*ton d'êmeibet' epeita* . . .). If the hero making the reply was Odysseus, the poet could then elegantly end the line with the expression 'much suffering Odysseus' (*polytlas dios Odysseus*). If Achilles was making the reply, the poet could use another frequently repeated formula, 'swift footed Achilles' (*podarkês dios Achilleus*). If Agamemnon was to speak the expression 'Agamemnon lord of men' (*anax andrôn Agamemnon*). The poet could similarly use the words 'the cow-eyed lady Hera' (*boöpis potnia Hêra*), 'the owl-eyed goddess Athena' (*thea glaukôpis Athênê*) and so on, as required by the context. These sets of formulas provided ready-made systems for composing well-formed verses, on the spot, as it were.

Parry further noted that for each 'essential idea', such as 'Odysseus' or 'Achilles', one could find in Homer a range of several distinct formulas, each slightly different in length or 'shape' from the other. Thus, for example, one could express the idea of 'Odysseus' by means of the short expression *dios Odysseus* ($-\;\smile\;\smile\;-$ x), the slightly longer expression *polymêtis Odysseus* ($\smile\;\smile\;-\;\smile\;\smile\;-$ x), the yet longer phrase *polytlas dios Odysseus* ($\smile\;-\;-\;-\;\smile\;\smile\;-$ x) and so on. Parry called this feature 'extent'. The resulting sets of expressions meant that one could construct a line of epic poetry more or less in the way one puts together a row of children's 'Lego' blocks (Parry did not himself use the Lego-block analogy). Wherever needed, a singer could slot the same idea into different parts of the verse.

If the singer wanted to say 'Odysseus', he had at his disposal a range of preset expressions of different sizes to fit the exact 'space' required and complete a well-formed verse. The poet could use the same principle to name other heroes and gods and to express other 'essential' ideas.

Parry pointed to one more important feature of systems of formulas. They were, he suggested, also characterized by 'thrift' or 'economy'. This meant that in principle, within each group of formulas expressing an essential idea (the idea of 'Odysseus' or of 'Achilles'), each individual expression would fit one particular 'space' (what Parry called 'metrical conditions'). Crucially, the number of phrases that could fit into exactly the same space but which expressed the same idea was kept to a minimum. The system was 'economical': It created the smallest number of preset expressions that could perform the task of making verse effectively.

Parry's argument, then, was that the system as a whole was extensive, yet economical; it was flexible, yet easy to use; it comprised a repository of stock expressions which was available to poets at a time when writing was still not used as a means of composition. As Parry and especially his student and colleague Albert Lord argued, a poet who trained in this special language of formulas from childhood could simply speak in epic verse as one would any other language. The system of Homeric formulas made possible a rapid, smooth, yet extensive process of composition-in-performance. The formulaic mechanism explained how traditions of such vast poems as the *Iliad* and *Odyssey* could be formed without the use of writing and without the need for prodigious feats of verbatim memory (modern studies have shown that such feats of memory are highly uncommon). At every performance, a poem will have been recreated from ready ingredients. And yet, Parry argued, this stock of formulas was too large and too highly evolved to have been invented all at once by a single individual over one lifetime. Parry thus concluded that it was created by many singers over several generations working within a tradition of song. This was the idea underlying 'oral-traditional poetry' and what is sometimes also known as oral-formulaic theory or the Parry–Lord theory. It has been revised, modified, adapted, challenged and disputed over many years, but it still reverberates today, among followers and opponents, in the field of Homer studies and beyond, wherever questions of orality and large poetic compositions are raised.

We need to stress one further important point. According to some versions of oral-formulaic theory (sometimes known as 'Hard Parrysm'), the purpose of formula systems was strictly to provide different sized expressions for a single essential idea, so as to keep the rapid flow of verse in performance. It was therefore argued by Parry and some other scholars that 'traditional' formulas were used primarily for their technical utility (i.e., to fill 'spaces' in the line) and not on account of their finer shades of meaning. Thus, for example, the formula *podas ôkys Achilleus*, 'swift footed Achilles', could be a way of expressing no more than the essential idea 'Achilles' and of completing the rhythm at the end of the verse.

This kind of argument provided a compelling, systematic description of Homer's traditional language, but it also stripped the words of much of their poetic resonance. There is some indication that Parry himself was aware of this and, had he not died so young, may have modified some of his earlier views (see Russo 1997, Kahane 2005). Indeed, there are many other scholars who believe that Homer's formulas carry deeply resonant, intricate meaning, even if utility is an important force in their development. Achilles, for instance, is 'swift footed' because the chase on foot in which he captures and kills Hector is a fateful element of his actions in the *Iliad*. Numerous critics argued for specific meaning in other formulas, too. At a more basic level, some scholars have suggested that when considering the development of Homer's poetry ('diachronically') over time, metrical form, the 'shape' of formulas and the hexameter itself, was the result of traditional phraseology. Words were not shaped to fit the meter, but the metre evolved out of the way traditional words were shaped (see in Clark 2004 with reference to the work of Gregory Nagy). Thus, formulas, even when they acted as metrical building blocks, could retain the rich detail of traditional meaning.

In the absence of comparative ancient material with which to test their ideas (and in the spirit of scientific 'experimentalism'), Parry and Lord sought evidence in the contemporary world. In the early 1930s, they conducted extensive fieldwork in what was then Yugoslavia, paying special attention to living Serbo-Croat traditions of oral poetry which they recorded, documented and analysed.

This material is now archived in Harvard University's South-Slavic collections and much of it is available online (http://chs119. chs.harvard.edu/mpc). The South Slavic tradition (sadly limited as a living tradition today) of *guslars*, singers who accompanied themselves with a stringed instrument called the *gusle*, provided many analogous illustrations of the process of composition and performance as well as the thematic structuring and formulaic arrangement of epic song (see, esp. Lord 1960).

Parry's studies formed the beginning of an intensive debate. Scholars, including Brian Hainsworth, Arie Hoekstra, Joseph Russo, Michael Nagler and others, showed that the Homeric formula could be modified, made more flexible, reconfigured and expanded in a variety of ways. Also, important objections to the neat completeness of formulaic systems were put forward. David Shive, for example, in a technical but important work (1987), showed that even the most prominent formulaic systems in Homer, for example, those naming Achilles, were less than perfectly economical. Other scholars have sensibly argued for a more nuanced approach to the semantics of Homeric language, defining, for example, fixed 'core' and more flexible 'peripheral' elements which possess stronger or weaker functions of both metrics and meaning in the formulas. Ultimately, as one important survey by Joseph Russo (1997: 259) points out, 'the word formula proved to be a poor thing, hopelessly inadequate to cover the different *kinds* of formulaic realities in Homeric diction'. Nevertheless, the idea of 'formulaic realities' remains. It is today almost universally accepted that the process of the making of Homeric verse involved elements of orality, that these elements can be observed in the many repetitive phenomena manifest in the *Iliad* and *Odyssey*, and that they are essential for our understanding of the poems.

We need to stress, however, that all we have possessed for at least two or two and a half millennia are written texts. A crucial question, then, is how the poems were transferred from voice to writing. Parry's and Lord's work on the South Slavic tradition put forward the argument that the oral poems were dictated, and thus written down, a suggestion which was later accepted, with various adjustments by many, but not all other scholars. Barry Powell (1991) argued that the Greek alphabet, and in this sense Greek writing itself, were first adopted (from Semitic scripts) and developed for the express purpose of recording Homeric verse. Some scholars, especially Unitarians and Neoanalysts, prefer to associate Homer more closely with written culture. Milman Parry's son, Adam, himself a prominent Homer scholar (who, like his father, died young, in a motorcycle accident with his young wife Anne Amory Parry, who was also an important Homer scholar), argued forcefully for a literate poet at the end of a long tradition, and other important Homer scholars, such as Martin West, have made similar or variant claims. Could an oral poet have acquired the skill of writing and used it to record his own poems or adapt the poems of others, then? Did one or more transcribers write down the poetry of one or more non-literate singers? Was the process rapid and dependent on a single person of genius, or was it, as hinted by the Pisistratean recension and suggested by Vico, Wolf and others, a slow process involving many individuals? In recent years, Gregory Nagy (1979, 1990, etc.) has argued for gradual 'crystallization' and a transition from fluid oral tradition to canonical text over centuries, a process that ends only in the Hellenistic era with the canonization of the written text of the Homeric poems. Amidst a wide range of views, what is almost universally agreed is that the *Iliad* and *Odyssey* are, as John Foley usefully suggests (e.g. 1991), 'orally-derived' texts.

What wider conclusion does the history of the Homeric Question, of Homeric scholarship and of Homeric tradition offer us as readers of Homer? To the ancients, as we have seen, Homer was the figure of a real person who nevertheless possessed multiple characterizations. The Homers (note the plural!) that emerge from oral-formulaic theories are altogether more scientific, yet they too preserve, indeed enhance the element of plurality and tradition. Using contemporary discourses of science, anthropology, anthropological fieldwork and linguistics, the modern history of Homeric scholarship preserves a continuity of characterization in the very process of change. Here too, we find in Homer a single tradition of multiplicity.

CHAPTER FOUR

Homer's poetic language

Poetic style and oral style

We have just seen some of the more technical aspects of Homer's text and its style and the possible implications of formulaic language for our understanding of the process of the composition of the verse. But how do such repetitions and formulaic language operate at the level style, poetry and meaning? A generation ago, an important student of Homer, Jasper Griffin, in his influential *Homer on Life and Death* (1980: xiii–xiv) wrote:

> It has been claimed that 'at a deeper level, all literary criticism of the Homeric poems must be radically altered by the Parry-Lord hypothesis', and even that a new 'oral poetics' must come into existence before we can, without absurdity, presume to tackle the poems at all. But the production of a new 'poetics' has proved difficult, and some recent writing on formulaic utterance has contributed less to our aesthetic understanding than might have been hoped.

Can we, then, speak of Homeric 'oral poetics'? Do Homer's technical patterns of repetition change the poetry of the verse? If the range of phenomena which are involved in formulaic style is as wide as many scholars suggest, there can be no single answer to the question. Some prominent features are, however, worthy of note.

Rhythm and music

Let us first, very briefly, note again the rhythmic and metrical framework of Homer's verse and consider its stylistic consequences. As we have already seen, each of the lines that make up the *Iliad* and *Odyssey* is composed in the same formal rhythm. This rhythm, the hexameter, is uncommon in some modern languages such as English. We can, however, grasp its flow in a poem such as Henry Wadsworth Longfellow's *Evangeline: A Tale of Arcadie* (1847; see Longfellow 1992). Here are the last three lines of the poem (the stress is marked in **bold**):

And by the evening fire repeat Evangeline's **story,**
While from its **rocky caverns** the **deep**-voiced, **neigh**boring ocean
Speaks, and in **accents** dis**con**solate answers the **wail** of the forest.

Here, and in much modern poetry, the rhythm is created by stressing certain syllables and words ('**And** by the . . .' stressed–unstressed–unstressed). Ancient Greek, as we noted in the previous chapter, creates the rhythm by different means, distinguishing between 'long' and 'short' syllables. To study this rhythm today may require technical analysis, but we must remember that originally this system was created, not by scholars and not for scholars. It was song, a form of music in words, created by singers for the pleasure of listeners. Early Greek and even later classical audiences would have been exposed to public performances of epic verse at regular events, such as the great festival of the Panathenaia in Athens, and to shorter performances in public and perhaps even in the home. The physical beat of the poetry would have had immediate impact on listeners, all the more so when it was performed to the accompaniment of a musical instrument.

Rhythm, then, is the musical container of Homer's poetry. The flow of the verse is rapid and effortless. The meaning of the words and of units of meaning fall smoothly into the line and its parts, just as the meaning of the words falls into form in popular songs or in opera and is parsed by the rhythm and the tune. This is something we can find in almost every line of the *Iliad* and *Odyssey*, for example, in the following lines from the beginning of the *Iliad*, just after Apollo shoots his arrows and spreads a plague in the Greek camp (1.53–6. The **long** syllables are again highlighted in **bold**):

Ennêmar men ana straton ôicheto kêla theoio,
têi dekatêi d'Agorên de kalessato laon Achilleus.
Tôi gar epi phresi thêke thea leukôlenos Hêrê.
Kêdeto gar Danaôn, hoti 'ra thnêskontas horato.

Nine days the god's arrows fell among the host,
but on the tenth Achilles called the army to an assembly.
Hera, the goddess of the white arms, put this into his mind.
She pitied the Danaans when she saw them dying.

Apart from changes to word order (to retain the flow in English), the phrases in each line of translation above match those in the Greek original. We can see how each line encloses a single sentence and a well-rounded idea: 'The arrows fell for nine days' // 'on the tenth Achilles called a meeting' // 'this was Hera's idea' // 'she pitied the Greeks'. The singer will have performed each verse, perhaps paused for an instant, and resumed the flow of song, accompanying himself on the lyre. Apart from these pauses, there are also often shorter 'pauses' inside each line (called *caesurae* and *diareses* – these too are arranged in highly formal patterns). Such pauses mark off smaller units of meaning and allow for finer gradation of the rhythmical movement and the music. For example, the last line above (*Iliad* 1.53) begins *kêdeto gar Danaôn*, 'She pitied the Danaans', and concludes, *hoti 'ra thnêskontas horato*, 'when she saw them dying'. In performance, a short pause or a plucking of the lyre between these phrases has the power to stress Hera's pity in a manner that is entirely traditional (since such pauses are found at fixed points in the line), and yet entirely of the moment. The epic bard is thus a musical interpreter, like a modern pianist, violinist or opera singer in concert.

Music and meaning neatly overlap in many of the lines in the *Iliad* and the *Odyssey*. But many verses also demonstrate another simple, yet effective rhythmical feature, known as 'enjambment' or a kind of verbal dovetailing, whereby the sentence in one line spills over into another, as in the following verses (*Iliad* 1.68–9):

ê toi ho g' hôs eipôn kat' ar' hezeto: toisi d' anestê
Calchas Thestoridês oiônopolôn och' aristos,

He [Achilles] spoke thus and sat down again, and among them
stood up
Calchas, Thestor's son, by far the best of the bird interpreters,

The first line contains two parts and two ideas, 'Achilles spoke
and sat down', and 'another got up [to speak]'. The person who
has risen is the seer Calchas. Yet his name is held back for a brief
moment, and only 'dovetailed' onto the sentence in the next line.
The result offers the possibility of dramatic silences, emphasis,
characterization and contrast between the mighty and impulsive
hero Achilles and the old seer Calchas.

A few lines later, Calchas says in an even more startling example
(*Iliad* 1.74–5):

ô Achileu keleai me Diï phile muthêsasthai
mênin Apollônos hekatêbeletao anaktos:

O Achilles beloved of Zeus, you ask me to speak of
the wrath [*mênin*] of Apollo the far-shooting lord.

Here too, enjambment separates two important parts of the idea
between the two lines. It provides the singer with the opportunity
to 'punctuate' his song and create emphasis and surprise. 'You ask
me to speak of . . .' says the seer. Speak of what? We the audience
are waiting to hear. The first word of the next line gives us the
answer, of 'Wrath' (*mênin*).

Repetition and poetic style

Words, sentences and countless other elements of Homeric
formulaic language fit smoothly into Homer's lines. 'The easiest
and best ways of showing the place the formula holds in Homeric
style', says Milman Parry, 'will be to point out all the expressions
occurring in a given passage which are found elsewhere in the *Iliad*
or in the *Odyssey*' (1971: 301). Parry provided a detailed example
of two short sections of the poems – the first 25 lines of the *Iliad*
and of the *Odyssey*, respectively, in which he marked repeated
phrases. Today, computers and the internet provide readers with
freely accessible, extended analyses of every single one of the

poems' 27,803 verses as well as in the Homeric hymns and the poems of Hesiod (see the *Chicago Homer* project at http://digital. library.northwestern.edu/homer/ – texts can be read in parallel transliterations, translations and the original Greek). Parry's analysis was very technical, but it is important to stress that, in fact, we are dealing with a vibrant poetic phenomenon. Repeated elements in the lines above and in almost every line in all other parts of Homer resonate (intratextually) with other parts of the verse and (intertextually) with occurrences in other epic poems. Such repetitions have the capacity to recall for accustomed audiences and readers the inherent multiplicity of Homer, the resonance of what John Foley (1991) has called 'traditional referentiality' of epic words and the vast, open-ended tradition of epic.

No two repetitions have exactly the same effect. But to demonstrate the effect of Homeric repetition, we can choose examples from almost any part of Homer's poems. For instance, in the verses cited above from the *Iliad*, in line 53, we find the words *kêla theoio*, 'the god's arrows'. These words recur a little later in the poem, in line 1.383, as Achilles, complaining to his mother, the nymph Thetis, retells the story of the quarrel. The words 'the god's arrows', and the whole of Achilles' speech, which contain many other repetitions (see further below), echo the poet's description of the opening scene of the poem. Through such repetitions, the troubled Achilles becomes a surrogate narrator of the poem while we, the audience, are provided with another perspective on the *Iliad*'s catastrophic opening events.

In the next line in the opening of the *Iliad* (54), we find Achilles calling the Greeks together and the formula *agorên de kalessato*, 'called . . . to the assembly'. With small variations, these words are often repeated elsewhere in the poem. Calling an assembly thus becomes, not simply an ad hoc practical event, but an act that resonates with the tradition as a whole, one of the conventional, almost ritual actions of the heroic world that defines the range of a hero's activities.

In the following verse (55), the formula *thea leukôlenos Hêrê*, 'the goddess of the white-arms, Hera', is an often-used regular expression for Zeus' sister and wife (the phrase always appears in exactly the same position, at the end of the line). The epithet *leukôlenos*, 'white-armed', like many other epithets in other name formulas, creates an idealized image of this important member of the cast of characters in the *Iliad* and paints a little recurring (visual) vignette of the goddess. If this were a modern film, we might expect to recognize the goddess by an iconic close-up of her lovely arms. As we already know, similar, frequently repeated expressions naming other gods abound in the poems, for instance, 'cloud-gathering Zeus', 'high-thundering Zeus', 'Zeus, whose might is greatest', 'grey-eyed Athena', 'far-shooting Apollo'. Heroes too are characterized in this way: 'Odysseus of the many stratagems', 'bright Odysseus', 'bright Achilles', 'Hector, tamer of horses' and more. Common expressions such as 'Achilles son of Peleus' or 'Odysseus son of Laertes' combining the name of a hero and the name of his father (the latter element is known as a *patronymic*) are, on the one hand, a means of reference, in this case, Homer's way of identifying a hero by his 'surname'. But, on the other hand, they provide us with a constant background reminder, here of the theme of fathers-and-sons, which is a central epic theme.

The number of repeated elements in Homer and their varied resonance, even if we restrict ourselves to the few lines cited above, is too long to list in full. Let us, however, briefly turn again to just one more echo which concerns the word *mênin* in *Iliad* 1.74–5, the verses we have just considered in the previous section. I will, for convenience, repeat both lines. Calchas says:

ô Achileu keleai me Diï phile muthêsasthai
mênin *Apollônos hekatêbeletao anaktos:*

O Achilles, beloved of Zeus, you ask me to speak of
the wrath [*mênin*] of Apollo the far-shooting lord.

Any hearer or reader familiar with the *Iliad* will of course at this point recall the very first word and the first line of the poem, which is perhaps the single most famous verse in the whole of Greek literature, where the word, 'wrath', the theme of the poem, appears in exactly the same place, at the very beginning of the line (*Iliad* 1.1. The translation below retains the exact word order of the Greek original):

mênin *aeide thea Pêlêïadeô Achilêos*

The wrath [*mênin*] sing Goddess Son-of-Peleus, Achilles

In line 75, then, Calchas is not merely proposing to speak of the wrath. Using this vastly resonant word, he and the singer of the *Iliad* are invoking the whole of the poetic and thematic tradition of the poem and almost 'compressing' the whole of the epic tradition into this one single word. This example may have particularly strong resonance, but the essential mechanism is operative in almost every verse of the *Iliad* and *Odyssey*.

Although far less frequent than the repetition of smaller units, we sometimes also find whole passages recurring in the poems. Just now, we have pointed out that line 1.53 is part of a larger narrative repeated later in Book 1 in Achilles' speech to his mother Thetis. When Achilles tells Thetis about the priest Chryses' visit to the Greek camp and the beginning of the quarrel, he retells the earlier narrative by the poet. Achilles' words in 1.376–9, for example, are a word-for-word repetition of the narrator's original description (*Iliad* 1.22–5):

Then all the rest of the Achaeans agreed and called out
to respect the priest and to accept the shining ransom;
This, however, did not please the heart of Atreus' son
Agamemnon,
But he drove the priest away, harshly, hurling strong words
at him.

Does such long, exact repetition facilitate the composition of the verse in performance? Is the repetition in some way related to an editorial process and to the process of writing down sung verse? As a poetic device, it underscores the association between Achilles, the greatest warrior, and the narrator, 'Homer', the greatest poet. Here they speak, quite literally, the exact same words. Repetition also has an important truth function: Having heard the story only a few hundred lines before from the poet, we the audience/ readers know that Achilles' words are a true rendition of events. Repetition may suggest to us that this is a story told again and again – in this sense, a traditional story which may yet be retold in the future, too.

Furthermore, inside longer repeated passages, we can find shorter phrases each of which recurs either fully nested or partially overlapping in yet other contexts. Each individual expression may have its own patterns of repetition and may appear more frequently than the longer units and thus in more diverse contexts. The first words, in lines 22 and 376, 'Then all the rest . . .' (*enth alloi men pantes*) are repeated more widely in other contexts in Homer. Their contents may not be dramatic, but the very act of repetition creates a highly traditional pattern for resuming a heroic narrative. Another phrase, 'and to accept the shining ransom' (*kai aglaa dechthai apoina*), which appears in the two contexts above, in lines 23 and 377, is also repeated outside of the *Iliad* and *Odyssey*, in the *Homeric Hymn to Aphrodite* (140); an even smaller part of this group of words, 'to accept the ransom' (*dechthai apoina*), appears with a minor variation in other places in the *Iliad* (6.46; 11.131; 24.137; 25.555), especially in the context of Priam's ransoming of Hector at the end of the poem. The *Iliad*, as we have noted, begins and ends with acts of ransom, the first of a living captive woman (Chryseis), the last of a dead warrior (Hector). These and other repetitions create a world of dense echoes, both direct and ghostly, each one connecting to others, each one having the potential to recall other parts of the narrative, other contexts and other meanings.

Typical scenes

Repetitive echoic structure is common in Homeric verse at yet higher levels of theme and content, and its presence is often associated with the oral provenance of Homeric poetry. When, for example, we look at the description of scenes of battle and fighting, speaking in the assembly, scenes of feasting and hospitality, arming, supplication, bathing scenes and more, we find sets of highly organized recurring motifs.

In *Iliad* Book 5, one of the great fighting books (describing Diomedes' *aristeia*) of the poem, we find a scene in which Diomedes faces two Trojans, Phegeus and Idaeus, who are the sons of Dares, a priest of Hephaestus (5.9–26). Bernard Fenik has analysed this and other fighting scenes in the *Iliad*. He outlines the action of the passage as follows (1968: 13–14):

1   Diomedes, on foot, is attacked by two Trojans in a chariot.
2   The first Trojan's spear-cast fails.
3   He is then killed by Diomedes.
4   The second Trojan turns to flee.

5 He is rescued y Hephaestus.

6 Diomedes captures the Trojan's horses.

As Fenik points out, a later scene describing Diomedes' fight against Aeneas and his charioteer Sthenelus (5.275ff.) is structured using the same motifs. Fenik outlines this second scene as follows:

1 Diomedes, on foot, is attacked by two Trojans in a chariot.

2 The first Trojan's spearcast fails.

3 He is then killed by Diomedes.

4 The second Trojan leaps down to defend the body of the first.

5 In the ensuing fight, he is wounded, but then rescued by Aphrodite and Apollo.

6 Sthenelus captures the Trojan horses according to Diomedes' instructions.

These two sets of events contain distinct elements of parity and divergence. In both cases, Diomedes is first attacked by two enemies; in the first scene, the surviving Trojan turns to flee, in the second, he turns to fight and so on. We are dealing with an elaborate set of typical narrative units, which can be identified in many other fighting scenes in both the *Iliad* and *Odyssey* (see, e.g. Edwards 1992).

The first to point to such 'typical scenes' was Walter Arend (1933). Shortly afterwards, Milman Parry reviewed Arend's work and suggested that the phenomenon could be explained in the context of oral composition and traditional discourse. Somewhat like shorter formulas, the recurrent motifs provided structural building blocks for the narrative – a modular system for putting together traditional scenes. As Parry suggested, an oral singer, having to compose his poem swiftly and without pausing, could do so by 'telling each action as it comes up in more or less the usual way, and in more or less the usual verses which go with that way' (Parry 1971: 406). As with formulas, Parry's view stressed the advantages of this practice in the process of composition, and he played down aesthetic functions. Thematic variations, Parry suggested, were *not* a question of finding 'falsely subtle meanings in the repetitions, as meant to recall an earlier scene where the same words are used' (1971: 407).

By the time Parry's review was published, in 1936, he himself was no longer alive. As with formulas, there is some evidence to suggest that, had he lived, he might have eventually allowed more flexibility in his arguments. Parry's student and successor Albert Lord moved in exactly this direction. Lord describes, for example, an instance where the famous Serbo-Croat guslar Avdo Međedović (1875–1953) was invited to sit in on a performance by another singer, Mumin Vlahovljak, of a long song which Avdo himself did not know. Afterwards and without forewarning, Avdo was asked to perform the song. Lord (1960: 78) reports that:

> Avdo began, and as he sang the song lengthened, the ornamentation and richness accumulated, and the human touches of character, touches that distinguished Avdo from other singers, imparted a depth of feeling that had been missing in Mumin's versions.

> The analysis of the first major theme in Mumin's and in Avdo's text . . . illustrates how well Avdo had followed his original and yet how superbly he was able to expand it and make it his own.

On the evidence of the living tradition, thematic patterns provide a framing structure that facilitates the composition; they reflect the 'traditional' portrayal of action, but are also a means of introducing variations, tailoring the composition to the moment and enriching it.

Ring composition

Another notable feature of Homeric poetry is 'ring composition'. There are many types of ring structures in discourse but, as anthropologist Mary Douglass notes, the most fundamental feature of this form is the ending which comes back to the beginning and thus signals completion (2007: 31–2). Ring composition often also involves the arrangement of words or themes in a 'Russian doll' structure on either side of a central element or in mirror formation ('chiasmus'). Whether ring composition originates in pre-literate oral cultures, or with early literacy and memorization, as Jack Goody, another famous anthropologist, suggests, with 'natural' ways of organizing materials, as some literary scholars and linguists have claimed, or is simply a generic social construct, it is, Douglass stresses, a way of controlling meaning, placing emphasis and defining relations between ideas. In Homer, in the *Iliad*, for example, we find Nestor describing the battle between his own people, the Pylians, and their enemies the Epeans. The narrative is arranged as a structured set of themes:

(732–36) A – Battle begins; prayers to Zeus and Athena.
(737–46) B – Nestor kills his first victim, the Epean Moulion. He captures the horses.
(747–49) C – Nestor pursues and captures 50 Epean chariots. He kills two men in each.
(750–52) D – Only the two Epeans escape. They are rescued by Poseidon.
(735–38) C' – The Pylians pursue and massacre the Epeans.
(759–60) B' – Nestor kills his last victim. The Pylians capture the horses.
(761) A' – The Pylians give glory to the gods and to Nestor.

In the scene, then, prayer (A) is matched by prayer, killing (B) by killing and capture of horses and by (C) pursuit and massacre. Some of these recurring elements, the killing, the capture of the horses or the rescue by a god, are familiar from our discussion, above, of aspects of typical scenes in Homer. Homer's style is not a series of isolated tropes, but an integrated phenomenon.

Ring composition characterizes larger segments of narrative but it can also be detected in the arrangement of smaller units of Homeric poetry. When Patroclus appeals to Achilles to help the Greeks, the angry Achilles first responds with pitying words (*Iliad* 16.7–11):

(7) A – Why are you crying
   B – Patroclus
      C – like a little girl?
        (8) D – A foolish one, who runs after her mother
           and begs to be picked up and carried
          (9) E – And clings to her dress and holds her
             back when she tries to hurry
        (10) D' – And gazes tearfully into her face, until she is
           picked up?
      (11) C' – You are like her,
   B' – Patroclus,
A' – dropping these soft tears.

The words 'like a little girl' in line 7 are matched by 'like her' in line 11; likewise, in the same line, the calling of Patroclus' name, and the reference to crying/tears; in line 8, the request to be picked up (in Greek, *anelesthai*) is matched by the exact same request in line 10 (*anelêtai*); the focus of the speech is the image of a clinging child (Patroclus) and a hurrying mother (Achilles), which is perhaps a little ironic, since it is Achilles who sits fast in his hut while Patroclus is the one in a hurry to go and help the Greeks.

Ring composition is not a mechanical opening-and-closing movement, but rather an organic compositional structure. The emotions are immediate, the scene homely, but the arrangement is meticulous, stately and formal. This is one of the ways in which Homeric poetry stands back and reflects on its themes.

Metaphor and simile

Our last example is a rhetorical comparison between two completely different objects or descriptions, the hero Patroclus in his agitated state over the suffering of the Greeks and a weeping little girl. Such comparisons, both metaphors and similes, sometimes brief, at other times extending over several verses, are not exclusive to oral poetry, but they are a noticeable feature of Homer's poetic style.

Metaphors, mostly brief, comprise some of the most famous expressions in Homer's language, such as the 'wine-dark sea', 'winged words', 'honeyed words', 'rosy-fingered dawn', 'ships, horses of the sea', the 'watery ways', 'the sleek veil of Troy' and the 'black cloud of death'. Metaphors are part of the names of many gods and heroes, for example, 'owl-eyed Athena' or 'Agamemnon, shepherd of the people'. As with 'winged words', the force of many metaphors is immediate. Words with wings are rapid and agitated words. A sea dark as wine is an unknown, threatening but also an intoxicating and attractive place. The complex nature of metaphor forces us to reflect on both the thing described and the description in new ways. Many Homeric metaphors, especially those that comprise a noun or a name and an epithet (or epithets) are, technically speaking, also formulas. Parry was of the view that they were used because of their 'metrical utility': 'rosy-fingered dawn' is simply a convenient means of expressing the essential idea of dawn. 'The sleek veil of Troy' would thus mean simply 'Troy'. Many translations simplify metaphors, for example, rendering this latter expression 'the sleek battlements of Troy'. Yet, as Michael Nagler (1974) has shown, formulaic expressions describing the loosening of a woman's headdress and the destruction of the walls of Troy are associated by a kind of 'family resemblance' (a distinct resemblance which nevertheless does not depend on any single common feature. Nagler borrowed this important term from the philosopher Ludwig Wittgenstein). Traditional phraseology, in this case as in many others, amplifies and enriches the poetic resonance of Homer's words.

Like metaphors, similes are also a common means of poetic comparison in Homer. In the simile, of course, comparison is openly acknowledged by such words as 'like', 'as' or 'as when . . .'. Some Homeric similes are short and frequently repeated, as, for instance, when heroes are compared to gods in the phrase 'godlike Achilles' (*theoeikel' Achilleu. Iliad* 1.131, etc.) or 'equal to a god' (*daimoni isos. Iliad* 5.438). Such comparisons work partly as standard means of reference. Achilles is a great hero. He is almost like a god. Yet closer scrutiny of both specific contexts and more general patterns of Homer's repetitive language often reveals more interesting nuances. In *Iliad* (1.131), for example, we find Agamemnon saying: 'Do not thus, mighty though you are, *godlike Achilles*, seek to deceive me with your wit.' This is the moment when the dispute between the two heroes over honour, which is the theme of the *Iliad*, comes to a head. 'Godlike' is a generic term of praise, yet in this verse, it underscores Agamemnon's very particular resentment and contributes to one of the most forceful displays of contempt in Greek literature. Similarly, in *Iliad* 5.438, the expression *daimoni isos*, 'equal to a god', is used to describe Diomedes, a hero well deserving of praise. He is, as some scholars have suggested, a younger version of Achilles himself. Yet, in Book 5, Diomedes reaches the limits of heroism. Having killed a series of Trojan enemies, he directs his fury at the immortals. He charges so vehemently, so 'like a god', that Apollo must in the following verses check him, brusquely warning (5.440–2), 'take care, Son of Tydeus, and give way, and do not strive to make yourself like the gods in mind, since the race of the gods, who are immortal, and of men who walk the earth is not the same'. Heroes are indeed 'equal to the gods' but the more Homeric poetry stresses the comparison, the more it also underscores the disparity, the essential condition of mortality, and the glory and tragedy of heroic death.

It is, however, the longer and more formal similes that are most distinct in Homer's style. The similes describe a wide range of scenes and activities, but the majority are drawn from the world of nature, agriculture, hunting and craftsmanship. As a whole, they represent a world more 'ordinary' and familiar than the past world of heroes and heroic exploits. We find themes of wild beasts, wolves, boars, fawns and lions in the wilderness and alongside men, for example, in hunting scenes (see a listing in Scott 2009: 193–7). Menelaus meeting Paris is compared to a lion who finds the carcass of a stag or a goat and is hunted by young men (*Iliad* 3.23–7). The two Ajaxes carry off the Trojan Imbrius like lions snatching a goat from the hounds (*Iliad* 13.197–201). Odysseus emerges from the thicket to face Nausicaa and her handmaids, like a hungry mountain-raised lion (*Odyssey* 6.130–5). We find similes describing sea eagles and hawks; insects including bees, wasps, flies and locusts; domestic animals like bulls and oxen, donkeys and goats, mice and more; as well as natural phenomena and the elements, such as wind, fire, the stars and the moon (e.g. *Iliad* 8.555–61). We find similes describing smoke, rocks and trees, towers and walls. In Book II of the *Iliad*, following Agamemnon's proposal of abandoning the campaign (a test that nearly ends in disaster for Agamemnon), the Greek assembly stirs like waves on the Icarian sea (*Iliad* 2.144–6), and a line later like tall sheaves of grain shaken by the Western wind (*Iliad* 2.147–52). Nature and the elements appear again as Odysseus is carried into the sea by a wave, like thistles blown over the plain by the northern wind in late summer (*Odyssey* 5.328–30). We also find descriptions of weeping women, of a sausage turning on the spit and other varied scenes of domestic life.

Of the total number of longer similes, about 200 (the exact count depends on our definition) are found in the *Iliad*. The rest, about 40, appear in the *Odyssey* (Edwards 1991: 24 [volume V of Kirk 1985–93]). This is a notable disparity in number between the two poems. Some scholars have suggested that the difference reflects deeper thematic and tonal distinctions. The world of the *Iliad* is essentially one. The poem is an austere image of war focused on heroic combat and the siege of Troy. The changes in pace and perspective affected by the simile offer welcome variety and make better sense in the narrative of the *Iliad*. In contrast, the *Odyssey* depicts a wider range of worlds, many of which (notwithstanding the fantastic parts of the *apologue*) are closer to the realities depicted in the similes. The *Odyssey*, it is argued, is less accommodating to similes, or perhaps, being varied itself, has less need of them. This is a compelling explanation of an undeniable statistical difference between the *Iliad* and *Odyssey*, which does not, however, alter the basic ways in which similes work in both poems.

As in metaphors and short similes, many of the images and scenes in the longer similes can be read as straightforward extensions, expansions, contrasts, intensifications or illustrations of the object, action or idea at hand. But there are always also more resonant and more complex elements in the similes that alter our perspectives, temporarily freeze the rapid pace of events and force us, for a moment, to reflect on heroes and heroic epic.

In Book 4 of the *Iliad*, for instance, the Trojan Pandarus breaks the truce agreed between the warring sides, shooting Menelaus with an arrow (an unheroic weapon, in the world of the *Iliad*). The shot is not lethal, but the arrow grazes Menelaus' thigh and draws blood. There follows one of the most famous similes in the poem (*Iliad* 4.141–7):

> As when a woman colours ivory with purple
> A Maeonian or a Carian, making it a cheek-piece for horses;
> And it is kept in an inner room, and many riders
> long to have it, but it is kept as a king's treasure,
> both an adornment for the horse, and a prize for the horseman:
> So, Menelaus, your shapely thighs were stained with the colour
> of blood, and your legs also and your ankles below them.

Some of the effects of the simile and its meanings are straightforward. Stained ivory is an inanimate, 'deathless' object. It is a prized thing of beauty, the product of valued skill, an object that belongs in ordered and essentially peaceful life. In contrast, Menelaus is a mortal whose life could be extinguished by an arrow. His injury marks the chaotic breaking of order by a perfidious and unheroic act and the essential turbulence of the war. Agamemnon's concerned speech later in the book reminds us how much is at stake here: if Menelaus dies, the Trojan expedition loses its purpose. Only minimal slowing of the pace of the narrative is affected here. We are in the midst of a story and the simile, although it extracts us from the linear progression of events and their time and place, allows for smooth alignment between the new image and its surrounding context. Indeed, this simile, like many others, is based on a direct visual analogy between the red blood and red or purple-stained ivory (Greek colour terminology is notoriously flexible). Early scholarship on the simile sometimes speaks of the *tertium comparationis*, the 'third element of comparison', in our case, the colouring – which is neither the thing compared nor the comparator. In this sense, the simile provides what we could describe as a 'parallax' effect. We see the same image from two different positions and thus (as in stereoscopic vision) gain a sense of depth.

The resonance of the comparison is, however, a little more complex. The stained ivory simile does not fully overlap the context. Many of its details remain outside the analogy and the contrastive framework. A complete comparison is difficult, if not impossible. Why is the maker of the ivory cheekpiece in our simile from Maionia or Caria? Why is the maker a woman (and not a man)? Ivory may resemble (white) human flesh in colour, but why specifically a cheekpiece for horses? Why is it important that this is a high-status item (some similes describe perfectly pedestrian objects or scenes)? What is the analogue or the contrast in the world of the warring Greeks and Trojans of the keeping of the stained cheekpiece in an inner room? What is the relevance of the fact that the cheekpiece adds beauty to both the horse and the horse's rider? The problem of the relevance of the details in the simile is an old chestnut. Some of the details of this simile and many other similes remain outside of any relation of comparison. The similes, we should add, sometimes also use a language which is distinct from other parts of the narrative and which, on the whole contains less 'traditional' repetition than elsewhere in Homer.

Viewed on their own, that is, not as analogies, many of the similes describe perfectly plausible worlds. For instance, actual carved ivory objects like those described in *Iliad* Book 4 have been found in early Iron Age Mycenaean graves. H. L. Lorimer in her study of material objects associated with Homer (1950: 508), records various equestrian decorations from Nimrod. In other words, some of the simile's details seem to strengthen the impression of an independent world that is closer to later historical reality, perhaps the Iron Age, and is at some remove from the

martial activities of the heroic world. These details can contribute
to the characterization of the heroic activities and put them into
relief, but they resist complete incorporation/interpretation within
the terms of the world of the epic past. Similes embedded in the
narrative thus present us with an amalgam of poetic and historical
presents and pasts.

In the *Odyssey*, when Odysseus and his men blind the Cyclops,
we are told that they thrust a great sharpened stake into the
monster's eye and press and twist 'as when some man bores the
beam of a ship with an auger, while others below rotate it with a
strap, grasping at both ends, and it turns continuously' (*Odyssey*
9.384–6). Immediately after this description, we find another simile
that makes reference to iron and metalworking (*Odyssey* 9.391–4):

As when a blacksmith plunges a great axe or an adze
in cold water and it hisses loudly as he tempers it,
for this is how the iron gains its strength,
so his [the Cyclops'] eye sizzled around the olive-wood stake.

Mention of iron, clearly important to the broad dating of the poems
(see above discussions of history), is not exclusive to the similes.
However, iron does appear in several other interesting domestic
contexts, in important similes which sharply contrast with the
surrounding heroic settings. In *Iliad* (4.482–9), for example, the
death of the Trojan Simoeisius is compared to the felling of a tree:

He fell down in the dust, like a black poplar,
that grows in the land that lies by a great marsh,
a smooth-barked tree, yet with branches growing at its very
top:
One whom a man, a wheelwright, cuts down with the shining
iron, to bend it into a wheel for a well-wrought chariot,
and the tree lies growing hard and dry by the river banks.
Such was Anthemion's son Simoeisius whom godly
Aias killed.

The effect of the simile is powerful and immediate. Yet some
details of the scene seem independent of their surrounding
context. It would require heavy-handed interpretation to fit the
great marsh, the tree's smooth trim or the chariot wheel precisely

into the heroic battle scene and the death of Simoeisius. The simile conjures up a partly self-sustained world, closer to the Iron Age and, in principle, to the world of the poem's performance (in general, the fitting of wheels has sometimes been associated with the name Homer and with the making or fitting together of poetry).

In some cases, the links between the similes and the performance world are even closer. Consider again the simile of the stained ivory. As the singer's comparison is brought home, in *Iliad* 4.146–7, he says:

> So, Menelaus, your shapely thighs were stained with the colour of blood, and your legs also and your ankles below them.

These lines employ a unique rhetorical/poetic trope. The singer in the world and time of the performance (cf. the contrastive expression 'the men of today', e.g. in *Iliad* 5.304; 12.383; 12.449; 29.287) is directly addressing Menelaus, a character whose time is in the distant past inside the poem. This powerful appeal, known as *apostrophe* or 'direct address', is only rarely used in Homer, here directed at Menelaus, elsewhere only in addresses to Patroclus (in the *Iliad*) and Eumaius (in the *Odyssey*). Homeric apostrophes usually occur in moments of crisis. Significantly, the great heroes Agamemnon, Achilles and Odysseus are never addressed in this extraordinary manner by Homer. Why are Menelaus, Patroclus and Eumaius approached in this way? Some critics have suggested that they represent weaker, more fallible and more 'ordinary' doublets of the greater heroes, and are thus closer to the non-heroic world of poetic performances (Menelaus/Agamemnon; Patroclus/Achilles; Eumaius/Odysseus). If this is true, then the apostrophe in the simile of the stained ivory, which itself establishes a world more ordinary, provides yet another point of contact between the present and the world of the heroic past. Homer seems to bring these worlds together, yet he keeps them apart. Such paradoxical encounters are one way of keeping the fame (*kleos*) of the past alive, in other words 'imperishable' (*aphthiton*).

One simile makes this connection between worlds and times, between song and performance and the world of heroes clearer than the rest. Consider these lines from the *Odyssey*, describing Odysseus' actions in the decisive contest of the bow (21.406–9).

Odysseus picks up the weapon and is about to prove both his strength and his identity:

> As when a man who has mastered the lyre and song
> easily stretches a new string around a peg
> grasping the well-twisted sheep's gut at both ends
> so Odysseus effortlessly strung the great bow.

The link between this climactic moment in the plot of the *Odyssey* and an ordinary moment in the world of the performance is decisive and telling. What is particularly interesting is that here there is a strong overlap between the details in the simile and the details of Odysseus' actions in the heroic world (lyre = bow; lyre-string = bow-string; peg = nocks [the nocks are the notched ends of the bow], the twisted sheep's gut, stringing 'at both ends', etc.). It is, precisely at the moment of the greatest apparent disparity between heroic feats of the past and epic performance in the present (presumably by a feeble, perhaps blind bard . . .), that these two worlds come most closely together. But then, by successfully shooting the arrow in the contest of the Bow Odysseus affects his homecoming to the 'ordinary' domestic world of Ithaca. His triumph, his return and his *fame* are also the present return of the past and the triumph of epic song.

CHAPTER FIVE

Proems, tales and plots

The proems

Homer's poetry and art have many other stylistic, thematic and poetic features, some of which we will consider in the subsequent chapters in our 'commentary', as we consider aspects of the poems in their narrative order. Before we do so, we need to reflect on a few of Homer's important principles of storytelling. I want to look at how the poems are introduced; at the manner of the telling of tales from the past; at the relation between event, word and truth and at the general outlines of the plots of the *Iliad* and *Odyssey*. My purpose is not to provide a complete survey of approaches to these weighty and complicated questions (which would require a very long book), but to expose something of the underlying premises of the narrative.

First words are always important, and the first words of the *Iliad* and *Odyssey*, which are, after all, the first words in Western literature, are particularly so. How, then, does the singer introduce his tale? Where does the song come from? How does the poet know what he knows? Can we the audiences and readers trust the poet and his songs?

Homer's traditional epics do not simply begin to tell a story (compare, e.g. Thomas Hardy's *The Mayor of Casterbridge*: 'One evening of late summer, before the nineteenth century had reached one-third of its span, a young man and woman, the latter carrying a child, were approaching the large village of Weydon-Priors, in Upper Wessex, on foot' Hardy 1886 [1998]). Both poems open with formal introductions or *proems* (for the

Iliad, cf. Redfield 1979; for the *Odyssey*, in Pucci 1987 and 1998: 11–29). As we have already seen, the first things stated are the poems' themes, condensed into a single word. This is followed by brief outlines of the plots, or part of the plots of the poems. The *Iliad* begins (1.1–6) as follows:

> Of the wrath [*mênin*] sing, goddess, of Peleus' son, Achilles,
> that destructive wrath which brought countless woes upon the Achaeans,
> and sent down to Hades many valiant souls of heroes,
> and made them their bodies spoil for dogs and every bird;
> Thus the plan of Zeus was fulfilled,
> from the time when first they parted in strife,
> Atreus' son, the king of men, and great Achilles.

The *Odyssey*'s proem follows a similar pattern (1.1–10):

> Of the man [*andra*], tell me, Muse, the man of many ways
> who wandered much after he had sacked the sacred citadel of Troy.
> Many were the men whose cities he saw and whose mind he learned,
> and many were the pains he suffered in his heart at sea,
> yearning to preserve his life and the return of his companions.
> Yet even so he did not save his companions, much though he strove,
> for they perished by their very own folly,
> the fools, they feasted on the cattle of Helios Hyperion;
> but the god took from them their day of their return.
> Of these things, goddess, daughter of Zeus, beginning where you will, tell us too.

By the time we reach the actual story, we have, in a manner of speaking, already heard the tale. The proems' summaries are not, however, as plain as they seem. For example, what exactly is the will of Zeus in the *Iliad*'s proem? Is it the destruction of Troy, which, although briefly noted, is never described in the poem? Or does the plan of Zeus refer more specifically to the wrath of Achilles? To the killing of Hector? What relation does Zeus' will have to the vast tale of the Trojan saga, which, as other poems in the *Epic Cycle* show, begins much earlier, with the abduction of Helen, and extends well past the fall of Troy? Why, in the proem of the *Odyssey*, are Odysseus' adventures in Ithaca, his dealing with the suitors and especially his relation to his wife Penelope, his son Telemachus and his father Laertes barely noted? These 'unaccounted' events occupy the latter half the *Odyssey*. They are neither brief nor incidental to the plot. Although the names of the poems, the themes and the summaries in the proems provide us with some indication of what we might expect to find in the following long poems, the first few lines of the *Iliad* and *Odyssey* are both less than and more than proper summaries.

The proems of the *Iliad* and *Odyssey* introduce not only the narrative but the narrator, too. Homer, as Marcel Detienne says, is one of the 'masters of truth' of ancient Greece (Detienne 1996). Telling a traditional story like Homer's requires the assertion of both authority and a certain kind of continuity; it raises questions about transmission and sources of knowledge. And indeed, both the *Iliad* and the *Odyssey* begin by addressing these issues, making special *invocations* by the narrator to the Muse, goddess of poetry, asking her to sing of past events. These are, however, rather special acts.

Many authors and texts in antiquity begin with some form of appeal or special address which stakes their claim to knowledge and sets the scene for what is to follow. In the fifth century BCE, Herodotus begins his narrative of the wars between the Greeks and the Persians with the words 'Herodotus of Halicarnassus, his researches ["researches" in Greek – *historiai*] are here set down to preserve the memory of the past by putting on record the astonishing achievements of both our own and of other peoples' (*Histories* 1.1). Herodotus first describes the events surrounding the Trojan War and there is important shared ground between his work and Homer's. The *Histories*' narrative, exploring the identity of Greek 'self' versus Persian 'others' can be seen as a continuation of the Homeric narrative about a Pan-Hellenic army of Greeks fighting non-Greek 'barbarians'. Yet we must appreciate how different Homer's introductory manner is from Herodotus'.

Herodotus begins by stating his name, 'Herodotus', and his provenance, 'Halicarnassus' (a famous centre of learning in Ionia – now the western coast of Turkey), and by laying claim to his own work. When we the readers ascribe the *Histories* to Herodotus, we are, in an immediate sense, simply agreeing with the text. Homer does things otherwise. On the one hand, the Homeric narrators clearly mark their presence. The *Iliad* and *Odyssey* are not stories that 'tell themselves'. On the other hand, both the narrator of the *Iliad* and the narrator of the *Odyssey* remain anonymous. Apart from the bare marking of his existence, neither narrator discloses any detail of identity in the proems nor anywhere else in Homer's poems (see Richardson 1990). Many other poets are mentioned by name in the *Iliad* and *Odyssey*: Phemius, Demodocus and Thamyris, Achilles himself, who sings in the *Iliad*, and Odysseus who tells his tales like a poet in the *Odyssey*. Yet it is entirely up to us, the audiences and readers, to make the association between the unidentified but distinctly present narrators of the poems at large and the name Homer. To ascribe the *Iliad* and *Odyssey* to Homer, therefore, is not to agree with anything the poems openly tell us. We ourselves must play an active part in the tradition. We must 'accept' the poet's identity on trust from the past and 'pass it on'. In general, tradition claims for itself the status of truth, but it is not empirical truth. Whether a tradition is actually transmitted from the distant past or 'invented' and retrojected into that past (as Eric Hobsbawm [Hobsbawm and Ranger 1992] and others have argued), it and its source are by definition removed from immediate experience. However, the essential element in traditions is not quite their 'inventedness' or the occlusion of an invented source, or even their real sources in the past that underpins the truth of traditions, but commonly the acts of trust which accompany them. Traditions are social performances in which we accept something as having been handed over from a distant past which we ourselves cannot access, or visit, or see directly. We carry this sense of past with us to the future without quite knowing what it is. Looking back to Homer's elusive introduction, our point is this: The first lines of the poems pull us in, demand and affirm 'traditionality'. They affect the presence of an unknown but 'certain' original speaker. We may think of our Homer as a historical figure (as the ancients did), or we may argue that he is a cultural construct (as modern critics have suggested). Yet, precisely, in such acts of interpretation and acceptance, we define the traditional elements of Homer and Homeric poetry.

In the *Histories*, Herodotus takes ownership of his own work. Many other texts in antiquity begin with such acts of possession.

Virgil's *Aeneid* begins 'I sing of arms and the man' (1.1). In a gesture of homage to Homer and Homeric tradition, Virgil too does not name himself – although in his case, there exists ample external historical information to link him to his poem. In a further gesture towards Homeric tradition, Virgil appeals to the assistance of the Muse in following verses. Yet in stark contrast to Homer, Virgil speaks as the one who is doing the singing: '*I* sing', he says and claims the poem for himself. At the beginning of the *Iliad* and the *Odyssey*, neither of the unnamed yet-present narrators makes a claim to sing or speak himself. Instead, each asks the goddess of song to tell the story. The narrators thus seem to 'transfer ownership' of the content of the poems to another, or rather to never take possession of it in the first place: These songs belong to the Muse. To themselves the narrators of the poem paradoxically assign merely the role of hearers.

Needless to say, the same person making these introductory appeals to the Muse is the person who sings the rest of the poems. One of epic's distinct generic features is that, despite its large cast of characters and frequent direct speeches by characters, it was performed by one singer, who sometimes narrates the story in his own persona and sometimes imitates his characters and speaks in their voice. Yet through the special act of an appeal to the Muse, the singer eschews possession not only of the first line, but of everything that follows. He may be the one who speaks, but within the conventions of epic, it is the Muse who animates his voice and whose knowledge is responsible for the words. The narrator, who portrays himself as the hearer, is merely a mouthpiece, an instrument for the handing-over and passing-on, a link in the chain of tradition.

At any individual performance of these poems, there will have been a particular singer, bard or rhapsode performing the song. He may have been called Homer, he may have been another singer, such as Ion – the professional performer of Homeric poetry in Plato's dialogue by the same name. Or indeed, the singer may have been one of the Homeridae. Yet the force of the invocations at the beginning of the *Iliad* and *Odyssey* defines the Homeric narrator only as the voice of the Muse. The singer is listening, as it were, to his own voice speaking words whose origin he himself claims to be elsewhere. The first lines of the poems implicitly suggest that different singers can perform the 'same' song.

It is significant that this act of handing-over is portrayed in almost exactly the same manner in the first lines of both the *Iliad* and the *Odyssey*, suggesting that this is a deliberate feature of Homeric poetry. As if to affirm the importance of the act of withdrawal and transference, we find similar ideas also expressed in several other places in the Homeric poems (*Iliad* 11.218; 14.508; 16.112). Most prominent among them is an invocation in the second book of the *Iliad*, just before the 'Catalogue of Ships' (for the Catalogue, see Chapter 2). The narrator, unnamed as before, calls upon the Muses for assistance (*Iliad* 4.484–93):

> Tell me now, Muses who have their dwellings on Olympus,
> for you are goddesses, and are everywhere, and know
>   everything,
> while we hear only rumour and know nothing:
> Who were the leaders of the Danaans and their lords.
> Their multitude I cannot speak nor name,
> not if I had ten tongues, and ten mouths
> or an unbreakable voice and a bronze heart within me,
> unless you Olympian Muses, daughters of Zeus
> Master of the Aegis, call to my mind all those who came to
>   Ilios.
> But I will now tell of the leaders of the ships and all the ships.

Here, in even greater detail than at the beginning of the poems, the singer has through his own words become an anonymous listener. As a mortal, he 'hears rumour' and himself 'knows nothing'. The narrator is without doubt the one who speaks and will continue to speak ('I will now tell of the leaders of the ships . . .'). But he has eschewed his own powers of knowledge, and thus also possession of the song and the words – as if he were merely the means of transfer, a vehicle for the voice of the Muses who are 'everywhere' and 'know everything'.

The importance of these lines, then, is in the principles of poetic transmission they embody. If the words that preserve the deeds of great heroes are to remain 'undying', they must be presented in the poems as truth that can be transferred from one poet to another, from one performance to another, from one generation to another. The narrator's paradoxical declaration ('I know nothing') carries the force of these lines. Resisting possession by 'mere mortals', the poems offer themselves to all those who would pass them on. The performance of the poem at any one time and place by any one singer and the text of the poems are aligned, in principle, with the words of the Muses who 'know everything'. Reading these verses, we are now better equipped to understand claims such as those made by the *Greek Anthology*'s epigram (16.295, discussed above). Homer may have a single name, but he is not one person. 'Not the field of Smyrna gave birth to divine Homer, not Colophon, the star of luxurious Ionia, not Chios, not rich Egypt, not holy Cyprus, not the rocky island homeland of Ulysses . . .' Homer is not one person, not a man born of the earth. He has come to embody the whole of Greece.

Retelling the story of the past

But what, in fact, happens in Homeric epic when an event from the past is converted into words, told and retold? In addition to the poems at large – which are repeated 'traditional' stories – there are, inside the *Iliad* and *Odyssey*, countless other stories of many different kinds. Some are presented as hearsay, others as eyewitness accounts, some as truth, others as obvious lies. We can illustrate something of the essential qualities of Homeric storytelling by considering one such tale: the 'imperishable' story of the fate of Agamemnon. The events of this tale lie midway between the two Homeric poems, in the *Iliad*'s future, after the sack of Troy, and in the *Odyssey*'s past, before the return of Odysseus. Agamemnon's fate is not mentioned in the *Iliad*, but the story is repeatedly retold, by several different narrators, in the *Odyssey* (1.29–30, 35–43, 298–300; 3.193–8, 234–5; 255–77; 4.91–2, 514–37; 11.409–34, 452–3; 13.383–4; 19.96–7, 199–200. See also 1.46–7, 326–7; 4.546–7; 10.387–9 = 24.20–2). Indeed, in the *Odyssey*, the narrative is offered as an *exemplum*, a salutary tale from the past that serves as a model for future action. More importantly, Agamemnon's story is told as a model for events that will be retold. By looking at it closely, we can understand something of epic poetry and the way it creates repetition and continuity.

The core of the tale is well known (to later audiences, above all through Aeschylus' fifth century BCE dramatic trilogy, the

Oresteia): Upon his return from Troy, Agamemnon is killed at the hands of his treacherous wife Clytemnestra and her lover Aegisthus, and is avenged by his son, Orestes, who kills both his mother and her accomplice. Already in the *Odyssey*, this story is presented as a famous tale. In Book 1, Athena, speaking to Telemachus, says (298–300):

> Have you not heard what fame [*kleos*] great Orestes won
> among all mankind, when he killed his father's murderer
> the guileful Aegisthus, who killed his illustrious father?

A little later in the *Odyssey*, the old hero Nestor says to Odysseus' son and the assembled company (3.193–4):

> Even you yourselves, although your live far away, heard
>   of the Son of Atreus,
> how he came back and how Aegisthus planned his bitter
>   destruction.

One critic rightly points out that the tale 'must have been the rumour *par excellence* in Achaean society' (Olson 1995: 24). Yet, as he stresses (1995: 27),

> the story of Agamemnon's death is not the same each time
> it is told . . . individual narrators routinely adapt it to their
> own purposes, while the characters who listen to these tales
> understand and interpret them in accord with their own plans
> and preoccupations. The poet himself, meanwhile, uses the
> accumulating force of these various Oresteias to deceive,
> mislead, frighten and intrigue his audience.

What is important for our general understanding of the use of stories in Homer is that although each version or telling of the tale functions within its context, they are not quite made-up stories or variants in opposition to a single truth.

Let us briefly see how versions of the same tale change and how each fits in its context. In Book 1 of the *Odyssey*, Athena offers advice to Telemachus. She presents the tale of Agamemnon's death as an example everyone should know, as recollected truth that should guide Telemachus' future behaviour ('you too, be valiant', 1.301–2). While Agamemnon is away, Aegisthus devises 'woeful/bitter work' (3.303) and slays him upon his return, but after 8 years, Orestes appears and slays his father's killer (3.307). The analogy between Orestes' story in the past and Telemachus' situation in the present is useful. In both cases, outsiders pose a threat to the father's rightful place within the marital union and they must be stopped. But the analogy has to be managed carefully. Athena must fashion her tale with only specific goals in mind. Unlike Agamemnon's wife and Orestes' mother Clytemnestra, Penelope, Odysseus' wife and Telemachus' mother, is a paragon of fidelity and faithfulness. If Athena, speaking to Telemachus, were to lay the blame of Agamemnon's death on Clytemnestra, the mother of the 'avenger', and if this story were to serve as the model for action and to be repeated in Odysseus' house, Telemachus might get the wrong idea. Would he then try to kill his mother Penelope? It is hardly surprising that in this version, Athena places the blame of Agamemnon's death squarely on Aegisthus and leaves Clytemnestra entirely out of the tale.

A different version of this narrative appears later in the *Odyssey* (11.409–34), when the ghost of Agamemnon tells Odysseus how he died. Here blame is placed a little more clearly with Clytemnestra. Agamemnon says (409–10):

Aegisthus planned death and doom for me
He, with my destructive [*oulomenêi*] wife, called me to his
house and killed me.

Clytemnestra is described as 'destructive/accursed'. The poet uses exactly the same word which also describes the wrath of Achilles at the beginning of the *Iliad* (1.2). Clytemnestra, like the wrath, is a 'thematic' cause of events of epic proportions.

The ghost of Agamemnon adds (421–2):

I heard the most piteous cry of Priam's daughter,
Cassandra, whom scheming Clytemnestra killed.

In this version, Clytemnestra is a murderous villain. The story's moral emphasis has changed for the benefit of its immediate situation and also in order to build up tension for future action within the plot of the *Odyssey*. Odysseus must reach the shores of his home in Ithaca not knowing if, like Agamemnon, he too will die at the hands of a destructive wife. The *Odyssey*, let us add, takes a particularly complex view of a wife's fidelity and more generally of the question of scheming, truth and survival. Like her husband, Penelope is a wily character. Like Odysseus, she uses her tricks in order overcome the many perils of her world. Yet her cunningness also gives her a potentially dangerous power. The whole point, however, is that, unlike Clytemnestra, Penelope remains true to the hero of the *Odyssey*.

The message of these and other changing versions of the narrative is that stories belong in the moment of the telling, where they must be managed carefully. Repetition is a useful device, but what in a scientific world we would call 'exact repetition', a reappearance of the past, could, in the world of traditional heroic epic, lead to disaster and to consequences that are 'untrue' to the ethical values of the narrative and to the events of the plot at large. Each moment of acting and telling is informed by the models of the past, but is also unique because, paradoxically, only in such uniqueness can fidelity to the stories of the past be maintained. The *Odyssey*, and the *Iliad* too, as poems that effect the fame of their characters are dependent on this idea for their successful preservation of memory. Continuity through change is an important principle of traditional narrative in Homer.

Stories like the death of Agamemnon are often described in Homer as *muthos*. The Greek word is the origin of our modern word 'myth', but there are important differences between the two. As Richard Martin has shown in his influential work *The Language of Heroes*, in Homer, *muthos* denotes a unique type of 'speech-act', an utterance closely associated with the speaker of the words and 'indicating authority, performed at length, usually in public, with a focus on full attention to every detail' (1989: 12). *Muthos* in Homer refers to various types or genres of speech, but especially to stories recollected from memory – in other words, to stories from the past. Such *muthos* implies authority and power by the speaker (it is opposed, as Martin argues, to *epos*, which implies shorter, more 'ordinary' utterances, often accompanied by gestures. The emphasis in *epos* is on how it is perceived by the addressee. See 1989, esp. pp. 12, 21). Picking up on this discussion, Gregory Nagy has suggested that indeed in Homer's time, the word *muthos* carried a unique sense of authority. This earlier kind of Homeric 'myth' is, as Nagy says, 'special speech' in that it is 'a given society's way of affirming its own reality' (1996: 130). It is the myth of stories which Homeric characters tell each other and no less the myth of the *Iliad* and *Odyssey* which the singers of epic enact in performances that are precisely tailored to present moment, yet retain the truth and fidelity of the tradition as a whole.

Outlines and plot structures

The story of Orestes and other stories from the past of the Homeric heroes reveal important principles of truth and narration, but they are dotted elements within the larger narrative design of the *Iliad* and *Odyssey*. What, then, is that larger design? Each poem describes well-defined events along a distinct timeline: a dispute between kings, the deaths of heroes, adventures at sea, a journey home. Yet, the closer we look at the plots of *Iliad* and *Odyssey*, the more we realize that although they tell a simple tale, the figures of their long narratives refract in exuberant and not always fully controllable ways. As one recent scholar speaking of the *Iliad* rightly says, the poem is 'so vast as to defy ready comprehension' (Powell 2007: 65). The *Odyssey* is almost as large as the *Iliad*, and arguably the strands of its plot are more numerous and more diverse.

We begin, however, with the 'simple tale'. Formally speaking, the *Iliad* has not infrequently been seen as a well-structured narrative. It can be divided into three essential, interlocking sections, each comprising eight of the poem's 24 books. According to this division, the first section, Books 1–8, lays out the great themes of the poem against the backdrop of the Trojan War. These include the quarrel of Agamemnon and Achilles, Achilles' wrath and withdrawal from battle, the actions of Achilles' mother Thetis, themes of supplication and pity and Achilles' fate. The plot begins with Chryses, the Trojan priest of Apollo, who comes as a suppliant to the Greek camp, begging to ransom his daughter Chryseis. Chryseis is Agamemnon's captive prize, and he refuses to hand her over. Later, he is forced to do so, but seizes Achilles' captive and prize, Briseis, in her stead. The quarrel between these two heroes ensues, and Achilles, on advice from his divine mother Thetis (1.421–2), withdraws from the battlefield. Achilles' decision will mark his path between a long but unremarkable life and a short life of excellence that will carry with it imperishable fame.

This first part of the poem introduces the main Greek heroes, Achilles, Agamemnon, Menelaus, Odysseus, Ajax, Diomedes and the main character on the Trojan side including Menelaus' wife Helen and her abductor Paris, king Priam, the hero Aeneas and Hector, Priam's son and defender of Troy. The section contains important assembly scenes, broken truces and long descriptions of fighting between both mortal heroes and gods.

The middle part of the poem, Books 9–16, focuses on the immediate effects of the quarrel and on Achilles' wrath and withdrawal. This section deepens the resonance of major themes. Book 9 describes the 'Embassy', the long scene describing the meeting between Achilles and three comrades who have come to see him in his self-imposed seclusion and attempt to entice him to rejoin the fighting. Achilles refuses, but the speeches in this book outline important values, perspectives and states of mind. They not only lay out the codes of heroic action and thought in Homer but also challenge them. In the 'fighting books' that follow, the drama of Achilles' absence unfolds and the Greeks' position becomes more and more difficult. With Achilles refusing to fight, his comrade Patroclus sets out to help the Greeks, and heads for battle wearing Achilles' armour. Despite initial success, Patroclus is killed by Hector in Book 16.

The third and final part of the *Iliad*, containing Books 17–24, explores the fateful consequences of the previous sections and brings the *Iliad* to its climax and close. With Patroclus dead, Achilles must put aside is wrath and return to battle. He and Agamemnon are reconciled; their quarrel is resolved. Yet, seeking to avenge Patroclus, a new kind of frenzy takes hold of Achilles, and he is forced to re-confront his fate. His choice is precipitous death, which, however, is to occur beyond the end of the narrative of the *Iliad*. Much fighting among both heroes and gods follows Achilles' return to battle. The Homeric gods, often deeply affected by the death of their mortal favourites, cannot themselves die. For gods, the consequences of heroic excellence are limited. The brevity and fragility of mortal life, highlighted by the constant interaction between men and the immortal gods, as well as by the semi-divine parentage of heroes, is a constant background to all action in the poem. Achilles pursues Hector and, with the help of the gods, slays him. The *Iliad* concludes, as it begins, with a scene of supplication. Priam, Hector's father, comes to the Greek camp, meets Achilles, offers ransom and begs for the return of his son's corpse. A brief moment of communion passes between Achilles and Priam, and Achilles grants the suppliant's wish. Hector's mother Hecuba, his wife Andromache and Helen each offers a speech of mourning as the Trojans bury Hector.

The arrangement of events is the essence of the plot. It was, of course, also the main concern for Aristotle in the *Poetics*, antiquity's most prominent work of literary criticism. Well-constructed plots, Aristotle argued, contained a sequence of a beginning, middle and end linked by relations of cause and effect. A beginning is that 'which does not itself follow anything by causal necessity, but after which something naturally is or comes to be'. An end is that 'which itself naturally follows some other thing, either by necessity, or as a rule, but has nothing following it'. A middle is that 'which follows something as some other thing follows it' (*Poetics* section VII, 1450b.26–31).[1] In the *Poetics*, Aristotle describes the overall movement of such plots in terms of 'complication' (or 'binding', in Greek *dêsis*) of the themes, followed by their 'resolution' (in Greek *lysis*; 1455b.24–32). And indeed, it is not difficult to describe the *Iliad*'s plot in this manner. The poem first 'complicates' emotions, social relations and hierarchies as well as conceptions of the self and the world. It brings these themes to a point (or points) of crisis, and finally winds its way towards a resolution. We can speak of the quarrel that begins and ends, of the rise and subsidence of wrath, of a pattern of 'withdrawal and return' in Achilles' actions or, with a change of perspective, for example, of the tragedy of Hector or indeed of the tragedy of Achilles, which can be understood in Aristotelian terms. We can point to the correspondences between Agamemnon's rejection of Chryses' supplication in the first book of the poem and Achilles acceptance of Priam's supplication in the last book, and so on.

Yet the plot of the *Iliad* cannot simply be reduced to such an elegant form. Aristotle himself was among the first to draw our attention to the complexity of epic plots.

---

[1] The letters which follow the section numbers refer to the standard pagination ('Bekker numbers', following this scholar's edition) for the works of Aristotle.

He famously says (*Poetics*, 1450b.34–51a.6):

A beautiful object, whether it be a living organism or any whole composed of parts, must not only have an orderly arrangement of parts, but must also be of a certain magnitude; for beauty depends on magnitude and order. Hence a very small animal organism cannot be beautiful; for the view of it is confused, the object being seen in an almost imperceptible moment of time. Nor again, can one of vast size be beautiful; for as the eye cannot take it all in at once, the unity and sense of the whole is lost for the spectator . . . As, therefore, in the case of animate bodies and organisms a certain magnitude is necessary . . . so in the plot, a certain length is necessary, and a length which can be easily embraced by the memory.

Proper magnitude is a central concern for Aristotle. Of course, his main object of study in the *Poetics* is tragedy. Epic poetry, he realized, could not be judged by the same standards, if only because of its greater length. Sophocles' *Oedipus the King*, for example, is a long play, but at 1,530 verses, it is only one-tenth the size of the *Iliad*, which contains 15,693 verses (and almost one-twentieth the size of the *Iliad* and *Odyssey* combined!). Equally important is the inherent arrangement of events within the plot. Tragedy, Aristotle suggested, should have a single action and it should confine its action, as much as possible, to a single revolution of the sun. The *Iliad* and epic, he knew, extended over many days and in a deeper sense were 'not bound by limits of time' (*Poetics* 1449b.14). And 'epic structure' as he says, contains 'a multiplicity of plots' (1456a.10–19).

Is the *Iliad* really 'not bound by limits of time'? As we have already noted briefly, counting each rise of day and each sunset marked in the text and paying close attention to the passage of 'real time' in the plot, we find that the poem's events cover just 51 days of action during the final year of a war that lasted (as Homeric poetry itself tells us) 10 whole years. The *Odyssey*'s time counted in a similar way spans just 41 days in a period that covers 10 years of war and 10 years of wandering. Furthermore, the beginning of the *Iliad* is not independent of events that precede it. It certainly follows the Judgement of Paris and the abduction of Helen by 'causal necessity', as Aristotle would say. These earlier events are not told in the poem, but without them, the plot of the *Iliad* and the Trojan War would not exist. The beginning of the *Iliad*, then, is not quite an Aristotelian beginning, but rather, as Horace noted, a beginning *in medias res*, 'in the midst of things' (*Ars Poetica* 148). One modern critic extends this idea: 'the epic has no simple beginning; there is a range of possibilities which remain problematic' (Lynn-Georg 1988: 39).

The end of the *Iliad* is likewise 'un-Aristotelian' and occurs in the midst of things. The name *Iliad* suggests that this is the story of *Ilium*, the city of Troy, but the poem concludes well before the fall of Troy, an event which is not narrated in the *Iliad*. And even though it focuses on the wrath of the Achilles, the poem is not called the *Achilleid*.

The *Odyssey*, which is named after its hero, displays the comparable discrepancies. It too is not simply a snapshot of 41 days in the life of one man. Despite their immense size on the one hand, and the limited 'real-time' span of their plots on the other, both the *Iliad* and *Odyssey* are just parts of larger stories. These are stories which other, later and often shorter epic poems like the *Cypria*, the *Thebais*, the *Little Iliad*, the *Returns*, and perhaps even such poems as Virgil's *Aeneid* try to complete. Aristotle's suggestion that epic is 'not bound by time' and contains 'a multiplicity' of plots is not wrong.

Like the *Iliad*, the *Odyssey* is, in essence, a simple tale: As already Aristotle says, it can 'be stated briefly' (*Poetics* XVII, 1455b.17–23):

> A certain man is absent from home for many years; he is jealously watched by Poseidon, and left desolate. Meanwhile his home is in a wretched plight – suitors are wasting his substance and plotting against his son. At length, tempest-tossed, he himself arrives; he makes certain persons acquainted with him; he attacks the suitors with his own hand, and is himself preserved while he destroys them. This is the essence of the plot; the rest is episode.

This summary may be the essence of the plot, but it is not how events are presented in the actual narrative of the *Odyssey*, which is far more fractured and complex.

The *Odyssey*, as Longinus says, is 'a sort of epilogue to the *Iliad*'. Yet, if in this poem, we were expecting to go back and tie up all *Iliad*'s 'loose ends', we will, for the most part, be disappointed. The events of the *Odyssey* do occur after the events of the *Iliad*, of course, and knowledge of the fall of Troy constantly resonates in the background of the *Odyssey*. Indeed, even some events *not* told in the *Iliad* are not forgotten. Yet the *Odyssey* brings about a great change. At the end of the *Iliad*, Menelaus and Helen are still separated, he in the Greek camp, she behind the walls of Troy. When we reach the *Odyssey*, the two are back in Sparta, reunited in apparent conjugal harmony. At the end of the *Iliad*, Achilles, Agamemnon, Ajax and many other heroes are still alive and fighting. When they appear in the *Odyssey*, they are dead spirits in the underworld. We the audience/readers have only 'blinked' for an instant as we move from the last line of the *Iliad* to the first line of the *Odyssey*. Yet, in this brief moment of transition, the scene, the tone, the flow of time, the characters, some of their values and even some facts of life and death have changed. The main figures of the *Odyssey* are neither Iliadic warriors like Achilles, Patroclus, Hector or Agamemnon, nor are they quite 'dead-men-walking'. The *Odyssey*'s heroes are survivors. Odysseus suffers, but he is alive. The hero Nestor, already an old man in the *Iliad*, lives on happily. Menelaus and Helen live in Sparta and are busy with the marriage of their children – the next generation. Odysseus' son Telemachus escapes a plot by the suitors to kill him and comes of age. Laertes, Odysseus' old father, lives to see the return of his son from the war. The women of the *Odyssey*, Calypso, Circe, Nausicaa, queen Arete, Helen and above all Penelope, are likewise different from the women of the *Iliad*. Although many of them experience loss, they are much more active and self-willed (see further below, Chapter 8).

Comparing the two poems, Longinus (*On the Sublime* 9.13–14) says:

> . . . whereas in the *Iliad* which was written when [Homer's] genius was in its prime the whole structure of the poem is founded on action and struggle, in the *Odyssey* he [Homer] generally prefers the narrative style, which is proper to old age.

He explains:

> . . . Homer in his *Odyssey* may be compared to the setting sun: he is still as great as ever, but he has lost his fervent heat. The

strain is now pitched to a lower key than in the 'Tale of Troy divine': we begin to miss that high and equable sublimity which never flags or sinks . . . In saying this I am not forgetting the fine storm-pieces in the *Odyssey*, the story of the Cyclops, and other striking passages.

Whether the *Odyssey* really is a less sublime output of Homer's old age as Longinus suggests, *On the Sublime* rightly notes the more-complex nature and indeed the episodic structure of the *Odyssey*.

The first four books of the poem, traditionally known as the *Telemachy*, describe 'Odysseus' absence' and focus on Telemachus and Penelope. Books 1 and 2 describe how, with the assistance of Athena in disguise, Telemachus – seeking news of his father – prepares for a sea voyage. Over the next two books, he visits Nestor in Pylos and, joined by Nestor's son Pisistratus, visits Menelaus and Helen in Sparta. In Book 4, the last book of this section, the scene shifts back to Ithaca, to Penelope and to the suitors, who are planning to ambush Telemachus upon his return. The scene changes again in Book 5 where, for the first time, we meet Odysseus, who is stranded in the island of the Nymph Calypso, pining for his home and his wife. Towards the end of the book, he sets sail and is shipwrecked on the shores of the mythical Phaeacians. He meets the young princess Nausicaa and seeks the Phaeacians' help in getting home. Before they do so, however, the *Odyssey* takes a large detour into the past. In Books 9–12, known collectively as the *Apologue*, Odysseus tells the Phaeacians of his adventures over the 10 years of his wanderings – his encounters with the Cyclops, his stay in the island of the witch Circe, his visit to the underworld, the loss at sea of all of his companions and finally, his arrival on Calypso's island. The Phaeacians ferry Odysseus home and he reaches Ithaca in Book 13. He meets Athena, who will help him disguise himself and plan his revenge, and is reunited, first with his loyal swineherd Eumaius in Book 14, then with his son Telemachus, who has managed to avoid the suitor's ambush. In Book 17, Odysseus arrives in the town. He meets the suitors, and, while in disguise, encounters their arrogance. He meets Penelope, but does not disclose his identity. The decisive scene comes in Book 21, during the archery contest set up by Penelope to determine who of the suitors shall marry her. Odysseus picks up the bow, proves himself in the contest, casts off the rags of his disguise, slaughters the suitors and, in an interview which some see as the climax of the poem in Book 23, is finally recognized by Penelope as the two are reunited. The final book of the poem describes the ghosts of the suitors in the underworld and the reunion of Odysseus with his father Laertes.

What, then, is the design of this complex and varied narrative? A balanced tripartite division like the *Iliad*'s does not fit the *Odyssey*. One suggestion has been to view the poem in tetrads or groups of four books (see, e.g. Tracy 1990): the Telemachy in Books 1–4; Odysseus' adventures in Books 6–8; his stories to the Phaeacians in the *Apologue* in Books 9–12; Odysseus in Ithaca in Books 13–16; events in the palace – Books 17–20 and finally, Odysseus' triumph, his reunion with Penelope, and the conclusion of the poem in Books 21–24. This division works well in some tetrads, but not in all. For example, grouping Books 5–8 together can seem a little forced. These books bind Odysseus' last experience of wandering and wilderness on the island of Calypso and his first experience within the world of mortal civilization among the Phaeacians. Cutting into the middle of this section, then, is nothing less than Odysseus' symbolic rebirth (see 6.1ff.), a movement from death to life, from a timeless divine existence to mortal existence, and the re-emergence of an isolated individual into the social sphere. If these four books form a unit, they are a unit made of two diametrically opposite worlds.

Some attempts to trace the design of the *Odyssey* sensibly do away with the formal symmetry of parts with equal numbers of books (book divisions in Homer are in any case a relatively late phenomenon, dating probably not earlier than the Hellenistic period). Instead, we find suggestions of more organic ordering: Events in Ithaca before Odysseus' return form one part of the narrative (Books 1–2); Telemachus' journey another (Books 3–4); Odysseus and Calypso are described in the next section (Book 5); Odysseus and the Phaeacians (Books 6–12) and finally, Odysseus in Ithaca (Books 13–24) conclude the arrangement (Latacz 1998). Perhaps the only balanced structural division in the poem is the one that splits the poem more or less down the middle. As Oliver Taplin, for example, suggests (1992: 19):

> . . . the *Odyssey* is, at a fundamental level, divided into two parts. Until 13.92 the poem has told of the adventures of many

years and all of the 'real' and 'fantasy' world. From 13.93 it is set on Ithaca, mostly in Odysseus' house, and it takes up only six days of narrative time.

Whichever way we divide the *Odyssey*, its overall design is clearly of a different type from the *Iliad*'s. Likewise, the end of the *Odyssey*, in contrast to the end of the *Iliad*, which leaves the crucial event of the fall of Troy unspoken, provides us with a strong sense of closure. By the last words of the poem, Odysseus' homecoming is complete. He is back as the king of the island of Ithaca, husband to Penelope, father to Telemachus and son to Laertes. The end of the poem binds together the poem's many common themes: the return, both 'outer', as Odysseus traverses geographic boundaries, and 'inner', as Odysseus regains his identity and place at home and in society; further themes include survival, the one against the many, recognition and reunion, wit, truth and lies, and storytelling and song. And yet, as the poem's complex arrangement and its essential theme of 'return' suggest, Odysseus' tale, especially its end, which is so complete, also seems to 'go back' (return . . .) to a beginning. The *Odyssey* promises more journeys for its hero. This promise is expressed in Teiresias' words to Odysseus in the underworld in Book 11; and at least one verse from those prophetic words (11.134), while predicting Odysseus' death (the 'real end'), also seems to allude to another epic poem, the *Telegony*, and to Odysseus' accidental demise at the hands of his own son Telegonus. Indeed, already at the beginning of the *Odyssey*, the narrator concludes his proem by saying 'Of these things, goddess, daughter of Zeus, beginning where you will [*tôn hamothen g*' 1.10], tell us too.'

In antiquity, Aristotle suggested that many episodic elements in epic are 'inherent to their nature' (*Poetics* 1455b.13 – the Greek word used is *oikeia*), but he ultimately suggests that the structure of epic plots is too diverse to be judged by the standards of unity in tragedy (which he prefers of course). Modern critic Joachim Latacz, although he sees deep meaning in the *Odyssey*, says of its composer (1998: 35): 'It seems as though this poet has no definite plan.' Some modern scholars have argued that the *Odyssey*'s looseness of structure should be corrected, that elements which offend the unity of the plot should be erased from the text as inorganic intrusions. Others, however, have suggested that digressive material embodies precisely 'the substance of the narrative' and have stressed the differences between, for example, oral poetics and literate unity, between cumulative and hierarchical stylistic and linguistic principles: digressions and other features closely associated with oral culture, on their own or in conjunction with elements of formal order, are, in fact 'rich with meaning' (Martin 2000: 49). Whichever way we look at the structure of the *Odyssey*, whether as an accident of historical accumulation or as the result of a principle of poetics, we are faced with a diversity that marks both the poem as we have it and its poetic tradition.

CHAPTER SIX

The *Iliad*

The withdrawal of Achilles, prizes and fame

Having briefly looked at the overall structure of the poems, we need to consider some details of their themes and qualities as they appear, as the narrator wished them to be told, in the order of the plot. What follows, we must stress, is not a detailed commentary, but a discussion of key points and ideas as they appear in their traditional sequence.

The first third of the *Iliad*, Books 1–8, covers a period of 25 days in the ninth and penultimate year of the Trojan War (cf. 2.295). Following the proem, events begin, we recall, as Chryses, the Trojan priest of Apollo, comes to the Greek camp to plead for the return of his daughter, Chryseis (1.12ff.), who is Agamemnon's captive and his share in the spoils of war. Agamemnon, a harsh and inflexible leader, refuses to give her back and Apollo sends upon the Greeks a plague (1.44ff.) that rages for nine days. On the tenth day (1.54), Achilles summons the assembly. He and Agamemnon exchange heated words, but Agamemnon is eventually forced to release Chryseis (1.116ff). Unable to lose face, he seeks a replacement: 'prepare another prize for me, so that I should not be the only one among the Argives who is without a prize, for that would not be appropriate' (1.118–19), and takes Briseis, Achilles' prize and captive woman. The outraged Achilles decides to withdraw from battle and the *Iliad*'s thematic quarrel is launched.

There is a skilful build-up of emotion here, as the two heroes ratchet up their hostility towards each other. Achilles calls Agamemnon 'a man clothed in shamelessness, of a crafty and covetous mind' (1.149). Agamemnon returns the favour and says 'by all means, run away if your heart bids you so, I will not plead with you to stay for my sake. I have with me others who will do me honour' (1.173–5). Yet we are also dealing with a larger moment of crisis of values and the questioning of a world system. Prizes, and captive women in particular, are essential 'capital' in Homer's symbolic economy and world order: The prize is a material reflection of the hero's valour among his peers and, in a sense, it also embodies the status of the hero. We are dealing, in other words, with the basic codes of exchange, reciprocity, hierarchy and social order.

The quarrel between Agamemnon and Achilles is a single event, triggered by specific actions. Yet it is also an expression of persistent personal and social tensions and it is, in this sense, a conflict built into the structure of Homeric society. Agamemnon is a stern leader and the Greek overlord. Achilles is a hero whose individual excellence singles him out. He is *aristos Achaeôn*, 'the best of the Achaeans'. One hero holds the greatest power by virtue of his social standing. The other's source of power is his own superior martial prowess. Competition and eventual clash are part of their relative characterizations in a world in which the absence of equilibrium and the pursuit of excellence (*arêtê*) are a constant.

The importance of the prize goes further still. Without the symbols of status, a hero would not be singled out among his peers and he may thus also not become the subject of song. Without song, the mortal hero's fame would be lost in time after his death, and the hero himself would be condemned to remain one of the 'wretched mortals'. The quarrel between Agamemnon and Achilles is thus over the body of a woman, over a powerful symbol of exchange and social hierarchy, over inherent tensions in the social structure of the world of the *Iliad* and ultimately also about existential and poetic first principles. This, then, is the inaugural moment of the quarrel of Achilles and Agamemnon.

Although the indignant Achilles at first thinks of killing his opponent, Athena intervenes (1.194ff., see our comments earlier, too) and Achilles eventually allows Agamemnon to take Briseis (1.318ff.). He then meets his mother, the nymph Thetis, and tells her of his grief (1.384ff.), and she advises him to stay by the ships and withdraw from battle (1.421–2). Since the beginning of the quarrel, 11 days have now passed (1.477). Several more days pass rapidly in only a few verses, as Chryseis is taken back to her father and Achilles' anger mounts. Here, we see the fluidity of Homer's time. It is not homogenous empty time, but a flexible narrative element that contracts and stretches according to need and helps the narrator assert his response to mortal finitude.

On the twelfth day (1.493, since the meeting of Achilles and Thetis, cf. 1.425), 21 days into the narrative events, Thetis pleads with Zeus to strengthen the Trojans, so that they have the upper hand and the Achaians give honour to her son. The poem weaves an intricate relationship between Achilles and Thetis – a combination of intimate filial and maternal emotions, powerful anger and, especially on the divine Thetis' part, a sense of ultimate helplessness in the face of her mortal son's fate (on Thetis, see especially Slatkin 1991). Zeus agrees to Thetis' request (1.518ff.), although it brings him into conflict with his wife, Hera (1.536ff.). There is an important point here. The *Iliad*, and epic in general, are large poetic creations that bear public, indeed 'cosmic' meanings, yet their narratives are often carried forward through intimate personal relations: a husband and wife, not only Zeus and Hera, but of course Menelaus and Helen too, a mother and son, and elsewhere fathers and sons, and individual enemies, allies and friends, such as Achilles and Patroclus.

In Book 2, the Greeks hold another assembly. The *Iliad*'s martial narrative is studded throughout with assembly scenes, and more generally, with verbal exchanges and speeches, which take up about half of the total number of lines in the poem. Talking is a surprisingly frequent activity in the *Iliad*, considering that the poem is at heart a narrative of fighting. The emphasis on speech nevertheless makes sense as a central element in a poem that, as we keep stressing, self-consciously styles itself as a mechanism for preserving fleeting mortal action in words. To the Greeks, the divide between 'word' (*logos*) and 'deed' (*ergon*) has always been important. In the *Iliad*, the two domains are inextricable. Heroes, and above all Achilles, are not only great warriors, but great speakers too. Social status is not only manifest in leadership in battle, but also in summoning assemblies and in leadership in speech. Such speech is often prominently marked. Some of the most distinct phrases in both the *Iliad* and *Odyssey* are the lines introducing a character's speech, such as 'And to him/her said in reply . . .' (*ton' d'apameibomenos prosephê* . . .), followed by the name of a hero or a god – Achilles, Odysseus, Agamemnon, Diomedes, Hector, Ajax, Menelaus, Eumaius, Zeus, Athena, Iris, Aphrodite and more (for speech introductions, see Holoka 1983, Edwards 1987 and 1992, Beck 2005).

Zeus, acting on Thetis' pleas, sends a dream to Agamemnon, which prompts him to test the Greeks in a section of the narrative suitably called the 'testing' or *diapeira*: On the twenty-second day (2.48) of the *Iliad*'s plot events, Agamemnon summons the Greek host and, hoping to spur them on by negative suggestion, proposes that the armies go home. Catastrophe nearly strikes. Thersites, a man whose words have no 'structure and order' (*akosma* 2.213), 'the ugliest/most shameful [*aischistos*] man who came to Troy' (1.216), and an antithesis to the great heroes, incites the armies against Agamemnon. Alarmingly, his words, set in hexameters that are as structured and elegant as those of Achilles and the narrator himself, nearly take effect. Thersites is nevertheless subdued by a sharp response and a blow from Odysseus (2.243ff.). Aristocratic order is restored to the Greek camp, after which the leaders, ships and contingents of the Greeks are named and counted in the Catalogue of Ships (2.484–877), followed by a shorter Catalogue of Trojans. The violent action and powerful emotions that characterize the rest of the poem are not present in this 'factual' poetic list, but we must remember that for the ancients, Homer was rarely mere entertainment. We have already seen how the Catalogue, with its many named references creates the expectation of historical and geographic reality. We have also seen how, through the appeal to the Muses in the invocation that proceeds the Catalogue, Homer's unique 'truthfulness' and authority are invoked. The Catalogue, whatever its independent poetic merits, projects its 'facticity' onto the rest of the poem. The truth of the Catalogue is the truth of the wrath of Achilles and the *Iliad* as a whole (for the Catalogue, see Simpson and Lazenby 1970, Kirk 1985–1993, Latacz 2004, Dickinson 2007).

In Book 3 of the *Iliad*, a possible solution to the conflict over Troy and Helen seems to emerge, prematurely, of course. It is merely one of the foils of the plot. A truce is agreed between the Greeks and the Trojans. Menelaus, Helen's husband, and Paris, her abductor, are to fight in single combat which will determine the outcome of the war. We, the readers of the book, like modern cinema audiences, know that this will come to no effect – 21 books of the *Iliad* are yet to unfold. Ancient audiences of the poem also knew that this is not how the story ends. Yet in oral-traditional performances, the question is not 'what will happen in the end?' In the end, Troy must fall. Oral tradition, inherently fluid as it is, contains absolute narrative certainties, indeed so certain that they are left almost entirely unsung in both the *Iliad* and *Odyssey*. The question, rather, is 'what will happen before we get to the end, and how will we get there?'

Just before the duel between Menelaus and Paris, Helen and Priam view the Greek heroes from the walls of Troy in a scene known as the *Teichoskopia* (literally, 'the observation from the walls', 3.121ff.). Helen names the heroes for king Priam, and of course for us, the audience and readers. Shortly afterwards, the duel takes place (3.324ff.). It is an unequal match and Paris has to be rescued by Aphrodite (and whisked away to Helen's bedroom). Menelaus, the cuckold husband, is frustrated in his hope of revenge, the truce is broken and battle begins (Book 4). These events, and broadly the whole of this first section of the *Iliad*, provide a mapping of the heroes and heroic sensibilities as the main figures are pitched one against the other, placed side by side, and identified.

The most explicit measure of a hero is his martial excellence. We get a detailed view in Book 5, a major fighting book which highlights the exploits of the Greek hero Diomedes. The book begins 'Now Pallas Athena gave Diomedes son of Tydeus // courage and daring, so that he might distinguish himself among all // the Argives, and win great fame [*kleos*]' (5.1–3). As often in Homer, simple words like the ones in these opening lines also embody essential principles of heroic epic. Gods and mortals often interact in Homer. Some, like Achilles or Aeneas, boast divine parentage. Others like Diomedes, Paris (rescued by Aphrodite in Book 3) or Odysseus (helped by Athena) enjoy the patronage of gods, who often influence mortals and incite them to action. The nature of these relationships and their implication has always intrigued students of Homer. Earlier scholars such as Bruno Snell, Arthur Adkins and others had argued that representations of divine influence attest to an early 'underdeveloped' stage in the history of human consciousness, subjectivity and society in general (Snell's book is called, not surprisingly, *The Discovery of the Mind*), when motivation was not yet individualized and internalized and was thus represented in the form of external agency and influence of the divine (see Snell 1953, Adkins 1960). More recent scholars like Bernard Williams have argued against such 'progressivist' claims and have shown that aspects of the self we associate with modernity can also be identified in the Homeric poems. These scholars refused to reduce Homeric heroes to the state of passive actors and have shown how decisions, choices and responsibility can, in fact, be actively associated with the hero's cognition and thought (Williams 1993, Gill 1996). Whatever our view of the question of historical consciousness and the representation of subjectivity and the self, what is beyond doubt is that gods and 'godlike' heroes inhabit Homer's world together. The two groups maintain strong links and many similarities. These similarities, however, only underscore the essential difference between the immortal gods and heroes' condition of mortality (see further in Chapter 9, below).

In the opening line of Book 5, Athena gives Diomedes courage, not merely so that he should distinguish himself in battle, but, significantly, that he should win fame (*kleos*). The importance of fame is by now familiar to us as one of Homer's basic poetic themes. By performing great martial deeds, by gaining fame and, ultimately, through a narrative in poetry, Diomedes will draw nearer to immortality which he cannot otherwise obtain. The literal words of the *Iliad*, for example, the line we are discussing, since they are precisely words of fame that celebrate a hero's martial excellence and are available for audiences and readers, provide 'performative' validation (i.e. validation that occurs through the utterance or 'performance' of the words) of the poem's stated principles.

Book 5 is a long book that extends for more than 900 lines and describes heroic combat in detail. We see many heroes, but above all Diomedes, who fights, sometimes from his chariot, but often in single combat, the most common mode of warfare for epic heroes. Here violence and death, through precisely chosen words, are elevated to the level of sublime poetry. A spear strikes one hero 'in the chest between the nipples' (5.19), another 'between the shoulders' and rushes right through his body (5.41); one man is struck 'through the right buttock' and the spearhead drives 'under the bone and into the bladder' (5.66–7) and another is struck 'behind the head at the tendon . . . straight through the teeth and under the tongue' (5.73–4) while yet another's arm is cut clean off and 'falls bleeding to the ground' (5.82). As in the Catalogue, these dense, almost clinical descriptions, although they are not always anatomically correct, serve to underscore the facticity of the poems, as if confirming that Muses really 'were there', that they do 'know everything' and have passed it on to the singer. It is, as the text says, the *'right* buttock' that was hit. This detail creates a meticulously precise image. And yet, these verses are not acts of factual reportage or detached aestheticism. They do not gloss over human suffering and the horrors of death. Often, even otherwise obscure victims, who seem to be included in the poem only so that we can witness the moment of their death, are given brief, pathetic 'biographies' (see Griffin 1980): Hypsenor, killed by Eurypilus, was, we are told, the son of 'high-hearted Dolopion, who was made Skamandros' priest and was honoured throughout the land like a god' (5.77). The dead warrior is the son of a father who will grieve for him. The *Iliad* is a poem of heroes and of war, but the 'non-combatants', their pain and their loss are also present in the narrative. The father–son relationship is of particular importance to the thematics of the *Iliad*. An old father mourning the death of a young son is one of the pivotal and most poignant images of the poem. Such mourning, like the act of war itself, turns the natural order of human life on its head.

All of the *Iliad*'s battles so far take place on the twenty-second day of the plot. It is the first day of fighting and a very long day. It begins in Book 2 and runs on to the middle of Book 7. In the midst of this fighting sequence, in Book 6, we see one particularly interesting encounter, between Diomedes and the Trojan hero Glaucus (6.1–236). The two are enemies fighting on opposite sides. Yet, when they meet, through stories of the past which they tell each other, they learn that they are also bound by ties of guest-friendship (*xenia* – one of the most fundamental ritualized relationships in Greek antiquity. The word *xenos* means 'guest', 'host' and 'stranger'. See Herman 1987). Glaucus tells Diomedes about his ancestor Bellerophon, how through spiteful intrigue Bellerophon was made to carry with him secret 'painful/destructive signs' (*sêmata lygra* 6.168 – the only reference in Homer to visual signs that may be a form of writing) that order his own death, and how he only narrowly escapes. Diomedes realizes that his own ancestor had once entertained Bellerophon as a host. The two heroes do not fight, and instead exchange armour as a sign of friendship. Strangely, Glaucus hands over his gold armour in return for Diomedes' bronze armour. It is an unequal exchange: 'Zeus', says the poet, 'took away Glaucus' wits' (6.234). Elsewhere, the Homeric world seems to rest on relations of reciprocity and symmetrical exchange. Yet, as in this scene, as indeed in a much larger sense in the opening quarrel of the poem, we realize that good order and social equilibrium are precarious states, underneath whose surface potential violence always lurks.

The day's fighting continues in Book 6, yet in this book, we are also offered a glimpse of domestic life. We see Hector, before he heads into battle, in a scene with his mother Hecuba (237–311), with his brother Paris and with Helen (312–69), and finally, with his wife Andromache and young son Astyanax (370–502). Domestic narratives involving mortals are rare in the *Iliad* (see, e.g. the scene between Achilles and Thetis – Thetis herself is an immortal, of course). When they do occur, they are marked by sombre tones and a sense of urgency and commitment which contrasts sharply with domestic scenes among the gods. The gods cannot die. Their actions bear no final consequence and their interactions among themselves are often tinged with comic streaks.

In the last of Hector's domestic vignettes, Andromache begs her husband not to leave the city walls and not to make her a widow (6.429–31). Hector tries to comfort and reassure her and, shortly afterwards, attempts to embrace his son. The boy, however, recoils in fear at his father's bronze helmet and its terrible horse-hair crest (6.466–70). It is a singular light-hearted moment that also highlights the mournful underlying tones of the scene and its tragic forebodings. Hector will die. Andromache will become a widow. Astyanax, as Andromache herself presages, will be thrown from the top of Troy's walls and killed after the fall of the city (*Iliad* 24.726–38, also mentioned in an extant fragment from the *Little Iliad*).

These and many other narrative sequences carry with them the poem's preoccupation with mortality, with the fate of Troy and with other important themes. However, as Joachim Latacz, for example, in his useful introduction to Homer observes, they seem only indirectly associated with the story of the 'wrath of Achilles'. Latacz rightly points out that the story of Achilles does not encompass the entire *Iliad* (1998: 121). The poem as we have it is 'larger' than its theme, just as the poem's title, *Iliad*, 'the song of

Ilium', is 'larger' than the poem itself. Homeric tradition thus seems to declare that the monumental *Iliad* as we have it, canonical and vast, intact and complete, is still only a 'fragment', a part of the true larger whole. To cover the story in its entirety, we must turn back to such events as the 'Judgement of Paris' (only briefly mentioned at the very end of the *Iliad*. See 24.25–30), to the story of the sacrifice of Iphigenia, of which there is no mention in the *Iliad* (in 9.145, a living daughter named Iphianassa is mentioned. We have discussed the relation between myth and variant above), to mythological traditions about the birth of Achilles and more. To find versions of these narratives, we must look, in our extant tradition, into a wide range of post-Homeric sources, to the *Epic Cycle*, to Herodotus and Pindar, to Greek tragedy and to various later summaries such as Apollodorus' *Bibliotheca*, Proclus' *Chrestomathia* and more. Audiences and readers of the *Iliad* at various stages of the poem's long history will have been familiar with some versions or variants of these tales, some of which digress from the central theme of Achilles' wrath. Which? When? Where? We do not know what precise historical circumstances led to the *Iliad* being preserved as the particular segment of the larger narrative that it is. Even putting aside questions of the oral tradition, the digressive elements suggest to us that the *Iliad* is a poem that is only part of its own story, a story that cannot be described within the confines of strict thematic unity. The fact is that the poem's diverse narratives, even those that were suspected or rejected by scholars in antiquity and in modern times, have been passed on by the tradition (on 'digressions' in Homer, see Austin 1966, Scodel 2008). One critic recently described the *Iliad* as the 'eccentric centre of Western consciousness' (Lateiner 2004: 27). We, reading the basic lessons of the poem's plot, can perhaps use this paradoxical characterization more literally and extend its meaning: the compact narrative centre of 'wrath' in the *Iliad* aspires *outwards*, towards *Ilium*, and more generally, towards many other types of narrative and towards both the past and the future.

Book 6 ends with the parting of Andromache and Hector, as Hector and Paris head for the battlefield (503–529). Despite so many events and changes of scene, the twenty-second day of the plot, the first day of battle, has not yet come to an end. Battle narratives spill over to the beginning of Book 7 and continue until another truce between the warring sides is sought. It is only halfway through the book that we see the rise of a new dawn (7.381). Essential as this fluid approach to time is to the idea of ancient epic, it is also one of Homer's most 'modern' qualities. We often associate the flexible manipulation of time with contemporary literature such as James Joyce's *Ulysses* or Marcel Proust's *In Search of Lost Time* and with the fragmented experience of modernity. Many influential twentieth-century literary scholars (including Mikhail Bakhtin, Erich Auerbach, Georg Lukács and others) have attempted to contrast the dynamic modern experience of time, change and historical movement with what they regarded as the static perception of time in Homer and other early works. But as we have seen, and as many readers of Homer (including Bernard Williams, Michael Lynn-George, John Peradotto, Gregory Nagy and others) have shown, such exclusive historical characterizations are not supported by a close look at the text.

With the rise of a new dawn in Book 7, the previous day's dead are buried and the Greeks build a protective wall around their ships (7.433ff.). Following this, we see much fighting, which extends to Book 8. Midway through the book (8.470–6) Zeus finally decides to act on his promise to Thetis and to make the Greeks pay for Achilles' pain. Hector drives the Greeks further and further back. As the day ends and 'the bright light of the sun fell into Ocean drawing black night over the face of the earth' (8.485), the Greeks' difficult position becomes clear.

Achilles' dilemma and the death of Patroclus

From Book 2 of the first part of the *Iliad* to Book 9, Achilles is largely absent from the narrative. His withdrawal from battle puts the whole Trojan expedition in jeopardy and casts a dark shadow over the plot. Achilles' isolation and absence from action also bring the hero to reflection and eventually to a questioning of the very reasons for fighting and of the basic social and moral bonds of heroic society. The epic hero reflecting on his situation is also a means for the epic poem itself to look at its own position and values. Taking the principles of heroic action and fame to their limits, perhaps to excess, Achilles, the best of the Achaeans, learns what the hero can and cannot achieve.

The setting for this important reflection is the Embassy scene in Book 9. As we noted earlier, the Greeks decide to send three heroes, Achilles' old tutor Phoenix, the great warrior Ajax and the cunning Odysseus to plead with Achilles (the three, we noted in Chapter 3, are repeatedly referred to in the 'dual' form – a persistent critical problem of special significance for our understanding of traditional Homeric language). Various arguments are put forward by the ambassadors: The Argives are suffering, Hector's violence is raging, and Agamemnon, as Odysseus explains, has agreed to offer compensation several times over, to give back Briseis (9.273–4) and to give Achilles one of his daughters (Chrysothemis, Laodice or Iphianassa, 9.287) in marriage. Achilles' response is one of the key moments in the *Iliad*. His wrath and Thetis' advice have forced him out of the social sphere of his peers and into confrontation with everything he has known. In a famous passage, he points out that (*Iliad* 9.318–20)

> Fate is the same for a man who remains behind and even for one who fights with great force.
> We are all held in a single honour, the coward and the brave man.
> A man who has achieved nothing dies just like the one who has done much.

These are strong and puzzling words. If they express disappointment at a lack of past recognition – they also express complete and perhaps irrational disdain for Agamemnon's abundant current offer, which should make good precisely this lack. From this perspective, Achilles' response can only be explained as the mark of complete, blind fury which has broken the boundaries of sociality. Yet the exact words are also strangely 'rational'. They acknowledge that death is common to all and that life, once lost, cannot be regained. This leads Achilles with iron-clad reasoning to a startling thought: 'Why must Argives fight with Trojans? And why did the son of Atreus assemble the host and led it here? . . . Are the sons of Atreus alone among mortal men who love their wives?' (9.337ff.). Here we have a fundamental premise of social life – Achilles acknowledges a shared condition among men – but no less a radical challenge to the basic group identity of the Greeks, as distinguished from another group, the Trojans, without which the opposing camps described in the *Iliad* would not exist. Indeed, without discernible opposition between Greeks/Argives and Trojans, there would be no Trojan War and no *Iliad*. Achilles thus formulates some of the poem's fundamental dilemmas. He has been forced to consider the shared experience of all men and perhaps a deep truth about the value of human life. Paradoxically, these words also seem to suspend the foundations of his social ('shared') existence and his own position among his peers.

Achilles' speech is an extraordinary moment of recognition in Greek thought. It is the linchpin of his personal fate. He says (9.412–1):

If I remain here and fight over the city of the Trojans,
my homecoming [*nostos*] will be lost, but my fame [*kleos*]
    shall be
imperishable [*aphthiton estai*]
but if I return to my beloved homeland
my noble fame shall be lost, but my life shall be long
and the end of my days shall not come to me quickly.

Here too, Achilles' choice between noble fame and long life is more than a dilemma for heroes. At stake is *kleos* as the principle of epic song, which is placed in an opposite relation to life. Epic stipulates that the only mortal response to mortal finitude lies in an extension of life through fame, which is, however, only acquired in death, the very element of mortal finitude.

Achilles refuses to rejoin the Greek host and to fight. At first, he indicates his intention to go back home to Phthia. Towards the end of the Embassy scene, he relents, though only slightly. In response to Ajax' appeal, Achilles says he will fight, but only if Hector should reach the Greek ships and set fire to them (9.653). Within the *Iliad*'s own terms of reference, there seems to be no real solution to the basic dilemmas posed in this scene. If the *Iliad* were to endorse the views expressed by its greatest hero and his actions, which challenge some of the basic reasons for fighting, the poem would be suspending, not only many of practical codes of Homeric societal action, but more radically the poetic principle which underlines its claim to transcend mortality, its own raison d'être as song and thus its own 'voice'. If it were to reject Achilles' words and support the principles of martial excellence which brings fame, it would again be rejecting the voice of the greatest figure of its own creation, seemingly advocating its 'own' glory at the cost of a rapid lunge towards the death of its heroes. The poem, and we, its audience, would seem to be enjoying death for sport, like spectators in a gladiatorial show, like the Homeric gods watching their favourite heroes in battle. A poem like the *Iliad*, whose action culminates in profound scenes of pity, whose actions are an acknowledgement of human fragility, cannot choose this route. This dilemma comes to a head in the literal words of Achilles which, as influential studies have shown, overlap the language of the Homeric narrator (see Martin 1989: 223). How, then, can the narrator of the poem speak against 'himself'? The contradiction forces epic to reflection that has no easy solution. The result, we might say, is painful self-consciousness.

If there was a simple way to resolve this contradiction, the *Iliad* would not be the poem that it is. It would not have been an 'undying' formulation of conditions of being, but a statement of just one point of view. Part of the greatness of the *Iliad* is that although it offers a striking portrayal of the values of heroic life, it also always seems to offer more. Homer may be 'the Bible of the Greeks', but his views are not pronouncements of a closed set of beliefs (indeed, the Bible's pronouncements too are more than a closed set of beliefs). We are dealing with a poem that responds to the condition of mortality by creating a setting in which we as spectators can reflect on this condition and its values again and again.

Book 10 of the *Iliad* is dedicated to night-time reconnaissance missions by Diomedes and Odysseus on the Greek side, and by the Trojan Dolon, who is eventually captured and killed by the former two (hence, the scene is traditionally called the *Doloneia*). Dealing with 'unheroic' ambush scenes and night-time hostilities, this book has sometimes been regarded by critics with suspicion: Does it accord with the heroic ethos? Yet, as recent studies have convincingly shown, within the *Iliad*, a poem of frontal heroic confrontation, one can also trace an indirect 'poetics of ambush' (Dué and Ebbott 2010).

Sunrise in Book 11 (line 1), on the twenty-sixth day of events and what is only the third day of fighting, sees preparations for battle and a revival in the fortunes of the Greeks, including an *aristeia* of Agamemnon. But the Trojans and Hector in his own *aristeia* eventually have the upper hand and succeed in pushing the battle right up to the Greek ships (in Books 11–14, leading up to Book 15). This day too is a long fighting day which lasts for eight books, to Book 18. The Greeks get some respite in Book 14, when Hera seduces her husband Zeus and thus draws him away from the fighting. Here, as throughout the *Iliad*, gods' actions are inseparable from mortals'. But the contrast between the fatal consequences of heroic combat and the casual, sometimes comic everyday domesticity of divine actions, in this case of Hera and Zeus (Zeus falls asleep after lovemaking), underscores the tragedy of mortal conflict. In Book 15, Zeus awakes and, true to his role as the god 'whose strength is the greatest' (*hou te kratos esti megiston*) and whose 'will' is fulfilled through the poem's plot, he takes charge of events again and – as if he were the singer himself – plots out the narrative course of the *Iliad* and beyond: Hector will drive 'strengthless panic' into the Greeks and push them back; Patroclus will rise to their aid, but will be cut down by Hector; Achilles will kill Hector and the Greeks will fight on, 'until they capture tall Ilion, through the schemes of Athena' (15.71 – the 'schemes' are the wooden horse – not mentioned in the *Iliad* but described in the *Odyssey*).

This, indeed, is what happens. Hector's success, Achilles' withdrawal, and the plight of the Greeks at this midpoint in the *Iliad*'s plot prompt Patroclus to take pity on the Greeks and to ask Achilles to help (Book 16.1–45). Achilles refuses, but with Achilles' permission, Patroclus dons his companion's armour and heads for the fray. The poet now, at this fateful moment, calls upon the Muses to tell 'how fire first fell upon the Achaians' ships' (16.112–13). Advancing, Hector and the Trojans do indeed set one of the ships on fire, but after a long battle, Patroclus and the Myrmidons drive them back and scatter them. Following an *aristeia* (Book 16) in which Patroclus demonstrates his prowess and kills Zeus' son, Sarpedon, Patroclus is slain by Hector, with Apollo's help. As he breathes his last, Patroclus foretells Hector's death at Achilles' hands (16.818–67).

The end of the quarrel, the death of Hector, the ransom of his body and the end of the poem

The third and final part of the *Iliad* is a narrative in which the main characters must face the consequences of their past actions and the burden of their destiny. Patroclus has fallen, but his death does not escape Menelaus' attention (17.1). Hector strips Patroclus of Achilles' armour, and a fierce battle over the body ensues. By the end of Book 17, Menelaus and Ajax demonstrate great valour and eventually take back the corpse. The death of his companion, a surrogate wearing his armour, offers Achilles, yet again, a setting for contemplating *his own* death. Grief stricken and besides himself, Achilles must now 'come back to himself', rejoin the fighting, and avenge his friend, even as he is reminded again by his mother that this choice will doom him to a 'swift death' (*ôkumoros*, 18.95). Swift-footed (*podas ôkus* 18.97) Achilles is greatly agitated by Thetis' words, but he does not relent. 'May I straight away die, since I did not help my companion at his death' (18.98). As we noted, throughout the *Iliad*, he is named 'swift' and 'swift footed' because, in the final showdown, he pursues his opponent Hector and kills him (on the epithets, see Vivante 1982). Yet this simple, often-repeated idea foreshadows Achilles' future in more ways than one. The verbal preponderance of 'swiftness', in this passage and elsewhere, associated with the *Iliad*'s greatest hero, brings to our eyes a man who, as he will chase his enemy, will also be running towards his own death. Swiftness, we realize, denotes a concrete attribute of bodily excellence that allows heroes to aspire beyond the condition of mortality and defines Achilles at a specific moment in the plot, but it also represents the fleeting existence of a man and the fragile condition of heroic bodies.

Making his decision, Achilles has not forgotten his anger towards Agamemnon. Yet now, under compulsion (*anankê*) and for Patroclus' sake, he must leave behind wrath and the loss it represents (18.111–12). He chooses to die, but in the glorious deeds of his death, he will 'gain great fame': Both Trojan and Greek women will shed tears for him (18.120–4). Nevertheless, Hector is now in possession of Achilles' armour, and Hephaestus, the blacksmith of the gods, must make a replacement for the hero. In the scene known as 'the Shield of Achilles', Homer offers us an elaborate description of its artwork (18.462–617. This elaborate verbal description of a visual object is technically known as an *ecphrasis*. See Stanley 1993, Becker 1995). The shield is a well-wrought Homeric *mise-en-abyme*, a compressed means of reflecting the *Iliad*'s world from within the *Iliad*. It depicts a city at peace and a city at war, agricultural scenes, dancing and more. What is extraordinary about this verbal description of an inanimate object is its integrated depiction of living movement and action in time (e.g. 'young men were whirling in the dance', 18.494). In his famous work *Laocoon* (1766), Gotthold Ephraim Lessing discussed the virtues of the 'Shield' and the 'beauty in motion' it embodies, beauty which transcends the normal conventions of visual art and its temporality.

Twenty-seven days after Achilles and Agamemnon part in anger (Dawn rises again in 19.1), on the fourth day of combat, after 18 books of the *Iliad*, which by some estimates would have taken over 2 days to perform (if there ever was a complete performance of the *Iliad* in antiquity), a formal reconciliation takes place. Achilles and Agamemnon abandon their previously held positions and end the quarrel between them. Achilles declares the folly of 'raging in soul-destroying strife over a girl' (19.58); Agamemnon offers Achilles many gifts and admits to the blindness of mind (*atê*) cast upon him by Zeus. With these events, social order seems to have been restored in the Greek camp and the Iliadic theme of the quarrel of Agamemnon and Achilles concludes. This element of the plot has been developed, brought to its climax and resolved. Yet this is not the end of the *Iliad*. Five books of song, more than a sixth of the poem, and many fateful events, indeed the poem's most important and decisive actions, remain to be told. The poem 'itself' thus seems to tell us yet again that important matters lie beyond the end of its formal stated theme. Achilles, and perhaps even Agamemnon, are no longer fighting over prizes as they have before. Precisely in their reconciliation, in rejecting 'strife over a girl' and backing down from some of their competitive stances, they raise questions over the regulatory system of symbolic investment and exchange that seems to be the basis of their social world. This world is whole again, yet the harmony between the hero and the values of this world can no longer be taken for granted, as other forms of wrath – Achilles' wrath towards Hector and the wrath of the Greeks towards the city – are yet to be sung.

More fighting follows. The gods themselves fight each other (Books 20–21) amidst accounts of great martial feats by Achilles who in his own *aristeia* slays many heroes. Eventually, Achilles and Hector fight, and, with intervention from Apollo, Zeus and Athena, Hector is slain (Book 22). Achilles will earn great fame for his actions and he knows it. As in Diomedes' case, this fame is quite literally the *Iliad*'s narrative which we encounter as audiences and readers. Yet Achilles' wrath yet again seems to exceed all boundaries. As Hector is breathing his last, he begs Achilles to allow his body to be ransomed (22.338). In other words, if we momentarily put aside the powerful emotions and sublime effect of the words, Hector begs Achilles to treat his death and his body in accordance with the normative system of exchange, material and symbolic, that governs heroic society. Achilles angrily refuses. His wrath has taken him beyond the social, to the borders between human and animal. At the beginning of the scene, the poet likens Achilles chasing Hector to a hunting dog chasing a fawn (22.189–93). Achilles now moves a step further away from the realm of humanity, *adopting for himself* the identity of a wild beast. He says to Hector, 'Just as between lions and men there are no oaths of faith, nor do wolves and lambs share an understanding . . . so there will be no oaths between me and you' (22.262–6). A little later, he adds, 'I would cut out your flesh and eat it raw' (22.347), and eventually, Achilles devises 'shameful plans' for Hector (22.395) – he will deny his enemy a proper burial. The whole point, which eventually Achilles too will recognize, is that neither Hector nor indeed he himself are wild animals. In life, as in death, they are men. The tragedy of this moment is the crossing of the boundary between the human and the inhuman, a crossing which is born, paradoxically, not of insanity, but of human emotions such as care, guilt, grief and anger. Achilles ties Hector's feet to his chariot and drags his body round with Trojan's head trailing in the dust.

Patroclus is dead and the Greeks bury his body and hold funeral games in his honour (Book 23, days 28 and 29 of the plot events – see 23.109, 226). But Achilles persists – he drags Hector's corpse around Patroclus' tomb with unabated, helpless fury for 11 days, as if Hector's death has robbed him of revenge. He is now as incapable of killing his enemy (again) as he is of averting his own death. The poem makes it clear that the reasoned framework of exchange between deeds and prizes and perhaps even between death and fame has changed.

The *Iliad*'s plot is not a set of open possibilities. Events within the poem's narrative world are governed by an elaborate notion of fate (in Greek *moira*, a man's allotted share in life) and by mortality. Outside of these events, at the level of the narration, the plot is governed in the most practical sense by the end of the poem and by the familiarity of the audiences with the tradition of the Trojan War. Patroclus and Hector must die. Achilles himself is still alive by the final lines of the *Iliad*. Yet he, and we, and even his horses know he must die (see Book 19.404–24). He is a man whose actions have simply not yet caught up with his fate and in this sense a man for whom time brings no real change. Achilles is doomed because of the hand which he has been dealt by the fates and because he has been told so by his mother and by the dying Hector. He is also doomed because the conventions of his world have been shaken and cannot be restored to their original state: Achilles' rightful prize Briseis was seized and, in the course of events, his friend Patroclus has died; the prize has been returned, but nothing can bring back Patroclus from the dead. Achilles' place in the world and perhaps the underlying logic of his world too have been challenged, and, once challenged, cannot be as they were before, even when Achilles rejoins his comrades and is again fighting on the Greek side. Achilles offers us a uniquely Greek 'heroic' (and perhaps tragic) variation on the religious theme of the Adamic fall, one that looks less to man's relation with the divine and more to his relation with fate, mortality and himself. The *Iliad*'s world order, once challenged, can no longer remain as it was. The *Iliad* has turned Achilles' fated time, a time without change, a time in which each man has his own set future, into a time of absolute change, in which the moment of 'before', and the moment of 'after', even though they are moments in the life of a single man and are contained within one orderly poem, are separate moments of absolute contingency – each different from the other. It is the representation of the complete loss of the past, a loss which is keenly felt but which is perfectly preserved in sublime and 'imperishable' poetry, the fame and glory of Achilles, that is the *Iliad*'s and Homer's achievement.

Achilles is one of the pivotal figures in the West's canon of literary heroes, and its oldest (perhaps not the first, but the first recorded). As the hero at the centre of a poem that presages the tragic loss of a heroic world (a change from better to worse, as Aristotle, describing the best plots of tragedy, says in the *Poetics*), he is a very ancient figure. Yet he also cuts a strangely modern figure of change. Cultural critics and literary scholars like Erich Auerbach, Mikhail Bakhtin, Georg Lukács as well as important classical scholars of the twentieth century, such as Bruno Snell, Arthur Adkins, Werner Jaeger and others, have forcefully argued that the Homeric heroes like Achilles are essentially 'at one with their world'. Heroes live and die, but their existence, so this tradition of criticism argued, is contained within a world of unchanging values. Fate as the embodiment of continuity between one moment in time ('a hero's birth') and another ('his death') predominates in Achilles' history and almost everywhere in the Homeric poems. Yet we have just seen that lines of fate that so clearly connect the past and the future in Homer also seem to separate these moments in time. Achilles has achieved great deeds. His fate is to die. His fame will be imperishable. In this regard, he is the hero of an ancient epic. But can we understand all of his actions within the fixed existential framework of exchange of prizes and fame with which the *Iliad* begins? The *Iliad* which we ourselves read today is proof of Achilles' fame. Can we, however, understand his actions and response after the death of Patroclus, his anguish and his fury (and, as we shall see, his acceptance of Priam's supplication at the end of the *Iliad*) simply in terms of the heroic framework? The question has no simple, single answer. Achilles' actions as described in the *Iliad* seem to suggest, at least in part, a hero who lives in a world of *essential* change, one who can no longer live by his own ordered principles, a hero who can never go back to a previous harmonious existence and must, perhaps for this essential reason, die a 'second' death which compounds the biological death. This aspect of the hero of the *Iliad*, if we accept it, suggests an existential state of separation, a kind 'homelessness' (as the Romantic German philosopher Novalis [1772–1801] and others after him have called it) and a sense of melancholy which is often used to characterize, not the ancient past, but a specifically modern subjectivity, a modern historical consciousness and the condition of modernity itself. Here, it seems to me, we can detect Homer's capacity to preserve, precisely through change and multiplicity, a vibrant sense of existence and thus, paradoxically, also a continuity from past to present.

What remains of the plot of the *Iliad*, in the final book of the poem, describes the events surrounding Hector's ransom and burial. Zeus guides the events. He sends Thetis to tell Achilles to release Hector's body for burial and Iris to tell Priam to go to the Greek camp to take the body back. Priam meets with Achilles (in the night between day 41 and day 42 of the plot. See 24.31, 351). He offers ransom and begs for the return of his son's body (24.468–676) in a scene which we can only describe as the enactment of an impossible relation of kinship.

Priam is Hector's father – Hector is often called *Priamidês*, 'the Son of Priam' in the *Iliad* (e.g. 2.817). Achilles is 'the son of Peleus', *Pêleidês*. This too is a common patronymic, which appears already in the first line of the poem and is used throughout the *Iliad* (indeed, over 50 times). Here, as earlier in the case of *ôkus*, 'swift' or the word *sêma*, 'sign', 'tomb', 'portent', we can catch another glimpse of the *Iliad*'s intricate verbal texture, which marks both plain fact and the poem's deepest themes in the same expression. Achilles, Hector and many other Homeric heroes are described by means of their father's name. It is a practical denomination. A Homeric surname. Yet naming heroes in this manner constantly reminds us of the absent presence of the father in a hero's life and of the epic theme of fathers and sons (also noted, for example, in the brief 'obituaries' Homer gives to many otherwise anonymous fallen heroes). This is the theme that crowns the closing scenes of the *Iliad* and, in the final book, marks a climactic point of 'jarring symmetry', a moment of direct emotion but also of paradoxical reflection.

Fathers and sons are related by blood. Nothing could be more true in this scene. Yet the blood that unites Priam and Achilles is not the blood of life, but the blood of death. Priam embraces Achilles' feet and kisses the hands that killed his son (24.478–79). Achilles sees before him the father of the man who was his enemy and killed his friend Patroclus. If we think of Patroclus in Achilles' armour as Achilles' surrogate and of Achilles' conscious choice of fate, then Priam is the father of the man who, in a manner of speaking, killed Achilles himself and deprived Achilles' father, Peleus, of a son (24.503ff.). Thus, Priam and Achilles, 'father' and 'son', meet in an almost unimaginable relation. They are both bereft of the persons they love. They are completely bound to each other by their loss, separated and joined at the same time. Yet Priam, looking at Achilles, sees his own son, and Achilles, looking at Priam, sees his own father (24.507–12). On the one hand, there is between Achilles and Priam a relation of kinship which cannot exist in any society, time or place – such relations between 'killers' and 'victims' undermine every principle of social stability and continuity. On the other hand, Achilles and Priam are bound by an intensely and genuinely social relation, a moment of recognition of the true force and meaning of kinship, precisely because of who the two are. They realize what it truly means to be a father and a son.

The bond between Achilles and Priam exists in an singular point in time, dependent entirely on the circumstances of the moment, yet it also exists outside of time. It is an event, a relationship, that appears in an instant and which instantly dissipates (a moment like the 'now' time of the present itself, which, as Aristotle and other philosophers recognize, is gone the instant we try to grasp it). This moment and the relation between the two characters is not an abstract or transcendental moment, nor is it an idea free from material or temporal constraints or from the persons involved. Achilles and Priam have not ceased to be who they are. One is a Greek hero, the other is the king of Troy. There is no peace between them. The narrative of the *Iliad* makes this emphatically clear. Priam asks for the return of the body of his son. Achilles receives him kindly and consents. But then (24.559–70),

> looking darkly, swift footed Achilles spoke to him:
> 'Do not provoke me any more, old man; I myself am minded
> to give Hector back to you . . .
> Therefore do not stir my heart amidst my sorrows,
> old man, lest I should not spare you in my hut,
> suppliant as you are. . . .'

Priam, so brave in coming to the camp, fears and obeys (24.571. In a later tradition in the *Ilioupersis*, Achilles' son Neoptolemus eventually kills Priam during the sack of Troy). Achilles, who has earlier mistreated Hector's corpse now has it washed and anointed and gives it back. The Greek hero and the Trojan king share a meal and one last important moment. Priam marvels at Achilles' divine aspect and Achilles wonders at Priam's noble figure and words (24.629–32). This is not so much a moment of recognition of shared humanity as a recognition of the marvel and fragility of an 'other', of someone who is *not* of one's own blood and who is thus *not* one's self. It is a human moment which depends (in the scene) on specific bodily and material presence in a time and a place, but which can nevertheless only exist at 'absolute' points of observation (see the expression 'gazing at each other', *es alhêlous oroöntes* in 24.632). Achilles declares a 10-day truce, but this is not a treaty of peace. It is a finite period of respite, a social extension of the instant of recognition between Priam and Achilles. The truce is applicable to all, but it leaves the enmity between Greeks and Trojans intact and the downfall of Troy as certain as ever.

The next day (24.695), Priam brings Hector's body Home. Yet even this homecoming is not the end of the poem. Like opera, the *Iliad*'s war music subsides very slowly. At the beginning of the poem, we saw that the narrator handed over his first words to the Muse, the goddess of song. Now, at the end, he seems to hand over his last words to other female speaking figures, this time to the mortal women of Troy and their lament.

The women of Troy have a particular affinity to loss. They are doubly disenfranchised: first, because they are women in a world of men and of sharply demarcated gender boundaries, and second, because they are on the side of the vanquished. They will not be killed, but will be taken captive and become the 'prizes' and possessions of men. First speaks Andromache, Hector's wife and the mother of their son Astyanax (*Iliad* 24.718–45); Hecuba, Hector's mother, the woman who gave him life, speaks next (*Iliad* 24.746–59); the last, unique speech of the poem is by Helen (24.760–75), Hector's kinswoman (as the consort of Paris, Hector's brother) and friend, and also the woman over whom the war is fought, who has indirectly brought about Hector's death. The *Iliad*'s final speeches are thus not words of praise for the great deeds of the dead, but those voices that bear the painful burden of staying alive.

The *Iliad* concludes after 9 days of mourning (24.784) with Hector's funeral. Fifty-one days have passed since the action of the *Iliad* has begun (24.785). The very last line of the poem (804) says: 'So they were busy with the burial of Hector, Tamer of Horses', almost as if there should be more to come. We know, of course, that this is not the end and that the greatest suffering is yet to unfold.

CHAPTER SEVEN

The *Odyssey*

The opening books of the *Odyssey* and the *Telemachy*

As with the *Iliad*, it is important to look at the main themes and events of the *Odyssey* in context and in the sequence of the verse. The proem has offered us a brief partial summary of the poem's action: Odysseus' wandering, how he lost his men and how, finally, he came home. The verses that follow develop the poem's themes of homecoming and return, *Wanderlüst* and domestic life, family, fidelity, identity, coming of age, the passage of generations and time, the telling of stories, the power of song, disguise, recognition, lying and truth. Characters in the *Odyssey* tell many stories – for example, as we have seen, the story of Agamemnon, or indeed Odysseus' extended tales of his own adventures. These stories take us backwards and sometimes forwards in time in great jagged leaps over a long overall period from the narrative of Odysseus' birth and childhood (19.393–466) to a foretelling of his death (11.134). Like Odysseus himself, the narrative goes 'island-hopping'. It oscillates between Ithaca, Olympus, Calypso's island, the Cyclops' island, Circe's island and other islands and the land of the Phaeacians. Judging by the *Odyssey*, the Muses really do seem to be everywhere, as the invocation in *Iliad* 2.485 suggests. Yet when the plot's main events are unfolding in one location, time keeps moving, by and large uneventfully, in others (see de Jong 2001: 589–90, appendix B). The 'real time' of the

Odyssey's plot events moves, like the *Iliad*'s events, more or less in a straight line, following what is sometimes known as Homer's principle of continuity of time or 'Zielinski's law'. With very few exceptions – outside of tales told by characters in the poem – the event-time in the plot always moves ahead in sequence (rather than simultaneously – see, however, Scodel 2008).

As in the *Iliad,* in the *Odyssey*, linear time, spanning 41 days, is prominently marked, often by references to the rising and setting of the sun (2.1; 3.404; 4.306, etc.). Such natural time – natural both because it is marked by events of nature and because this is how we often intuitively grasp the 'nature' of time – is particularly important given what we have earlier described as the capacity and purpose of epic words as a response to the constraints of mortality and as words that aspire to reach beyond mortal lifespans. The *Odyssey*, even more than the *Iliad*, inspires a malleable sense of time. But without the backbone of a linear day-to-day temporal movement, we would have been dealing with a work of art much closer to hallucinatory fantasy. Part of the strength of the *Odyssey* is that it can be read as a 'simple' traveller's account. The contents of this account incorporate many fantastic elements: the enchanting and luscious island of the nymph Calypso, the mythical Phaeacians, the world of the dead, encounters with the man-eating Cyclops, the six-headed monster Scylla and the whirlpool Charybdis. But the most extravagant of these tales are contained within the stories told by Odysseus (the self-confessed trickster. See 9.19) and by other characters. Responsibility for fantastic accounts is thus partly shifted onto the main characters, their minds, their schemes, their words and their strategies for survival. The narrator's plot and its discourse seem to keep a firmer foothold in the real world. Keeping this world moving along a linear timeline in which the sun rises and sets as it does in our own world helps couch the poem in everyday experience. In other words, although the *Odyssey* contains many fantastic elements, it is not a fairy tale but an extraordinary poem for ordinary audiences.

As with the *Iliad*, the plot of the *Odyssey* begins well after the beginning of the larger story, not only of Troy, but also of the return of Odysseus, who has been wandering for 10 years. After the proem, the poem seems to pick up on the tale (1.11–21):

All the other heroes who had escaped sheer destruction
were by now at home, saved from both war and the sea.

But him alone [Odysseus, still un-named!], longing for a home-
coming
   [*nostos*] and for his wife,
a powerful nymph, Calypso, bright among the goddesses
kept in the hollow of her cave, hoping he would become her
husband.
But as the years revolved, there came at last the year
in which the gods had ordained that he should return home
to Ithaca, though even there he could not escape from his trials,
among his own. All the gods took pity on him,
except Poseidon, who continued to rage unceasingly
against godlike Odysseus until he reached his own land.

Following this introduction, we might have expected to hear about
the adventures of Odysseus and Calypso. Yet we find that, like
the first introduction in the proem, this 'second introduction' is
followed by another change in narrative tack (we must wait until
Book 5 of the poem to meet Odysseus and the nymph, while the
plot moves to a different location and a different part of the tale).
Poseidon, we learn, has gone off to visit the remote Ethiopians,
while all the other gods were assembled together in the halls of
Olympian Zeus (1.26–7). Only here, as we enter a divine assembly,
does day 1 of the plot begin.

The setting is significant. Just like the *Iliad*'s narrative of
heroic fighting, which begins with an exchange of words, so does
the *Odyssey*'s narrative of heroic adventure begin with speeches
and stories. First to speak is Zeus, who complains about the folly
of mankind and their self-inflicted pains, invoking the story of
Agamemnon's death and the destruction which Aegisthus brought
upon himself by his reckless actions. The precise ethical import
of this speech and its implication for the conception of justice in
Homer is a matter of heated dispute, but its thematics are beyond
doubt: Old scores are settled in the end, just as return in the
Odyssey is indeed a reckoning, a reconciliation of the past, the
present and the future. The goddess Athena, Odysseus' protector
(44ff.), now pleads with Zeus and reminds him of the hero's
plight: 'My heart is torn', she says, 'because of wise Odysseus,
ill fated man, who has long been suffering woes, far from his
friends, in a sea-girt island at the navel of the sea' (1.48–50).
She tells Odysseus' story: how he is held captive by the nymph

Calypso. We have heard all this before only a few lines earlier. As we keep stressing, the 'facts' of epic are known. What keeps changing are the contexts of the telling. Zeus, who (like us) has not forgotten (64ff.), now explains some of the background: The god Poseidon is angry with Odysseus, who had blinded the Cyclops, Poseidon's son. The blinding of the Cyclops is a story which, of course, the *Odyssey* will repeat in detail later on in the poem, narrated by Odysseus himself. Zeus now agrees that Odysseus should be allowed to go home. The will of Zeus (cf. *Iliad* 1.5), uncertain at times and susceptible to the wily influence of the women around him, Hera, Thetis and Athena, nevertheless guides the Homeric poems and their plots. Athena proposes that Zeus send a messenger, Hermes, to tell the nymph Calypso of the decision to bring the hero home (1.80ff.). She herself heads for the palace in Ithaca to meet Odysseus' son, Telemachus.

In the spate of less than 100 verses, the story which is yet to unfold seems to have backed up and rolled into itself. We have revisited stories we have heard before, we are told stories we will hear again and we are promised stories we have not yet heard, but which we may know through the tradition. Such back and forth movement embodies an important Odyssean principle: The same story in Homer is repeated and yet is somehow 'always new' (1.352, see further below). The *Odyssey* is a poem about return, fidelity and the reassertion of identity. But the closer we look at it, the more we realize that this identity, both of Odysseus, and of the *Odyssey*, is never simply a repetition of things past.

The divine assembly scene in Book 1 sets the trajectory of Odysseus' homecoming. Yet, as in the *Iliad*, the first part of the *Odyssey* is marked by the resounding absence of the poem's protagonist. These opening four books, aptly known as the *Telemachy*, focus on Telemachus, Odysseus' son. The first two books are set in the palace in Ithaca. Here, several important figures are introduced: Telemachus, who is no longer a child yet is also not yet a man nor yet capable of fending for himself; Penelope, beset by the suitors who seek her hand in marriage, a woman alone without a husband to protect her; the suitors, reckless and irreverent, are consuming the wealth of another man's house (1.160, 248), each praying to be the one lying by Penelope's side (see also in the final books of the poem, 18.212–13). These characters, linked by Odysseus' absence, are all set in a situation that teeters on the verge of change.

One of the main agents driving the *Odyssey*'s plot is Odysseus' patron, the goddess Athena. She not only endeavours to bring Odysseus home but also encourages his son, Telemachus, to set out on journeys of his own, thus enacting a kind of continuity of patronage across generations. Approaching Odysseus' palace in the guise of Mentes, king of the Taphians (1.105), Athena advises Telemachus to call an assembly, to bid the suitors to leave, and to sail to Pylos and to Sparta to seek news of his father. She departs, and we, the audience/readers, are left in the palace, where the suitors are making merry, entertained by the singer Phemius, who sings of the 'return of the Achaeans' (*Achaeôn noston* 1.326).

Phemius' performance is the first of many singing scenes in the *Odyssey*. It is a lively vignette which carries great significance. The contents of Phemius' song are not described, although they clearly relate to the contents of the *Odyssey*, which is itself the song of the return of one particular Achaean, Odysseus. Of special importance is the response of the singer's audience. His words bring pleasure to the suitors. To them, in their reckless state of mirth, songs of return are merely a diversion. We, the audience and readers, know better: For the suitors, 'songs of return' will eventually spell death. In contrast to the suitors, when Penelope hears Phemius' song from her room upstairs, she complains that it 'brings distress to her heart'. She bears 'unforgettable pains', always longing for Odysseus, 'whose fame [the word *kleos* again] has spread throughout Hellas and Argos' (1.344). We, the audience and readers, again know differently. 'Songs of return' will in the end bring happiness and solace to Penelope. In this scene, then, song is described as having the power to enhance in its hearers the emotions of the moment and to presage the future. It can underscore a false sense of security as well as real pain. It can carry with it passing pleasure or, indeed, a deeper truth.

It is tempting to see scenes of singing such as this as representations of the performance epic poetry itself. Yet we cannot assume that poetic descriptions provide direct evidence of actual practice. Poetry inevitably takes certain liberties. More fundamentally, poetry is speech, and speech is generally not identical to action. A verbal description of the plucking of the lyre may be beautiful, but it is not the sound of the lyre being plucked. And yet it is possible to describe the event of singing and its surroundings in words that, in themselves, are a song. This 'literal' parallel is important. In Homer, the overlap between song as described *inside* the *Odyssey* and the *Odyssey* itself *as song*, while not a reliable index of historical performance, gives the details of the singing scenes particular resonance (see, e.g. Mackie 1997: 77, Segal 1994: 126). Phemius' song provides a good example. In response to Penelope's complaint about the painful effects of song, Telemachus leaps to the singer's defence. Zeus, he says, not the singer, is responsible for the doom of the Danaans (the Greeks). Telemachus adds: 'for the newest (*neôtatê*) song is always the one which audiences praise the most' (1.351–2). This generalizing statement about the nature of poetry and its relation to the audience has often puzzled commentators of Homer's traditional song. Is Telemachus simply being naïve, as William Thalmann (1992: 126) thinks? Or is this an ironic comment? Homeric verse is the poetry of the past, yet here, as Andrew Ford (1992: 109) suggests, the audiences within the poem seem to prefer accounts of more-recent events. Is it simply that Odyssean audiences, in contrast to the audiences of the *Iliad*, have a particular preference for newer stories, as Hilary Mackie (1997: 81) argues? The *Odyssey* is the later poem, an 'epilogue' (as Longinus says) to the *Iliad*. Do audiences within the *Odyssey* have self-conscious preference for 'late' work?

There may be yet another option for interpreting this difficult verse and Telemachus' statement, related to our earlier suggestions about storytelling in general and to the conception of time in Homeric epic. Considering the link between contingent performance and general truth in Homer, Gregory Nagy cites the work of anthropologist Edmund Leach, who has argued that (Leach 1982: 5 in Nagy 1996: 130–1)

> The various stories [GN: i.e., the myths of a given society] form a corpus. They lock in together to form a single theological-cosmological [GN: juridical] whole. Stories from one part of the corpus presuppose a knowledge of stories from all other parts. There is implicit cross-reference from one part to another. It is an unavoidable feature of storytelling that events are made to happen one after another, but in cross-reference, such sequence is ignored. *It is as if the whole corpus referred to a single instant of time, namely, the present moment.* [my emphasis]

Social anthropology has heavily influenced the study of oral traditions and our understanding of early poetry. If we accept

Leach's view above, we must allow that all pasts, once sung, are compressed by traditional narrative into a single moment in time, into 'the present moment'. This present is the time of the performance, which, of course, is always 'new'. Phemius' song about the return and doom of the Greeks is a more-recent story relative to other narratives from the past, but we must view this past from the perspective of a performance that always makes things new.

The *Iliad* and *Odyssey* themselves, as poems, seem to provide unmediated illustration of this principle. They are the oldest poems in the literary tradition of the West and their themes are older still. Yet Homeric poetry continues to draw 'praise' from audiences and readers in the present and to serve as a model for 'new' literary, cinematic, dramatic and other versions of the tale. In this sense, Homeric poetry, like Phemius' song, possesses the quality of 'newness', which does not describe contents never heard before nor the age of their composition, but enacts a renewed existence in the 'new' moment of their (re)performance in the present. This quality meshes well with the idea of epic as a tool of memory that preserves the past in an imperishable state through flexible performance practices.

Book 2 of the *Odyssey* begins with the rise of a new dawn and the usual formula: *hêmos d' êrigeneia phanê rhododaktylos Êôs*, 'When rosy-fingered, early-rising Dawn appeared . . .' (2.1). Complementing the sunrises at the beginning of narrative action, we often find in both the *Iliad* and *Odyssey* phrases that close off narrative sections by describing the setting of the sun. In the *Odyssey*, one of the most common is *duseto t' hêelios, skioonto te pasai aguiai*, 'The sun set down, and shadows covered all the paths' (e.g. 2.388). As in the *Iliad*, in addition to 'punctuating' the flow of events and matching them to our ordinary temporal experience, these verses give the movement of time an explicit visual quality. Epic action normally occurs when we can 'see' it, in the light. Darkness and the end of the day indicate a pause in action (the night-time ambush scenes in the *Doloneia* in Book 10 of the *Iliad* are a notable exception and, as we noted, were sometimes suspected of being external additions). The visual element is important, since seeing in Homer implies that the observer is immediately present at an event and thus (like the Muses, for example) possesses unmediated true knowledge.

Knowledge is, of course, transferrable only by means of words – hence the importance of words for Homer in regard to memory and recollection and their power over the condition of mortality. Such recollection, however, often occurs away from the light: It is telling that poetic performance in the *Odyssey* often takes place in the 'shadowy halls' (*ana megara skioenta*, 1.365, etc.).

Telemachus summons the assembly (Book 2), but is mocked by the suitors and their leaders, Antinoos and Eurymachus. Antinoos complains that Penelope had raised the suitors' hopes in vain – she set up a great web in the hall, promising to marry when she completes her task of weaving a shroud for Laertes. But after 4 years, he says, her secret was betrayed by one of her maidens: she was weaving by day and unravelling by night (2.87–110). The practicalities of this story are odd (weaving one web over 4 years, whether unravelled or not, is plainly slow work!) and its historicity is problematic (there seems to be no evidence for shrouds in early Greek historical traditions). Yet it provides an effective introduction to Penelope's character, her wisdom (*mêtis*) and her capacity for intricate and deceptive action. This story, noted twice elsewhere in the poem (19.137–56; 24.129–48, with some variations), is also one of the useful emblems of the *Odyssey*'s plot: both a literal device for developing tension and a metaphor for the manner in which events are 'woven' backwards and forwards, as Odysseus comes closer to home, but is blown off course, reaches Ithaca, assumes his many disguises and narrates both fictional events and events from the past (see further, e.g. in Lowenstam 2000).

In Book 2, in preparation for his journey, Telemachus asks the suitors for use of a ship (2.212), but his request is ignored. Nevertheless, Athena, who assumes many guises in the *Odyssey*, has other plans. She obtains a ship and a crew and, disguised as Mentor, an old friend of Odysseus, sails away with Telemachus that night. On the morning of the third day (3.1 – the rise of dawn), the ship reaches Pylos. Here Telemachus meets Nestor, 'the Gerenian Horseman' (*Gerênios hippota Nestôr*, 3.102, etc.), the oldest of the Greek heroes who had been to Troy and an eloquent speaker (cf. *Iliad* 1.247–52), who tells him of the return of heroes from the war. Yet of Odysseus' fate Nestor knows nothing. The next day (3.404), Telemachus, joined by Nestor's son Pisistratus, sails on to Pherae, and a day later (3.491), these two young sons of Iliadic heroes reach Sparta, where (in Book 4) they meet Menelaus and Helen, the husband and wife whose former separation looms painfully over the *Iliad*. Menelaus and Helen are celebrating the wedding of their son and daughter, an event that emphasizes the peaceful normalcy of their own union in the Odyssean present. They live in apparent domestic harmony, with nothing but feasting and the telling of tales from the past to distract them.

As elsewhere in the *Odyssey*, when stories are told, the poem stresses the powerful effect of words which can bring pleasure, cast a spell of silence on the hearers, or enhance the effects of real-life pain. In Book 1, Phemius' song is distressing to Penelope, stirring memories of Odysseus. The scene in Sparta provides another perspective. Menelaus and Helen are their own narrators. Menelaus tells of his adventures with Odysseus, and speculates on the loss of his companion's homecoming (4.182). Menelaus, of course, is not a singer like Phemius, but an artless participant in the action he describes. His stories are presented as a report on direct experience – things he has seen himself – and thus bear the aura of truth. Yet in theme and substance, in language and style, Menelaus' words are, of course, very similar to poetry as it is portrayed both inside the *Odyssey* and in the form of the *Odyssey* itself. His narrative is like the words of the poets of the *Odyssey*, Phemius and Demodocus, and like the words used by the Homeric narrator, and, if we allow for the conventions of the prologue and the invocations, even like the words of the Muse. Not surprisingly, Menelaus' 'real' account pains his hearers and brings everyone to tears, including, on this occasion, Pisistratus.

Pisistratus is only a supporting member of the cast of the *Odyssey*, but his response is worth noting. Like Penelope in Book 1 and like Telemachus, he has a personal relation to the people in the story. Menelaus' words about Odysseus and about Troy bring the 'yearning for tears' (*himeros goöio*) to everyone's eyes, including Menelaus himself, and they do not fail to affect Pisistratus, too (4.184–8):

Argive Helen wept, the daughter of Zeus,
Telemachus wept, and Menelaus, son of Atreus,
nor were the eyes of the son of Nestor tearless.
For he recalled peerless Antilochus in his heart,
The one whom the glorious son of the bright Dawn had killed.

Like Telemachus, but unlike Penelope and Menelaus, for example, Pisistratus has no memories of Odysseus, nor even any direct recollection of Antilochus who was his own brother. 'I myself never met him, I never saw him, but they say he was above all others', Pisistratus notes (4.200–1). Our text thus seems to indicate that narrative has the power to invoke in the hearers the memory of true experience which they have never had. The words may even imply that memory itself is not the event as it occurred, but *the words men say*. Such words stir in Pisistratus genuine emotion and what we can only describe, paradoxically, as 'new emotions and new memories of the past'. Mourning and weeping, as he adds 'are the only due we pay to miserable mortals'.

If Homeric words claim to preserve mortal fame, then here Menelaus' words come close to achieving this goal, re-enacting a painful, mortal past so vividly that they draw real tears, even when no originary memory exists in those who weep. Aristotle, in the *Poetics* (1449b), famously speaks of the power of poetry and imitation (*mimêsis*) to induce emotion, 'pity and fear'. In Homer too, it seems, words have strong emotive power. We may, however, be left wondering if Menelaus' 'imitation' and perhaps more generally Homeric words contain an even greater, uncanny 'performative' quality which approaches the affective force of reality itself.

In response to everyone's pained reaction, Menelaus sensibly suggests that they turn to their supper and leave the stories for the morning. In famous lines that follow (4.219ff.), Helen rapidly acts to further sooth the emotions of her guests. She casts 'a drug to quiet all pain and strife and bring forgetfulness to every ill' into their wine (4.221). Helen's drug is clearly meant to take away the painful effect of words. Yet, disconcertingly, it also has the power to counteract experience and life as a social relationship of precisely the kind that has just been invoked in Pisistratus' thoughts (4.222–226):

> whoever should drink it [Helen's drug], when he had
>   mixed it in his cup,
> would not let a tear fall down his cheeks that day,
> not even if his father and mother should lie dead before him
> or if *his brother* or beloved son should be slain
> with the sword and *he were to see it with his own eyes*. [my
>   emphasis]

The Greek biographer and essayist Plutarch (c. 46–120 CE) thought that Helen's drug represented her powerful eloquence (*Moralia* 614.b). He is at least right in suggesting that words can have a strong, enchanting effect. Elsewhere in the *Odyssey*, the effect of poetry and its pleasures are likened to a magical charm. Pleasing though such charms may be, we here also observe something of the dangerous power of words.

Having administered her philtre, Helen herself begins to speak and to tell stories of the war . . . She is of course the woman on whose account the Greeks went to war against Troy and suffered so much. She speaks 'of what is fitting' (4.239) and declares that she cannot speak of everything – in words that closely resemble those of the narrator of the *Iliad* when he claims that he cannot speak without knowledge from the Muses (*Iliad* 4.484ff.). Yet, if anyone should know about Troy, that person is Helen. She is a deadly source of inspiration for both action and words, a mortal Muse. She tells of Odysseus' secret foray into Troy, and of how she herself had treated Odysseus kindly and aided his task. Is Helen now, from her retrospective position in the *Odyssey* and aided by the effect of her powerful drug, trying to redraw a more favourable image of herself? Should we compare the effect of her actions and words to the effects of poetry? The scene brings to the surface the double-edged relation of pleasure and pain which is part of the transition from a world of deadly action and finite consequence to the sublimated world of imperishable words (the literature on Helen's drug is extensive. See, e.g. Bergren 1981).

The scene in Sparta ends at sundown. On the following morning (the sixth day – 4.306 – again we see 'rosy-fingered Dawn'), we are back in Ithaca, where the suitors hatch a plot to ambush Telemachus and kill him upon his return (4.663ff.).

Odysseus' journeys: Calypso, the Phaeacians and the *Apologue*.

Books 5–12 of the poem, or to be precise, Book 5 and up to Book 13.93, describe Odysseus' last 22 days away from Ithaca and the beginning of the end of his journey. As we noted earlier, views among scholars differ about boundaries and the division of narrative units. The division into 24 books is probably no earlier than the Hellenistic period. And, more fundamentally, behind our fixed texts lie the fluid and resonant traditions of song. It is almost by definition difficult to parse these traditions within absolute boundaries.

Book 5 begins, as usual, with the rising of dawn (5.1), which is, however, described by a unique formula occurring nowhere else in the *Odyssey* (but see *Iliad* 11.1): 'Dawn rose from her bed beside illustrious Tithonus.' The goddess *Eôs* leaves her mortal lover. It is a fitting opening that encapsulates the theme of the book in which the mortal Odysseus is to part with his beautiful divine captor, the 'fair tressed' (*eüplokamos*) nymph Calypso (her name means 'the hider'). Calypso lives in a lush, fragrant cave full of clusters of grapes and chattering birds (5.59–74). She would have made Odysseus her husband, kept him with her and given him eternal life. Now Hermes, under orders from Zeus, visits her island and instructs her to send Odysseus on his way. She complains bitterly, but must comply with the order to release Odysseus, who has been in her island for 7 years (see 7.259), and is tearfully pining for his home and for his wife: 'the nymph was no longer pleasing to him', we are told (5.153).

Calypso is one of several exotic women whom Odysseus encounters on his journey home to Penelope. In Book 6, we meet the young princess Nausicaa and indeed her formidable mother, Queen Arêtê ('virtue'). Later we meet the sensuous witch Circe, the ghosts of infamous women in the underworld, the Sirens whose song is enticing but deadly, and more. Gender is a fundamental component of social meaning both in antiquity (Aristotle begins the *Politics* with a discussion of the structural unit of the family and the 'natural' division of roles between males and females) and among modern critics (from anthropologist Claud Lévi-Strauss' work on women and exchange and in its many readings, for example, by Gayle Rubin, to Judith Butler on performative gender and kinship, and more. See further below). In the first part of the *Odyssey*, we have already met two key female characters who define the narrative, and, we might say, also illustrate the effects of the absence of the *Odyssey*'s protagonist: Penelope, who steadfastly resists the suitor's onslaught and holds the dangers of the future at bay, as it were, and Helen, who represents the burden of the *Odyssey*'s Iliadic past. The women who occupy Books 5–12 of the poem are different. Their worlds are separated, thematically and geographically, from both Troy and Ithaca, from the world of Odysseus' past and from the world of his future. They are, nevertheless, each in her own way, partners to Odysseus, and they play important roles in his journey, at times as obstacle to his return, at others providing assistance. All possess strong sexual resonance that combines both attraction and threat (see further discussion in Chapter 8).

Odysseus builds a raft, and sails away from Calypso's island (5.228–389), giving up the nymph's offer of immortality, but gaining the hope of fame and renown among mortals. After 19 days at sea (5.269–87), Odysseus is shipwrecked on the shores of Scheria, the land of the Phaeacians. He lies overwhelmed with fatigue (6.1ff.), caked in brine and naked. At this point in the narrative, he has been stripped of all but bare life. But Athena, always thinking ahead, has made other plans for his return to the world. Disguised as a young girl, she appears in a dream to the young Phaeacian princess Nausicaa and reminds her that her 'bright clothes are lying unwashed' and her 'wedding day is soon to come' (6.26–7). Athena urges Nausicaa to go out to the shore with her handmaids to wash the laundry. On the beach, Odysseus hears the girls at play. Holding a leafy branch to cover his nakedness, he emerges from the thicket 'like a lion raised in the mountains, brimming with strength, lashed by the rains and the wind, his eyes blazing' and seeking his prey (6.130–4).

There is a great deal of innocent charm in the scene that follows, but equally, not far from the surface, the tension of sexual threat and excitement, a mix of the forces of nature and culture, of animal instinct and social constraint. Odysseus is an experienced man, Nausicaa is a young girl/woman entering sexual awareness. At this point, he is alone and has no place in the social world. She is an eligible young woman of high status who is constrained by the obligations of her position. Their meeting is a crucial moment in Odysseus' 're-birth' and his return to civilization.

The lion simile describing Odysseus, let us note, characterizes not only the scene and its actors Odysseus, Nausicaa and her maidens, but also a much wider narrative theme that spans the whole of Homer's poetry. Naked, isolated and wild, Odysseus is on the border of animal and man, in touch with an intense ferocity. As we have seen, in the *Iliad* too the hero is compared to a lion. Indeed, in

Achilles' crucial encounter with Hector, Achilles likens himself to
such a beast. He too has reached the limits of the human. Yet the
protagonists of the *Iliad* and *Odyssey* are as different in their animal
ferocity as are the two poems that preserve their fame. Achilles
is a paragon of martial excellence and a man of quick and fierce
emotion. In the course of the narrative of the *Iliad*, he becomes who
he is through the tragic event of his being, we might say, through
the boundless wrath that defines his existence and through his anger
towards Agamemnon, Hector, the social world surrounding him and
perhaps even towards life and death and himself. He wilfully chooses
his fate. Wrath and animal ferocity are *within* the hero, inseparable
from his innermost being. In the *Odyssey*, fierce emotion and wrath
also form a 'crucial arena', as one critic has put it (Clay 1997: 68),
but they are more the setting for action than an essential force from
within. At the very start of the *Odyssey*, we are told that Poseidon
'was ever wrathful' (1.20, *asperchês meneainen*) at Odysseus for
blinding his son the Cyclops. The Sea God's wrath is one of the
main driving forces of Odysseus' long absence from home, but it
acts on the hero from outside. Anger is, it is true, also found closer
to Odysseus himself. His name, as the *Odyssey* later explains, means
'the man of suffering/wrath' (in Greek, *odyssamenos*. See 19.407
and comments further below). But although Odysseus is often in
conflict with his surroundings, his emotions are always purposeful.
Like the lion in the simile, he seeks his prey in the pursuit of survival
and life. His anger is only rarely separate from rational thought and
the cunning use of words. In the *Iliad*, man looks into the abyss of
death and is tragically drawn towards it. In the *Odyssey*, man stands
on the edge of darkness, he has seen the borders of the human, but
his gaze is to the light and to life.

Meeting Nausicaa, Odysseus utters cautious and flattering
words: 'Are you a goddess or a mortal woman?' he asks, 'You seem
like Artemis to me' (6.149ff.). He wishes her 'all that your heart
desires . . . a husband [literally "a man" – the same word used to
describe Odysseus himself in the all important first line of the poem]
and a home' (6.181). Nausicaa instructs her handmaids to give him
a bath and to clothe him. Athena makes her own contribution to
Odysseus' appearance, giving him stature and adding the colour
of hyacinth to his hair. Thus restored, he does not fail to affect
the 'white armed' (*leukôlenos*) princess, and she, cautious (he must
follow at a distance behind her, she says) yet excited, takes him to

the palace to meet her parents, Alcinoos and Arêtê. Despite some initial suspicion ('Who gave you these clothes?' asks Nausicaa's mother in 7.238), Odysseus wins over the royal couple. He tells them of his 7-year sojourn in Calypso's island, his departure and shipwreck, yet makes no mention of his wife, nor, indeed, reveals his name. Impressed, Alcinoos, whose open enthusiasm is the inverse of Odysseus' wary reserve, says, 'I wish I had a son-in-law like you.' Here, and throughout his stay with the Phaeacians, Odysseus must use all his cunningness to attract sympathy but avoid a union with Nausicaa that will again prevent his homecoming. And, indeed, he deftly secures from Alcinoos the promise to send him, the very next day, back home.

Counting bedtimes (7.343ff.; 13.17) and 'rosy-fingered dawns' (8.1; 13.18), we can calculate that Odysseus is detained a day longer than promised (his ship sails off for Ithaca on day 34 of the plot). This one day nevertheless stretches over five books, as time is whiled away in the telling of stories which themselves span many past years, from the fall of Troy 10 years earlier (the Wooden Horse) to Odysseus' arrival in Scheria. These stories comprise songs by the blind Phaeacian singer Demodocus, and, above all, the tales told by Odysseus himself, who, Alcinoos says, describes his story, his *mythos*, skilfully and truthfully 'like a singer' (11.368). Thematically, these books are the most colourful in the poem, ranging from a comic tale of domestic infidelity among the gods to accounts of cannibalism and descriptions of other man-eating monsters. In a more abstract sense, this section is a particularly important discussion of general Odyssean themes such as poetry and discourse and the relation between words, memory, identity and truth. A prominent role among these is played by the theme of names and naming. Odysseus tells many tales, but does not disclose his name to the Phaeacians until Book 9, when he feels he has secured their sympathy. When he finally asserts 'I am Odysseus, son of Laertes', he also proudly adds 'I am of interest to all men because of my wiles [*doloisi* – 'cunning tricks'], and my fame reaches heaven' (9.19–20). Through his stories, Odysseus, an unabashed master of deception, re-establishes elaborate links with persons, places and ideas ('chains of reference', as philosopher Saul Kripke calls them in his discussion of identity and the act of naming). These stories constitute Odysseus' personal identity which, like poetry itself, is a complex web of past events and performance in its present contexts.

To describe in detail the many fantastic episodes in the *Apologue* would require a separate book and can provide only a dim reflection of the Homeric narrative itself. I will therefore merely outline these in the briefest way possible as I contextualize more general comments. In Book 8, before Odysseus begins his tales, Demodocus sings of the 'quarrel of Odysseus and Achilles' (8.73–82), an episode not attested elsewhere in extant Greek literature but clearly a kind of compact echo of the *Iliad*, which shifts the focus of attention to the hero of the *Odyssey*. Demodocus also sings of the adulterous affair of Ares and Aphrodite (8.266–366), a comic interlude that nevertheless highlights the question of conjugal fidelity and reminds us of the threat posed by Penelope's predicament: Among the gods, infidelity is a laughing matter. Among mortals, as we know from the story of Agamemnon and Clytemnestra, it is a matter of life and death. Finally, Demodocus sings of Odysseus' ingenious strategy of the Trojan Horse (8.499–520) that leads to triumph in the siege of Troy. It is a fitting introduction for a man who is about to tell his story and reveal his identity. Each of these songs establishes multiple temporal and thematic continuities and tensions with both Odysseus' Iliadic past and his forthcoming trials on Ithaca. The narratives underline the relation between Odysseus and Achilles as protagonists of their respective poems; they highlight Odysseus' quarrel with the suitors, the question of Penelope's fidelity, of Odysseus' trickery and the reclaiming of his palace.

Odysseus' stories in Books 9–13 of his own adventures begin when he tells the Phaeacians his name and the name of his homeland (9.19ff.), and immediately move on to the description of an ill-fated raid on the Cicones (9.39ff.) which results in the loss of many of his men. Odysseus next describes a visit to the land of Lotus Eaters. The Lotus is a plant that brings 'forgetfulness' (9.84ff.). For those who eat it, it bears the threat of a loss of fame and thus of a social death – comparable to Odysseus' fate on the island of Calypso, the 'hider', and to the effect of Helen's drug. The consequences of this kind of 'second' death are even more disastrous for heroes than those of the end of their biological life. As he recounts his trials, Odysseus loses his ships and his men one by one. By the end of his narrative, no one but himself will remain.

Odysseus' next adventure is one of the best known scenes in the *Odyssey*: his encounter with the Cyclops Polyphemus (9.105–566), a one-eyed cave-dwelling cannibal. Each one of the Cyclopes, we are told, lives by the laws he makes for himself and his family, almost outside of any social sphere. The story is a Homeric variant on a common folk tale, and is also widely depicted in ancient art – for example, in vase painting (see, e.g. Glenn 1971). The Cyclops has no respect for the primordial codes of hospitality. He greedily devours Odysseus' men, who are his guests. Yet even the Cyclops is not merely an animal in human form. Perverse as his behaviour is, he wants to know the identity of his guests. 'Who are you?' he asks Odysseus. The obliging reply is antiquity's most famous pun. My 'famous name', says Odysseus, 'is No-One' (in Greek *outis* – 9.364–6). When Odysseus succeeds in blinding Polyphemus, the Cyclops cries out to his neighbours for help. '*No one* is trying to kill me by trickery or force!' he says (9.408. See de Jong 2001: 239–49) thereby contradicting himself.

To have a name is to be a 'man'. The *Odyssey*'s preoccupation with Odysseus' name is a complement to its interest in 'the man of many ways' who has many identities and indeed assumes more than one name. Calling himself 'no one' is Odysseus' strategy for survival in a deadly world of monsters. Yet as he re-enters the sphere of civilization and attempts to regain his former self, he will have to slowly, warily, give up such tricks.

Having escaped from the Cyclops, Odysseus and his ships reach the island of Aeolus, master of the winds (10.1ff.). Aeolus offers the fleet the favourable West Wind and places all other winds in a bag which he gives to Odysseus. The ships sail for 9 days and on the tenth come within sight of Ithaca (10.28–29), but Odysseus' men, through greed and curiosity, open the bag and release the wrong winds. The ships are blown off course and back to Aeolus, who this time sends them away with nothing but words of contempt. Human folly is always a force driving the plot of the *Odyssey*, setting it 'off course' and, as already Zeus in the opening assembly in Book 1 says, bringing destruction to men through their own devices.

Odysseus sails on to the land of the Laestrygonian cannibals, where all but one of his ships are lost (10.80–132). From there, he and his remaining companions sail to the island of Aiaia, home of the witch Circe. She is another powerful woman who threatens to take away Odysseus' homecoming but ultimately offers assistance. At first, she turns all his men into swine, and indeed would do so to Odysseus, too. But with the help of Hermes and a magical herb called Moly (10.304) he prevails, restores his men to their human form, and, after a year's stay, is sent with instructions from Circe on to Hades and the Land of the Dead to consult the ghost of the seer Teiresias.

Book 11 is the *Odyssey*'s *nekuia* or 'song of the dead'. It describes an underworld of sombre rituals and doleful spirits. It is also an important component in the story of Odysseus' 'rebirth'. Here narrative visions of the past and future – the very idea of Homeric epic – prevail. Odysseus meets Teiresias' ghost as well as the ghosts of his mother Anticleia, Agamemnon, Achilles, Ajax and many other heroes and of famous heroines, too. Teiresias speaks of Odysseus' future, of the end of his journeys at a moment of mistaken identification, when, far inland, the oar on Odysseus' shoulder, the mark of a wandering sailor, will be thought of as a winnowing fan, the sign of a sedentary tiller of the land. And indeed, Teiresias also tells Odysseus of his (Odysseus') death (11.134). Odysseus' encounter with the ghost of Achilles is another seminal moment in the underworld. We get a glimpse of how the *Odyssey* interrogates and interprets the *Iliad*. 'Don't console me about death, brilliant Odysseus', says Achilles, 'I would rather be a farm labourer, slaving for another man who owns no land and has not much wealth than be king of all the withered dead' (11.488–91). As we noted already in the first chapter, these words pose a challenge to the basic values of Homeric, and especially Iliadic poetry. They point to inevitable change and to the end of the heroic age, or rather, to the end of the consciousness and value systems of the heroic world. Yet Achilles' statement is not an elision of the past. It is, rather, a mark of its 'pastness' and its glory *as past*. Both Achilles and Odysseus, different as they are, have, in fact, made their choice as heroes and have opted for fame.

Leaving the underworld, Odysseus describes to the Phaeacians how he sailed back to Circe's island – where he is told of the further trials that await him on the sea. He and his men will sail past the island of the Sirens, deadly creatures, half bird and half woman, who beguile and charm (*thelgousin*) unsuspecting sailors with their song and lure them to their deaths. Whoever hears their song never returns: 'his wife and little children don't ever stand beside him or rejoice when he comes home' (12.42–3). The Sirens' sweet song is a magical rout to oblivion that underscores the dangerous power of words, especially in the hands of female singers. In order to listen to the song but avoid death, Odysseus must stop his companions' ears with wax and lash himself to the mast as his ship sails past the Siren's rock. The bleached bones of other sailors that surround the Sirens tell us that they have sung their song before. Yet they tailor their song (always a 'new' song) to the moment and the man (12.184–191):

> Come over here, much-praised Odysseus, great glory of
>   Achaeans,
> and beach your ship so you can listen to our voice.
> For no man ever sails by our island in his black ship
> before he hears the voice of our honeyed mouths.
> He takes pleasure in it, then departs, knowing more.
> For we know everything, how in wide Troy
> Argives and Trojans toiled and suffered by the will of the gods.
> And we know everything that happens upon the fertile earth.

Odysseus survives. Sitting comfortably in the Phaeacians' shady halls, he has lived to tell the tale. Yet his story stakes a claim for the power of epic song (the Sirens sing of Troy!) over life, which is essential if poetry is to be portrayed as more than entertainment.

Odysseus tells his hosts of yet further adventures, of more monsters, of the man-eating Scylla and her six deadly puppy-heads perched on a rock face, of the whirlpool Charybdis (12.235ff.) and of the affair on the island of Thrinacia, where Helios, the sun, keeps his oxen (12.260ff.), and where, again, through their own folly, his men perish. By the end of Book 12, Odysseus has lost all his comrades and his one remaining ship has been smashed to pieces. Clinging to the ship's keel, he drifts for 9 days (12.447, here, as before, even the fantastic narratives retain a clear counting of time. See, e.g. 7.253; 9.82; 10.28 and 14.314) until he reaches the island of Calypso. Odysseus' narrative of adventure now comes to an end and returns full circle to the place where his journey to the Phaeacians began. This section of the *Odyssey* is thus an elaborate repetition. Yet it repeats stories that neither the Phaeacians nor we as members of the audience or as readers have heard before in this performance.

Are the stories Odysseus tells the Phaeacians 'true'? Alcinoos and Arêtê do not challenge them: 'you don't seem like a cheat and a dissembler', says Alcinoos, 'your words have form [*morphê*] and good sense. You speak knowingly, like a singer' (11.362–69). To us too, the words of Odysseus and Homer ring true, at least in the sense that they are masterful and well-formed (they have 'form', *morphê*) examples of storytelling and song, part of the canonical tradition of the *Odyssey*. Yet, quite apart from their fantastic content, these are the words of a trickster, who later invents what are patently false identities for himself (e.g. as a Cretan – an inaugural moment for the tradition of 'Cretan lies' in the West). Furthermore, given that Odysseus is compared by Alcinoos to a singer, are we to trust singers like Demodocus, or even 'Homer' himself? Could they too be masters of wiles? The structure of the narrative blurs the line between reality and the description of reality in words. Unstable and potentially bewildering as this move may be, it is also a strategic element in Homeric poetry's claim to enact 'imperishable' and in this sense 'living' fame. This requires a brief explanation.

The *Odyssey* is not a nihilistic poem, nor is it a poem of relative identities. The return of Odysseus raises basic ontological ('what exists?' 'Is this the real Odysseus?') and epistemological ('what is knowledge?' 'how do we know that this is the real Odysseus?') challenges. But the poem is unambiguous about the values of the social bonds of kinship, love and above all trust that link Odysseus, Penelope, Telemachus and Laertes when they are physically separated, bonds that are asserted again at the end of the poem. The *Odyssey* has a purpose, an end point, what Aristotle calls a *telos*. Nevertheless, the poem establishes the stability of its values precisely through emphasis on the fragility or precariousness of existence and knowledge and on the essential plurality of discourse, and, more practically, especially in the second half of the poem, through Odysseus' and Penelope's constant wariness of deception. In the end, as we shall see, the *Odyssey* seems to suggest that we possess, not certain knowledge, but rather trust. Trust as a force does not rely on absolute fact, but, in the *Odyssey*, we find that it can create the facts of human social bonds: relationships between a husband and a wife, a father and a son, a son and a father and, in the wider sense, our relationship, as audiences and readers, with memory, tradition and the past. Indeed, the lack of absolute knowledge is inherent to the idea of trust. In a world of absolute truth, when, like the Muses (*Iliad* 2.484ff. again), we have 'been everywhere and know everything', trust and mortal agency and, paradoxically, song, are unnecessary. This perspective ultimately provides a foundation for the positive claims of the *Odyssey* and perhaps of Homeric poetry too: Like Odysseus, mortals who possess mind (*mêtis* – a quality that marks both Odysseus and Penelope) and discourse (*mythos* – Odysseus is *the* essential man of words and Penelope is the one who is the ultimate judge of their truth) have the creative power to establish and preserve real, meaningful identities, relationships and traditions.

The return to Ithaca

Odysseus' stay with the Phaeacians ends with the rise of day 34 of the narrative (see 13.18), as his seafaring hosts ferry him back in their ship to Ithaca and set him down on its shore, asleep, in the Cave of the Nymphs. Numerous attempts have been made to identify this cave and indeed other locations in the *Odyssey*'s landscapes (see, e.g. Bittlestone 2005). The temptation of following in Odysseus' footsteps, like the attraction of finding Troy, is obvious. The ancient seafaring world and its geography have, beyond doubt, formed the backdrop to the *Odyssey*. And yet already in antiquity, the Cave of the Nymphs, like the cave in Socratic thought for example (see at the beginning of Plato's *Republic*, Book VII, 514a–520a), have marked precisely the limits of human knowledge (see comments by Hoekstra in Heubeck et al. 1988–92 [vol. II, 1989]: 171). It hardly seems worthwhile to try to reduce them to literal holes in the rock-face.

With the arrival in Ithaca, Odysseus' 'outer' homecoming comes to an end and a second, 'inner' homecoming begins. One homecoming, it seems, is not enough for a poem whose essential figure is the figure of repetition. Odysseus must now reclaim his position as king, recover his identity and reaffirm his social and personal ties with members of his household and his family, with his swineherd Eumaius and with the dog Argos, with his old nursemaid Eurycleia, his son, Telemachus, his wife, Penelope, and finally Laertes, his father. To do so, he must, paradoxically, assume many disguises and tell stories of his past, sometimes constructing elaborate false identities for himself. As a corollary of his words, he also displays several signs (*sêmata*) to his doubting interlocutors: He reveals a scar etched on his body; he strings a bow and completes the feat of shooting an arrow through 12 axe-heads; he describes a tree trunk that is the secret bedpost of the marriage bed he himself has made many years earlier; and he recounts the layout of an orchard which his father gave him when he was a boy.

In Book 13, on the Ithacan shore, Odysseus first meets Athena, who appears before him in disguise, this time as a youth (222). Odysseus too assumes a disguise in the encounter. He invents for himself the identity of a Cretan wanderer. Goddess and hero share a predilection for ruse. Athena reveals her true person and she and Odysseus together plan his comeback and the downfall of the suitors. Transformed by Athena into an old beggar, Odysseus reaches the farmstead of his faithful swineherd Eumaius, where he tells more of his Cretan tales (14.191–359). He will continue to do so right up to the end of the poem, promising Eumaius (and later Penelope, too) on oath that 'Odysseus shall return' (14.152). In spite of himself, he is speaking the truth and foretelling (almost 'like a poet') the plot of the *Odyssey*.

Throughout the course of these events, Telemachus has been staying with Menelaus in Sparta. In Book 15, he is brought back to Ithaca with Athena's help. Telemachus negotiates delicate diplomatic situations, offers help to a suppliant (15.22–5), and, sailing home, successfully evades the suitors' ambush. By the end of the poem, he will take his place in the battle against the suitors next to his father (cf. 24.514–15). Yet Telemachus will not replicate his father's character and actions. He is not a teller of his own stories. His journeys are not the existential wanderings of a restless man of many minds nor the quest for a homecoming. Telemachus' coming of age will come to mark, as one critic suggests, the end of a poetic tradition of Homeric song (Martin 1993). It is precisely the end of the heroic race, its 'pastness', that is the necessary precondition to the beginning of the tradition of the songs of the heroic past. This is not a play on words. The *Odyssey* itself as poetry of the past and its illustrious tradition of reception in the literary history of the West, the *Odyssey*'s pastness in relation to Virgil's *Aeneid*, to James Joyce's *Ulysses* and to the many recent *Odyssey*-inspired films, are an example of how this idea of a mortal past survives when it is no longer a living body.

Odysseus and Telemachus meet in Eumaius' hut and Odysseus reveals his identity to his son (Book 16). The two are now united against the suitors and head for the palace in Ithaca. The scenes

that follow focus on the suitors' reckless behaviour and the
mistreatment (by the goatherd Melanthius in 7.215ff.; by the suitor
Antinoos, who throws a footstool at Odysseus – 17.462ff.; in a
comic but gruesome fist fight with the beggar Iros – 18ff.) of the
stranger, the disguised Odysseus. Penelope's predicament too is
highlighted (e.g. 17.492–606).

Disguise and recognition are central themes in this part of
the poem, as Odysseus withholds his identity from the suitors
(with much dramatic irony) and reveals it to other characters.
A well-known pathetic vignette describes Odysseus' recognition
by Argos, his dog (17.290–327). Argos ('Swift'), once a light-
footed hunter, now lies neglected in the dung. Yet with his animal
instincts, he sees through Odysseus' disguise. The dog feebly
wags his tail in recognition of his master. 'Then the fate [*moira*]
of black death grasped Argos, as soon as he saw Odysseus, in
the twentieth year', says the narrator. Here again we see the
Odyssey's underlying sense of ending. It is a homecoming, not to
the house in a time gone by, but to a place that has changed with
time. Return in the poem and in the Homeric tradition at large
would be meaningless if epic time stood still, if Odysseus could
simply re-enter the palace he had left 20 years earlier, if the world
of the *Odyssey* and the *Iliad* were not affected by mortality and
irrevocable change.

In Book 18, Penelope appears before the suitors. 'Their knees
were loosened and their hearts were enchanted with desire'
(18.212). They bring her gifts under the approving gaze of the
disguised Odysseus. They dance and sing and dally with the maids
in Odysseus' house while the beggar suffers further indignities (by
the servant maid Melantho, 18.321ff.; by the suitor Eurymachus,
18.349). But now, practical preparations for the suitors' destruction
begin. While the suitors are away from the hall, Odysseus and
Telemachus with help from Athena remove their weapons and lock
the doors (19.1–51). The suitors return and Penelope observes their
continuing mistreatment of the stranger. A long interview between
Odysseus, still disguised as the beggar, and his wife follows. 'What
man are you, and from where? Where are your city and parents?'
asks Penelope (19.105 – the line is repeated several times in the
Odyssey, e.g. 1.170; 10.325, etc.). The right moment has, however,
not yet come. Odysseus is too cautious to reveal himself so soon,
although he repeatedly addresses his wife with the words *ô gynai*,

which can be playfully translated both as 'O lady', a formal address
to a superior woman, and more intimately as 'O wife'. Penelope too
is cautious. She is not yet ready to accept (or at least, according
to some critics, openly acknowledge) news that her husband is
back. Likewise, the *Odyssey*'s narrative is not yet ready to end,
and we ourselves are not yet ready to give up the *Odyssey*'s sweet
ironies. Odysseus spins off another Cretan story, making 'the
many falsehoods of his tale seem like truth' (203, like the Muses
in Hesiod's *Theogony* 27). He describes the clothes which, he says,
Odysseus was wearing on his departure (19.225–43), and promises
Penelope that Odysseus will return (19.306).

At Penelope's behest, the old nursemaid Eurycleia now washes
the stranger's feet. Eurycleia recognizes the first of several distinct
signs (*sêmata*) of identity – the scar left on his leg as a boy by a wild
boar (19.392–468) during a visit to his maternal uncle Autolycus.
We are taken back to a scene describing Odysseus' 'baptismal'
moment of naming and thus to the moment that originally
marks his identity. He is Odysseus, 'the man of suffering/wrath'
(*odyssamenos*, 19.407. See discussion above and Dimock 1963).
But this recognition too is premature. Eurycleia is silenced by
Odysseus on pain of death.

Washed and dressed, the beggar is given another audience with
Penelope. She tells him of her sorrows and asks him to interpret a
dream which she has had: an eagle with a crooked beak has come
down from the mountain and has broken the necks of her favoured
geese. In her dream, says Penelope, she wept bitterly for her loss.
The eagle then speaks to her in human voice and tells her that he
is her husband, Odysseus, who has come back (19.535–53). The
disguised Odysseus sitting in front of Penelope assures his wife of
the truth of her dream. 'Odysseus himself', he says, has shown her
this sign. She, however, remains sceptical. We are dealing with a
complex scene that, on the one hand, confirms its own meaning,
not once, but twice (internally – when the dream-eagle explains
that he himself is Odysseus; externally – when Odysseus affirms
that interpretation). Yet, on the other hand, the scene also generates
new difficulties. Readers have found it puzzling, in part because
of Penelope's sympathy for her geese, which seems to suggest
sympathy for the suitors. But a sense of lingering doubt may be the
verses' desired effect: At this point in the narrative, trust has not
yet been re-established between the husband and the wife. In its

elusive way, the scene helps to highlight the tensions, fears, risks and the hopes that a reunion carries with it.

The *Odyssey*'s plot must nevertheless move forward to a conclusion. Shortly after her interview with Odysseus, Penelope announces a contest that will decide her future and accelerate the closure of the poem. Whoever of the suitors will string Odysseus' bow and shoot an arrow through 12 axe-heads will win her hand in marriage (19.572–81). Omens which throughout the *Odyssey* foreshadow the future and foretell the events of the plot increasingly populate the latter parts of the *Odyssey*. They presage Odysseus' victory, for example, at the beginning of Book 20, as Zeus thunders from Olympus (102–4). Odysseus often understands these signs (in Greek, *sêmata* again – the same word that designates his scar and other signs of recognition). In contrast, the suitors fail to read them (e.g. a bird omen in 20.242–43). We, the audience/readers, too, are given a message through such omens: Those who can read the signs of epic will triumph, and those who cannot are destined for death and a loss of their fame.

The end of the poem

What remain of the *Odyssey*, Books 20–24, describes the climactic events of the last 2 days of the plot (days 40 and 41. The sun rises at 20.91 and 23.347): the contest of the bow (Book 21), the killing of the suitors (Book 22), the reunion of Odysseus and Penelope (Book 23) and, finally, the reunion of Odysseus and Laertes and scenes from the underworld (Book 24). The archery contest takes the narrative a step further towards the confirmation of Odysseus' identity. As the contest begins, Telemachus asks to try to string the bow (21.101–39). Three times he fails. On the fourth attempt, we are told, he would have succeeded, but is checked by a nod from his father (21.129). Odysseus and Telemachus here enact performative statements of their proper kinship roles, the former with a nod of paternal authority, the latter acknowledging the sign, in a gesture of filial obedience (In other words, Odysseus' and Telemachus' roles as father and son are not simply given. The text says that Telemachus could have strung the bow, and we may be left wondering, what would have happened had he succeeded? According to the terms of the contest, Telemachus would have won his own mother's hand in marriage. Fortunately, the *Odyssey* never pursues this route and its potentially tragic consequences). The suitors Leodes and Antinoos try to string the bow, but they too fail (21.140–87). Antinoos and Eurymachus, the leaders of the suitors, now try to postpone the contest to the next day, but the beggar asks to try his hand. He picks up the bow, strings it, 'as a man strings a lyre' (21.406–8 – see our discussion of this simile, above), and easily shoots the arrow through the axe-heads.

There follows the poetry of revelation and violent revenge. Odysseus casts off his beggar's rags and 'pours forth swift arrows'. 'Now, at last', he declares, 'this insatiate contest has come to an end' (22.5). The *Odyssey*'s plot, however, is not yet complete. Even now, the poem is not ready to give up its ruse or to reveal Odysseus' identity to everyone. Odysseus shoots and kills Antinoos as the narrative reverts to anatomical observations worthy of the *Iliad*: The arrow cuts 'clean through the soft neck . . . up through his nostrils came the thick jet of a man's blood'. Yet the suitors imagine it is all a terrible mistake by the stranger (22.31–2). Odysseus sets them right 'Dogs! You thought I would never come back to my home' (22.35). They try to protest and to defend themselves, but with the aid of Telemachus, Eumaius and Laertes, Odysseus kills them all. He then turns to the servant maids who have been sleeping with the suitors and hangs them one by one ('they writhed a little while with their feet, but not long', 22.473). The insolent and faithless goatherd Melanthius is given special treatment. Odysseus cuts off his nose and ears, rips out his genitals and throws them to the dogs, and severs his hands and feet (22.474–7). These are scenes of extreme violence by any standard. Only Phemius the singer and Medon the herald are spared. Some critics note defensively that Odysseus does not actually order Melanthius' savage treatment (the text simply says 'they' did it). It is rather a weak attempt at an explanation. Others have expressed the hope that Telemachus, at least, is not among the perpetrators. Some identify traces of ritual sacrifice in these descriptions. Others still have tried to excise these offensive bits from the text of the *Odyssey*. Notwithstanding, it is hard to deny the fact that Homeric tradition has accepted, preserved and transmitted these verses and their violence. We must remember that Homeric poetry, and even the *Odyssey* and its upbeat end of homecoming and reunion, is poetry of gravity and substance. It is not an '. . . and they lived happily ever after' fairy tale.

In Book 23, we finally witness Penelope's acceptance of her husband's return. She is, however, in every way a match for her wily husband, and indeed, plays an active role in restoring his identity (there is a large body of learned literature on Penelope. Has she recognized Odysseus? How much, exactly, does she know, and when? See, e.g. Murnaghan 1986, Katz 1991, Felson 1994, Clayton 2004). Eurycleia offers Penelope the sign of the scar as proof of Odysseus' return, but Penelope, as always, speaks in sceptical tones 'It's hard for you to comprehend the counsels of the everlasting gods' (23.81–2), she says to the old nursemaid. One commentator adds 'Penelope suggests that gods can manage scars too' (Tracy 1990: 135). She and we audiences and readers need more proof. Precisely because of the poem's playful nature, the prospect of ending on a false note is too bewildering to contemplate. Odysseus must come home as surely as, for example, Hector and Achilles are fated to die.

The climax of recognition is reached by means of a cunning and powerful sign (a *sêma*). Penelope sets a trap for Odysseus, asking Eurycleia to move the bed 'which he himself made' (23.178) and set it for him outside the marital chamber. Odysseus is finally outwitted by this ruse. He is angrily forced to reveal the secret of the bed – against his will and thus more reliably – and to confirm his identity to Penelope with a true sign. He himself, he says, fashioned one of the bedposts from the trunk of an olive tree (23.183–230) which is rooted in the ground and which is thus immovable. 'No other mortal has seen our bed', he adds, 'except you [Penelope] and I alone' (23.226–7), and 'one handmaid . . . who guarded the doors of this protected chamber for us' (23.227–9). If the bed can now be removed from its guarded inner space and placed outdoors, the implication is that Penelope's marital fidelity has been compromised (for a discussion, see Zeitlin 1995). It is now Penelope's turn to lose her balance. The marital bed and her fidelity are intact, of course. The sign of the bed has confirmed both Odysseus' identity and Penelope's powers of mind (we shall come back to this important topic in the next chapter). She tearfully throws herself into her husband's arms.

Penelope and Odysseus happily enjoy the pleasures of reunion (23.296). We too, as audiences and readers, enjoy the satisfaction of this moment. At least some critics have been of the view that this, quite literally, was the end of the poem. The ancient commentaries known as the 'scholia', in a note on verse 296, state that two of the most influential Homeric scholars of antiquity, both keepers of the great Library of Alexandria, 'Aristophanes [of Byzantium] and Aristarchus [of Samothrace] marked this as the end [in Greek the *telos*] of the *Odyssey*'. These views are also echoed later in the critical tradition by another illustrious Homer commentator, Eustathius of Thessalonica (twelfth century AD).

Is 23.296 really the end of the poem? Can we, for example, ever be completely certain about the identity of a trickster like the man just united with Penelope and say that his homecoming is now complete? Is the secret of the bed secure beyond the shadow of a doubt? Odysseus and Penelope may guard it jealously, but is it also safe in the hands of a handmaid (whose appearance here and nowhere else has puzzled commentators)? The end of the *Odyssey*'s plot and the reunion of Penelope are complete, even as the potential of the poem to 'exceed its own boundaries' remains. The epistemology of the *Odyssey* (in other words, its position towards the question of true knowledge), the identity of Odysseus and the essential plotline of the *Odyssey* were not challenged in antiquity (with a few exceptions, notably; traditions begun with Xenophanes of Colophon in the sixth century BCE have also cast doubt on Homer's description of the gods). But the poem, whose whole purpose, after all, is to resist the finality of life, may here implicitly acknowledge that happiness is not a matter of absolute, final knowledge, but of ongoing, living relationships. And of course, in terms of the received text, line 296 in Book 23 is not the end of the poem.

Three important scenes follow the reunion of Odysseus and Penelope. First, a description of the souls of the dead suitors (24.1ff.). Next comes a reunion between Odysseus and his father (another aspect of the past, 24.205ff.), in which the hero cruelly withholds his true identity from an old and downcast Laertes, and only reveals it later on by displaying a further sign of identity as he recounts the precise number of trees in an orchard that Laertes gave him as a child (24.336–42). Last, but not least, rumour of the killing of the suitors spreads through the city and the Ithacans assemble angrily to avenge their kin (24.412ff.). A swift battle ensues in which Odysseus has the upper hand. As the text says, he would have killed them all (24.528), but he is finally checked by Athena, who in the form of Mentor imposes a truce and brings the *Odyssey* to a close.

Where, then, does the poem conclude? One modern scholar quite rightly focuses the problem by asking 'In what sense did the Alexandrian scholars use [the word] *telos* ["end"]?' (Heubeck in Heubeck et al. 1988–92 [vol. III, 1992]: 343). Are we looking to the closure of major themes? To a rounding off of narrative structure? Are we simply recording a historical fact of the tradition? For some scholars, the debate has not yet ended. Yet epic tradition itself offers a clear answer. Although doubts about the end were never out of the sight of critics, the tradition never dropped Book 24 of the *Odyssey* from the canon. The 'true' answer, then, is simply that Homeric tradition, whose main concerns are precisely finality, the necessity of an end and the possible means of transcending it, here reflects its thematic question in the literal problem of 'what is the last line of the poem?' Homer leaves that question in the hands of all those who would perform, read and interpret the poem afterwards.

CHAPTER EIGHT

Boundaries and social worlds: Men and women

Gender divisions

Homer's world, like epic itself, its stories, and even the technical composition of its formulaic verse, is defined by boundaries that are at once clearly marked and yet movable. We have just seen how this affects the end of the *Odyssey*. We have also noted, for example, that the plots of the *Iliad* and *Odyssey* are confined to relatively short periods of 'real time', just 51 and 41 days respectively, yet both extend many years forwards and backwards to past events and to events not told in the poems. Similarly, in terms of geographic boundaries, the events of the *Iliad* are contained within a small space – the Greek camp by the sea, the Trojan plain and the city of Troy. Yet the Trojan War, the conflict of Greeks and barbarians, is an ancient 'world war'. If we recall the Greek contingents and the host of the Trojans and their allies listed in the Catalogues in Book 2 of the *Iliad*, we realize that the poem compresses the whole archaic world into a single 'geographic' site. In the *Odyssey*, narrative traverses the 'many cities' which Odysseus has seen in his wandering. It spans the island of Calypso, Phaiacia, the Cyclops and Circe, and gradually moves from the very end of the world, the river Oceanus, and Hades, the world of the dead, to Ithaca, to Odysseus palace, to the bedchamber he shares with Penelope and indeed, to their marital bed. For all its expansive breadth, it focuses on just one man.

Homer's social world is similarly marked by boundaries which structure the meaning of the verse, but which are nevertheless challenged and traversed. One of the most vivid and telling of these concerns images, groupings, roles, institutions and relations which separate the bodies, practices and identities of men and women respectively. Gender relations are, of course, essential to the regulation and structuring of behaviour, not merely sexual or domestic, but for the organization of society at large. In both ancient and modern thought, these relations have been viewed as basic elements of sociality. One of the fathers of modern anthropology and social thinking, Claude Lévi-Strauss, in his seminal work, *The Elementary Structures of Kinship*, argued that the exchange (or 'traffic') in women, by men, within and among social groups, constituted a basic human communicative medium or 'language' (Lévi-Strauss 1969). But already Aristotle, for example, in the *Politics*, began his discussion of social order and the state (the *polis* – for Aristotle, the most highly evolved form of a commonwealth), by describing the basic relations between males and females and the nuclear unit of the household (the *oikos*). Aristotle's world is a world with sharply distinguished roles (*Politics* 1252a.26–31):

> The first coupling together of persons . . . to which necessity gives rise is that between those who are unable to exist without one another, namely the union of female and male for the continuance of the species . . . and the union of natural ruler and natural subject for the sake of security.

Aristotle stresses the difference between the sexes (*Politics* 1254b.13–16):

> . . . the male is superior and the female inferior, the male ruler and the female subject.

Many of us today will, of course, vehemently object to such views, but they express a prominent ancient bias which is also significantly reflected in Homeric poetry. Yet the *Iliad* and *Odyssey* also contain other, more complex images of the relations between the sexes and, by extension, of the order of society at large.

Aristotle was of the view that the relations between men and women, as indeed more generally the relations between masters and subjects, are fixed and determined 'by nature'. Modern views allow, in greater or lesser degrees, that gender differences (and according to some views even sexual difference) are a social construct and depend heavily on historical, economic and political circumstances, despite the obvious bodily/biological element. True to the plurality we have been stressing throughout this book, there may therefore be in Homer, right at the 'heart' of antiquity, many elements that allow for a multiplicity of perspectives.

Despite the martial and heroic content of Homer's poetry, despite the fact that the *Iliad* is a poem about men's fighting and the *Odyssey* is a poem about a singular man, the most prominent actions and plot movements in both the *Iliad* and *Odyssey*, are motivated by women and are centred on the relations between men and women and on what the ancients called conjugal *homilia* (see, e.g. Maronitis 2004). These relations also underpin both the order and cohesion of predominantly male or overtly male-controlled societies and also the threats these societies face. The two poems do, however, differ considerably with regard to the portrayal of such relations. The *Iliad* places greater emphasis on the destructive consequences of men's disputes over women and of states of separation between men and women. The *Odyssey* is more optimistic and gives more weight to a positive and harmonious potential of reunion. Although an underlying hierarchy of gender relations is maintained in the transition from one poem to the other, the *Odyssey* provides stronger challenges to this hierarchy in a manner that is perhaps comparable to the challenge to the heroic code voiced by Achilles in the Embassy scene in *Iliad* Book 9 and in the world of the dead in the *Odyssey* Book 11.

The abduction of Helen by Paris from Sparta and from her husband Menelaus, the larger story underlying the *Iliad* (not openly mentioned, but see *Iliad* 24.25–30), is a story about the transgression of the socially sanctioned union of a man and a woman. Such unions establish basic patterns of social behaviour: the legitimacy of offspring, the rules of inheritance, social continuity and the division and transfer of wealth. The abduction (whether Helen was a willing partner or acting under duress) replaces a legitimized public framework with illicit association. It generates not merely personal, but above all political enmity between Greeks and Trojans and leads to the war and ultimately to the destruction of Troy. This point needs to be stressed: Antiquity's most famous (one might say 'foundational') war as it is portrayed in Homer is not fought over the control of territory or natural resources, over trade, security or the exploitation of populations and labour. It is fought by men over a woman. Furthermore, when the war is won, the Greeks take Helen and leave. They do take booty, prizes and women slaves with them, but do not attempt to control Troy and its territory.

It is also important to note that the epic conflict over Helen is a strong social binding force that brings men together. The Trojan expedition is the basis of an alliance – which did not exist before the war – between the many Greek contingents under Agamemnon's leadership. It is almost only Menelaus who is personally affected by Helen's abduction. The other Greeks may be fighting for their own share in prizes and glory. Yet, at least formally, their common objective is to bring back Helen, to punish the offending city and in this sense to reassert both normative practice and a general symbolic social order which is perhaps emblematic of their future ('Panhellenic', see further below) identity later in Greek antiquity.

The events that form the immediate plot of the *Iliad* can likewise be viewed as a narrative of the transgression and restoration of social order against the background of relationships between men and women. Achilles' wrath and the quarrel between the heroes are events framed by the seizing and return of Chryseis on the one hand and Briseis on the other. Chryses' daughter has been taken by Agamemnon as part of one kind of social order that involves the distribution of women (and other prizes) among the Greek heroes in accordance with the laws of war. Chryses' appeal to the sons of Atreus to return his daughter and accept the ransom and his prayer to Aollo afterwards, when he is rebuffed, are attempts to restore another, domestic order that belongs outside of war. When Agamemnon is forced to give back Chryseis, this second social order is asserted, while the social hierarchy represented through prizes in the Greek camp is challenged. Agamemnon, as we have seen, stresses that his status depends on the possession of a war prize: 'Prepare another prize for me, so that I should not be the only one among the Argives who is without a prize, for that would not be appropriate' (*Iliad* 1.118–19). When he seizes Briseis, Agamemnon upsets another component of social order. The poem's many cycles of disruptions and restorations of social orders and codes begin . . .

Possession of the female prize is in part a practical concern, but the woman as prize is above all a powerful symbol within the social structure of the Greek camp and the world of the *Iliad*. Agamemnon's speech protesting the loss of Chryseis is coy and dissimulating. Yet there is truth to his words. As we have already seen (above, Chapter 6), the so-called heroic code and the hierarchy of heroic society depend on socially sanctioned allocation and exchange of symbolic goods and prizes, and above all women, between men. It would thus indeed be inappropriate, as Agamemnon suggests, for the leader of the host to be without a prize. We can now see how a localized dispute between Achilles and Agamemnon over the possession of women becomes the thematic focal point of the *Iliad*, which is, after all, an epic representing wide political and social identities.

Gender is not merely a key thematic element of the *Iliad*. As a symbol, it is also an important vehicle for thought. Achilles' recognition of the limits of the heroic code and the framework of the exchange of mortal life for imperishable fame is set off by the seizing of Briseis. But his very reasoning, just like Agamemnon's initial complaint, is articulated, not simply in political or moral terms, but in terms of gender (9.334–6):

> To the nobles and the kings he [Agamemnon] gave prizes.
> They have kept their prizes. But from me alone of the
>   Achaeans,
> he has taken and keeps for himself the consort of my heart.

The object of Achilles' words is Briseis. Yet the consort of Achilles' heart (*alochon thymarea*) is used to state a general principle: Agamemnon has transgressed the underlying codes of a heroic honour system and has arbitrarily singled an individual for unfair treatment. Achilles thus adds (9.337–9. See also above, Chapter 6):

>   . . . Why must Argives fight with Trojans?
> And why did the son of Atreus assemble the host and let it
>   here?
> Was it not for the sake of fair-haired Helen?

The words 'for the sake of fair-haired Helen' are eroticized shorthand for a whole series of social obligations that involve

Agamemnon's fraternal commitment to Menelaus, the legitimate position of women (and ultimately royal marriage) as a symbol of political stability, and much more.

When Achilles finally asks (9.340–3),

> Are the sons of Atreus alone among mortal men the ones
> who love their wives? Since any man who is good and wise
> loves his own woman and honours her, as I too loved Briseis
> with my heart, although she was only a captive of my spear.

he is exploring abstract principles of epic social order through the applied notion of men's love for their wives and indeed his own personal emotion. Looking back to Aristotle's characterization in the *Politics* of the male as 'natural' 'master' and the female as 'subject', provides us with one way of politically unpacking this reasoning (there may be other ways, of course – there is, for instance, no reason to assume that Achilles' emotions in this passage are not genuine, but even emotions are not universal – they are generated and felt within the conventions of specific historical contexts). In caring for his wife or female war-prize, a man is also asserting mastery over what is effectively his own proprietary domain. To separate the hero from his rightful female consort – whether we are thinking of Achilles, or Agamemnon, of Menelaus, or indeed in the *Odyssey*, of Odysseus – is, from this perspective, also to upset the hierarchy of the world.

Actions and roles

Violent martial action is the essence of the *Iliad*'s war poetry and of both its destructive and creative forces. As Seth Schein (1984: 71) puts it,

> The very activity – killing – that confers honour and glory necessarily involves the death not only of other warriors who live and die by the same values as their conquerors, but eventually, in most cases, also of the conquerors themselves. Thus, the same action is creative or fruitful and at the same time both destructive and self-destructive.

These activities are arenas of competition and are in Homer widely portrayed as exclusive to men. Indeed, in the *Iliad*, competition itself is male practice, through which men exercise, assert and compare their excellence (*arêtê*) and ultimately acquire 'imperishable fame'. In contrast, mortal women in the *Iliad* are neither combatants nor competitors. They do not engage in men's 'zero sum' competitions (i.e. competitions where one man's triumph is another man's defeat). Iliadic women do not kill enemies in battle, nor are killed by them. After the war, most of the women in the *Iliad* (with some prominent exceptions, for example, Cassandra) will remain alive, suffering captivity. They do not rescue companions nor are they rescued by allies or gods. Goddesses such as Athena, Hera, Leto, Aphrodite and Artemis, apart, only the Amazons, daughters of Ares, engage in fighting. (See brief mention in *Iliad* 3.189 and 6.186. There was, however, an *aristeia* of the Amazon queen Penthesilea in one of the poems in the *Epic Cycle*, the *Aethiopis*.)

Competitive action and indeed competitive speech too provide the context for a range of emotions such as anger, fear, bravery and friendship – which lead to further action. These are almost exclusively in the male domain. Achilles' stance towards Briseis motivates his response to Agamemnon and his wrath. Patroclus' feelings for his comrades drive him to put on Achilles' armour and eventually lead to his death. Achilles' emotions after Patroclus' death guide his return to battle and the killing of Hector, and his pity in response to Priam's pleas is the focus of the ransoming of Hector's body which brings the *Iliad* to a close. In contrast, women's emotional responses when portrayed in the *Iliad*, for example, in Andromache's complaint to Hector in Book 6, in Briseis' lament for Patroclus, or in the laments by Hecuba, Andromache and Helen over Hector's corpse at the end of the poem, have little or no consequence in action.

Aspects of Homeric poetry's male bias are openly stated throughout the poems and we have already seen some instances. In the meeting between Hector and Andromache in Book 6 of the *Iliad*, Andromache begs her husband not to head for the battlefield. It is, we noted, a unique moment of intimacy. Hector anticipates the fall of Troy, 'there will come a day when sacred Ilion will be destroyed and Priam and the people of Priam the master of the ash spear' (6.448–9). However, what troubles Hector more than the destruction of the city or the death of his bothers is the thought of 'an Achaean in bronze armour' leading Andromache off and 'taking away her days of liberty' and that she, unwilling but under compulsion, will have 'to work at the loom of another and carry water from the spring Messeis or Hyperia' (6.455–9). There is genuine emotion in these words, but Hector's speech remain centred on his male perspective as a hero. Andromache's future captor will one day say 'This is the wife of Hector who was best in warfare among the Trojans, the masters of horses.' Hector concludes (464–5):

> May I be dead and may earth piled high hide me
> before I hear you crying as you are dragged to captivity.

Despite his emotional concern, it seems Hector cannot quite bring himself to recognize a woman's pain. Shortly afterwards, Hector attempts to embrace his young son Astyanax. The fear he inspires in the boy (6.466–81) brings both a smile to Andromache's face and tears to her eyes. But Hector's response is quickly contained by his own assertion of gender boundaries (6.486–93):

> Strange woman [*daimoniê*], why do you ache in your
>   heart so much for me?
> No one will hurl me to Hades unless it is fated
> . . .
> Go back home, inside, and get to your own work,
> the loom and the distaff, and order your handmaidens
> to take up their work. War is a concern for men [*polemos
>   andressi melêsei*]
> all those who are the people of Ilion, but mostly for me.

Weaving may be the duty of a captive woman who works under compulsion (*anankê*). But as these and other lines stress, it is also the proper work of a wife who must obey her husband's firm instruction and leave all concern for fighting to men (on weaving, see Lyons 2003: 100).

Being excluded from martial activity, Iliadic women are by default left with roles as observers and to some degree as commentators. Paradoxically, but in a typical Homeric manner, the women of the *Iliad* thus possess a certain degree of power. As observers of heroic action, they share at least some qualities with audiences and perhaps even with poets and gods. The

Teichoskopia, the 'Observation from the Walls' is a notable example (3.161–244). Helen and Priam look on the duel between Paris and Menelaus, a duel which is emblematic of the Trojan War as a whole. She is the one who, not unlike a poet, introduces Agamemnon (3.178), Odysseus (3.200) and Ajax (3.229) to the Trojans and indeed to us.

More complicated in this regard is women's role in mourning and lament. Non-verbal response apart, words of lament commemorate the dead and keep the 'fame' of the past alive. They thus perform a function that is in part similar to epic poetry (see also discussion in Chapter 2 of the funerary inscription from Kamyros) and endow their speakers with important powers of expression. Some scenes of lament in Homer describe the performance of 'funeral dirges' (*threnoi*). These seem to be more-formal occasions at which the song is performed by professional male singers (*aoidoi* – at the funeral of Hector, *Iliad* 24.720–2), by Achilles (lamenting Patroclus, *Iliad* 18.324–42) or by the Muses themselves (at the funeral of Achilles, *Odyssey* 24.60–1. There is an obvious analogue between the Muses singing such a funerary song and Muses' epic songs about heroes of the past who die for glory). Yet, as we noted, in Homer, we also find occasions of more intimate mourning, weeping and lamentation, denoted by the term *goös*, which is given over to mortal women, prominently, for example, in the speeches over Hector's corpse by Hecuba, Andromache and Helen at the end of the *Iliad*. Paradoxically, such words both affirm women's subject position and provide them with their own voice. Andromache, for example, in her lament for Hector, complains: 'You did not die in bed reaching your arms out to me, nor speak any close-set word [*epos*] to me, one that I could remember always, by nights and by day as I weep for you' (24.743–5). The implication is, on the one hand, that even in death, Hector exerts authority over Andromache. Yet Andromache is the one speaking. In the absence of words from her husband, she is, we assume, by necessity speaking her own words, and may also do so in the future.

Shifting borders

The relations between the *Iliad* and *Odyssey* reveal both considerable continuity and significant change, a unity in multiple form. The basic gender boundaries attested in the *Iliad* can also be observed in the *Odyssey*, and yet the latter poem introduces important modifications. During the first gathering in Odysseus' palace in Book 1, when Penelope speaks, Telemachus orders her to go back into the house. 'Attend to your work, the loom and the distaff', he says. These words are identical to the ones used by Hector when he addresses Andromache in *Iliad* Book 6. In the *Iliad*, however, Hector explains that 'war [*polemos*] is a concern for men, all of them, and mostly for me'. Telemachus uses the same formula, but with an important change. 'Speaking [*muthos*]', he says, is a concern for men, all of them, and mostly for me, who holds power in this house' (1.358–9). On a second occasion, towards the end of the *Odyssey*, when Penelope speaks to complain about the suitors during the contest of the bow, Telemachus again intervenes, claiming authority for himself. Again he sends off his mother to her work at the loom and the distaff (21.350–1) using similar formulaic language, but again with a slight change. 'The bow [*toxon*]', he says in this version, 'is a concern for men, all of them, and mostly for me, who holds power in this house' (352–3).

The change of terms in this repeated formula is indicative of the different boundaries in each of the poems. The crucial word 'war' used in the *Iliad* is replaced in the *Odyssey* by the 'speech' and the 'bow'. By the time the *Odyssey*'s plot begins, the Trojan War (an emblem of all wars) has ended and its disputes have been resolved. Hector, Achilles and Agamemnon, the quintessential Iliadic heroes, are dead. Women are no longer allocated as war-prizes. Helen has been restored to Menelaus and Troy has been sacked. The quarrel over Briseis, the struggle between Achilles and Hector and even the Trojan War are now only a song. Needless to say, in the *Odyssey*, the characterization and allocation of power is a little different relative to the *Iliad*. Telemachus may be using a formulaic variation of the words used by Hector in the *Iliad*, but he is not a second Trojan prince. Hector's use of the expression 'war is a concern for men . . . and mostly for me' is precise and unambiguous. He really is the man to whom war (*polemos*) and Troy's defence are entrusted. In contrast, Telemachus at the beginning of the *Odyssey* is still a helpless young man who, even in the assembly, is not yet treated with the respect he deserves. The claim that words (*muthos*) are his concern since he 'holds power in the house' is unexpected. It must be read either as an ironic emphasis of his present predicament or proleptically, as a foreshadowing of his future. Telemachus' claim about the bow in Book 19 is similarly ambiguous. The bow, inasmuch as only one man, Odysseus, can rightly possess it, is *not* Telemachus' concern. In both cases, the differences should indicate to us that Telemachus and the *Odyssey* may speak with the *Iliad*'s (formulaic) language of heroic authority, but that verbal repetition is not necessarily a repetition of function, and that the orders of that past world and its values may have changed.

One of the features that characterizes the *Odyssey*, already in the first lines that follow the proem, is its emphasis on the individual (1.11–15):

All the other heroes who had escaped sheer destruction
were by now at home, saved from both war and the sea.
But him *alone*, longing for a homecoming and for his wife,
a powerful nymph, Calypso, bright among the goddesses,
kept in the hollow of her cave, wishing him to be her husband.
[my emphasis]

The *Odyssey* is not a story about the suffering of 'countless' heroes (*Iliad* 1.2). It has more to do with the struggles of a single man and it gives greater prominence to more-private worlds, including, for example, aspects of domestic life – not only in the scenes in the palace in Ithaca, but also in the narratives describing Calypso, Circe and Nausicaa and her parents. In domestic spaces, in the household (the *oikos*, contrasting with the commonwealth, the *polis*), relationships between men and women are different from those that characterize public spaces and the battlefield. In these domestic spaces (within the conventions of Homer's world), women play more-active roles which help define the *Odyssey*'s social spheres.

The actions of the *Odyssey* are motivated by the idea of return to the 'inner' space, by Odysseus' travels to Ithaca, by the reassertion of identity and of ties with members of the household (Eumaius, Eurycleia and Philoitius), by Odysseus' reunion with Telemachus and Laertes. Reassertion of control in the palace in Ithaca and the reaffirmation of a natural sequence of generations is a crucial aspect of social order. (In the *Iliad*, we stressed, sons often die, unnaturally and tragically, before their fathers.) Yet more prominent than all of these returns and reaffirmations is, of course, Odysseus' reunion with Penelope, a union of male and female, which combines elements of identity, sexuality, economic well-being and social functions. At the beginning of the poem, we are told that Odysseus is filled with 'longing for his return and his wife' (1.13). And, as we noted earlier, the Hellenistic critics Aristophanes and Aristarchus marked the end of the *Odyssey* at the point (23.296) when that longing is satisfied and Odysseus and Penelope consummate their reunion. In other words, some of Homer's most important critics regarded the re-establishment of order between man and woman, husband and wife, as the moment at which general order of the *Odyssey*'s world is reasserted in the poem and 'return' becomes closure, the point beyond which the poem needs no other words. This suggests that we should look a little closer at the relations of men and women and especially at Odysseus' encounters with women, Calypso, Circe, Nausicaa (and her mother, Arêtê), and consider their place in the *Odyssey*'s world view. Each first poses an obstacle then provides assistance to the return of order. Their stories are part of the background of traditional picaresque narratives, but also constitute a series of instructive variations that structure a Homeric idea of a legitimate and socially productive union between a man and a woman and the foundations of social order in the *Odyssey*.

The nymph Calypso offers Odysseus everything – marriage, luxurious surroundings and immortality. Odysseus, of course, is always after gain (see Athena's comment in *Odyssey* 13.299). Why, then, does he prefer the mortal Penelope who, as he openly admits, is inferior to Calypso (*Odyssey* 5.215–20)? The *Odyssey* is a story of longing, fidelity and return. Had Odysseus accepted Calypso's offer, we would have had a different poem, perhaps a story of how one man becomes immortal and enters the realm of the gods. Furthermore, in a world that revolves so completely around the idea of *fame*, Calypso, 'the hider', offers immortal oblivion. Yet what Odysseus and Homeric poetry seek is not the overcoming of death, but rather a transcendence of mortal existence that comes precisely through being mortal. Calypso is an unsuitable consort for a hero like Odysseus. She offers death by exclusion from memory. If Odysseus' fame is hidden (cf. *Odyssey* 9.19), he might just as well have never lived. Furthermore, to have stayed with Calypso would have meant life without a kingdom, outside of a day-to-day social hierarchy. Odysseus would have lived, not as a master and king but as the lesser partner and subject of Calypso, a powerful divine mistress (*dia theaôn*, see 5.78, etc.). Indeed, Odysseus, who is often described as a kind 'father' to his people (e.g. *Odyssey* 2.234), would have become a disempowered and politically 'childless' man. Within the framework of Homeric poetry and its values, this is an unacceptable position.

Odysseus' other female associations, we could argue, similarly help shape aspects of the hero and the social order of his world. Nausicaa is young, resourceful and mortal. She does not live in isolation, like Calypso, but in an orderly social world. Yet the Phaeacians inhabit a distant 'fairy land', away from ordinary human society. Remaining in Scheria, Odysseus' renown would be confined within his immediate surroundings and would again not reach 'all men'. More importantly, when we meet young Nausicaa in Book 6 of the *Odyssey*, she experiences the very first awakening of sexuality. Her innocent youth may make her an unsuitable partner in a poem whose main theme is the hero's *return* to something he has known before, in other words, the essential epic theme of establishing a 'continuity' with the past. Without a return, away from home, from the past and from memory, Odysseus risks being reduced to the state of an animal, as indeed the lion simile describing his state at the beginning of Book 6 (130–6) suggests. He risks becoming a 'nobody' (*outis*, like the name he gives himself when he speaks to the Cyclops. See 9.366). Odysseus only becomes the man he was when he is in society, and he can only properly do so when he is back in his rightful place as the king of Ithaca.

Encountering Nausicaa, Odysseus offers her a blessing (6.180–5):

> May the gods give you such things as you wish in your heart,
> A husband and a home and may they provide noble
> like-mindedness [*homophrosynê*] too, for nothing is better or stronger
> than when two, like-minded in thoughts [*homophroneonte noêmasin*], keep a house,
> a husband and wife. [This shall bring] many sorrows to their enemies,
> and joys to those who wish them well. And they themselves know it best.

As this idealized portrayal makes clear, conjugal harmony is primarily about 'keeping a house' and about finding a place within the general social order. It is, in fact, a gendered version of one of the most basic political principles of Greek thought, the idea that one should help friends and harm enemies (see Blundell 1991).

Given the importance of conjugal unions as reflections and embodiments of Homeric social order, we may ask, exactly what kind of 'like-mindedness' does the *Odyssey* here have in mind? Nausicaa and her father Alcinoos are heavily in favour of a matrimonial union between Nausicaa and Odysseus. The hero himself wants to gain the princess's help, but not to marry her. 'Like-mindedness' is thus here discussed in a situation where, in fact, speaker and hearer are thinking wholly different thoughts. Let us also bear in mind that this scene depicts Odysseus, a crafty master of words, and Nausicaa, an inexperienced young woman who has only now been subject to manipulative suggestions by Athena in her dreams. Somewhere in the background to Odysseus' eloquent rhetoric of harmony and 'like-mindedness', there seems to resonate, not a relationship between equals, but rather – to go back to the Aristotelian idea of a 'natural' union – a harmonious agreement of purpose between a 'master' and a 'subject', perhaps a like-mindedness that might form the basis of a relationship of the kind we see between Hector and Andromache in the *Iliad* Book 6.

Yet the *Odyssey*'s Nausicaa is not a passive subject figure. When the naked Odysseus emerges like an animal from the thicket, she does not flee, but stands her ground. The scene maintains high decorum, but is sexually charged. Nausicaa herself notes that any help she offers the stranger may trigger unkind rumours among the people (6.273–83). Yet Nausicaa controls both her meeting with Odysseus and later the scene in the palace with masterful confidence. She shows the promise of great *mêtis*, wisdom that is likely to lead her eventually to an empowered position, like her mother Arêtê, both in matrimony, and as a decision-maker in the royal court. Nausicaa's emerging *mêtis* also hints at the *Odyssey*'s prime example of a confident woman, Penelope, of course, whose wiles, wisdom and presence of mind, her *mêtis*, are a worthy (if 'un-Aristotelian') match for any husband. Penelope's most common epithet in the *Odyssey* is *polyphrôn*, 'of *many* thoughts', 'ingenious', stressing the ability of her mind and, of course, echoing the most common element *poly-*, 'many', in Odysseus' epithets. Together with Odysseus, Penelope will re-establish a house (*oikos*), and their 'like-mindedness' will indeed bring 'many sorrows to their enemies and joys to those who wish them well' (see Felson 1994: 18–19).

To what degree, then, do Odyssean female figures like Nausicaa or indeed Penelope move away from the Iliadic gender biases and types? Opinions vary, but their roles as women, their relationships and consequently something in the underlying conception of social structure and balance of power in the *oikos* and in the world of the *Odyssey* at large do clearly differ from the structures and relationships portrayed in the *Iliad* – for example, from the relationships between Agamemnon and the women close to him, Chryseis, Briseis and Clytemnestra, between Achilles and Briseis, Paris and Helen, or even Hector and Andromache.

The story of Agamemnon and Clytemnestra, an emblem of violent gender relations and of the destructive potential of a strong woman in the Iliadic world, is, as we have seen, a constant backdrop to relations between Odysseus and Penelope and to the world order of the *Odyssey*. 'There is nothing trustworthy in women', the ghost of Agamemnon tells Odysseus in the underworld (*Odyssey* 11.456. Cf. Zeitlin 1995: 48). That other emblematic Iliadic couple who appear in the *Odyssey*, Menelaus and Helen, in their re-established 'pre-Iliadic' state, are also part of the *Odyssey*'s perspective on social order. Part of the force of the *Odyssey* relies on its attempts to re-establish an image of peaceful social life in full view of the dangerous potential of domestic order (Aristotle, *Poetics* 1453b.19–22, says that domestic plots make the best tragedies), but – amazingly for a poem that places so much emphasis on fame and the past – without quite seeking to preserve the former values of such life.

Penelope, as Froma Zeitlin points out (1995: 44), is characterized by two contradictory positions:

> The poem presents her in such a way as to assure us of her fidelity. At the same time, it endows her actions with sufficient ambiguity to arouse the need for interpretation, often with diametrically different readings.

Penelope has been steadfastly waiting for Odysseus for 20 years. While she waits, she must apply her wits to survive and to resist her suitors (108 in number), using, for example, the ruse of the shroud she prepares for Laertes, weaving by day and unravelling by night (*Odyssey* 2.87–110. Cf. 19.138–56; 24.125–90). The ultimate proof of her *mêtis* and the seal of the *Odyssey*'s return to its proper, former social order, is, of course, Penelope's other ruse, the secret of the bed in Book 23 (see our discussion in Chapter 7). Against the background of the suitors' increasing frustration at her obstinacy, Penelope assures Telemachus that she and Odysseus have 'secret signs' (*sêmath' . . . kerummena . . . ap' allôn*, 23.110). Suspicious almost to the end, when she does meet Odysseus, Penelope duly asks Eurycleia to move the marriage bed to the porch, outside the bed chamber 'making a trial of her husband' (23.181). The point, as we have already explained, is that the bed itself, set within the protected surroundings, is the hidden sign – since one of its feet is the immovable stump of an olive tree. Penelope is testing Odysseus, but is also herself being tested. To have moved the bed is to suggest, symbolically, that she has betrayed the secret of the bed and has thus been potentially unfaithful. It all ends well. Odysseus remonstrates, his identity is proven, the bed has not moved and Penelope's fidelity is asserted. Yet through her crafty test, Penelope has also demonstrated that she is more than an obedient subject to Odysseus' mastery. She has reaffirmed the order of her old world and Odysseus, but that order is not quite the social and gendered order of their Iliadic past.

Nowhere is this better expressed than in the moment of reunion, in one of Homer's finest similes (*Odyssey* 23.232–39).

He [Odysseus] wept as he held his beloved wife, whose heart was true.
And as when the land appears welcome to men who are swimming
after Poseidon has smashed their fine ship on the open water, pounding it with wind and heavy waves
and only a few escape the gray sea landward
by swimming, with a thick scurf of salt upon them,
and gladly they set foot on dry land, escaping their ills;
So welcome was her [Penelope's] husband to her as she looked upon him.

The verses begin by speaking of Odysseus. By the final verse, however, we realize that in fact the simile itself describes Penelope. This 'reverse simile' and several others like it (especially *Odyssey* 19.108–14, comparing Penelope to a king) match Penelope to Odysseus and

> seem to suggest both a sense of identity between people in different social and sexual roles and a loss of stability, an inversion of the normal . . . Penelope does not take inappropriate advantage of her opportunity to wield power in Odysseus absence, yet to maintain his kingship she must come close as a woman can to doing so. (Foley 1978: 60)

Penelope and Odysseus live within a world ruled by men and kings not by women and queens, but their relationship attests to other possibilities. A further glimpse of the potential for 'alternative orders' within the *Odyssey* can be seen, for example, by looking not at those powers gained by Penelope as a woman, but at those powers ceded by Odysseus, by Homer and by the *Odyssey* in the course of the narrative. In the Phaeacian court, Odysseus asks the singer Demodocus to sing of the war in Troy, and of the Trojan Horse. Odysseus' response to the song is captured in another famous 'reverse simile' (*Odyssey* 8.522–31). Odysseus

> melted away, as tears from under his eyelids washed his cheeks.
> As a woman weeps, when she flings herself at her dear husband,
> who has fallen in front of his city and people,
> warding off the pitiless day from his town and his children,
> and she, when she sees him at his death, gasping his last,
> throws her arms around him, and wails loudly, but men behind her
> strike her back and shoulders with their spears
> and lead her to captivity, to bear hard labour and misery,
> and her cheeks waste away with the most piteous grief,
> so Odysseus shed a piteous tear from his brows.

What's striking about this description is not simply that it turns gender positions upside down, illustrating Odysseus through the image of a weeping woman whose warrior husband has died.

Equally important are the affinities and contrasts which the simile invokes between the *Iliad* and the *Odyssey*. Odysseus is here responding to Demodocus' (epic) song retelling Odysseus' greatest moment as an Iliadic hero of the past, a moment which itself is untold in the *Iliad*. Yet the Odyssean simile recalls at least one famous moment that is described in the earlier poem, the encounter between Hector and Andromache, and their anticipation of Troy's (fated) future scenario: Hector will die, precisely as the Odyssean simile suggests, 'warding off the pitiless day from his city and his children'. He imagines his wife weeping, again as the simile would say, and 'being led into captivity to bear labour and misery' (cf. the description in *Iliad* 6.459). As we have seen, in the *Iliad*, Hector's words are heavily inflected by his male perspective. Yet the very same image and the very same gendered relationship, once they are placed in the hands of the poet of the *Odyssey* and used to describe the response of the hero of the later poem to an 'Iliadic' past and the order of that past's world, have turned gendered roles and positions of power around. Andromache, as a woman, will live past the destruction of Troy as a captive and will become the tearful survivor of the *Iliad*. In the *Odyssey*, Odysseus, a man, *is* in the future of the *Iliad*. He *is* the tearful survivor who is listening to an account of the past. Yet by the time we have reached the *Odyssey*, the age of Iliadic heroes and Odysseus' own time as a hero of the *Iliad* have ended. With them, a certain world order has ended too. All that remains are the songs, the words of Homeric poetry, which, as the Odyssean simile comparing Odysseus to a weeping hero's wife powerfully demonstrates, allows us to revisit the past.

CHAPTER NINE

Mortality and the divine

Gods

Death is an essential presence in Homer's poetry. It is a boundary which even the greatest of Homer's heroes cannot cross, separating 'men who live by toil' (*andrôn alphestaôn, Odyssey* 1.349, etc.) and the 'blessed gods who are forever' (*theoi makares aien eontes, Iliad* 24.99, etc.). Yet in many ways, Homer's mortals and immortals are in close contact. Outwardly, they look the same and are often portrayed as acting, feeling and speaking in similar ways. Gods and men thus provide both important mirror images of each other and sharply contrastive reflections that ultimately illustrate the human condition as it is perceived in Homer's poetry.

Homer's world is populated by both the major Olympian gods and lesser deities, almost all of whom possess individualized personalities. As Herodotus says, Homer and Hesiod '. . . were the ones who created a theogony for the Hellenes, who gave epithets to the gods, who distinguished their merits and influence, their arts and abilities and described their forms' (*Histories* 2.53.5–8). Zeus in Homer is the 'father of men and gods' (*patêr andrôn te theôn te, Iliad* 1.544, etc.) and the one 'whose power is the greatest' (*hou te kratos esti megiston, Odyssey* 5.4, etc.). 'Far shooting' Apollo (*hekêbolos, Iliad* 1.43, etc.) is the god who, true to his epithet, strikes the Greek camp with his arrows, setting off the plague in the beginning of the *Iliad*. 'Grey-eyed' or 'owl eyed' (*glaukôpis, Odyssey* 1.44, etc.) Athena is a patron of Odysseus in the *Odyssey* and of Diomedes in the *Iliad*. She is a key agent of plot action in both poems. The wrath of Poseidon, the 'earth-shaker' (*enosichthôn*, *Odyssey* 1.74, etc.), over the blinding of his son the Cyclops is the underlying force that hinders Odysseus' homecoming. Hermes, Argeïphontes (*argeïphontês*, *Iliad* 2.103, etc.), is the messenger of the gods. His epithet is sometimes translated as 'the Slayer of Argus', but its precise meaning was obscure already in antiquity. Aristotle (*Poetics* 1458a.21) speaks of this obscurity as creating a numinous 'estrangement effect'. Artemis, who supports the Trojans, is, like her brother Apollo, an archer, the 'shedder of arrows' (*iocheaira*, *Iliad* 5.53, etc.). 'Man-slaughtering' Ares (*brotoloigos Arês*, *Iliad* 5.31, etc.) is the god of war. Hephaestus, the lame blacksmith of the gods, is 'famed for his skill' (*klytotechnês*, *Iliad* 1.571, etc.). 'Laughter loving' (*philommeidês*, *Iliad* 3.424), 'golden' (*chryseê*, *Iliad* 3.64, etc.) Aphrodite, and 'white-armed' (*leukôlenos*, *Iliad* 1.55 – the epithet is applied to mortal women, too, such as Helen and Nausicaa) Hera, Zeus' sister and wife, are important goddesses who use the power of sex to seduce men and influence the course of events. Demeter and Dionysus make brief appearances in the poems, although neither actually takes part in the action. These major divine figures appear in Homer in many settings, including assemblies, domestic scenes and battle scenes. They are portrayed as conversing and acting among themselves and also in contact with mortals. The gods' actions, although often terrifying and sometimes deadly, are also frequently tinged with humour and are on occasion overtly comical (as in Demodocus' song of the adulterous affair of Ares and Aphrodite – *Odyssey* 8.266–343) or even undignified, as some early critics such as Xenophanes of Colophon thought (see further below).

The *Iliad* and *Odyssey* portray many lesser deities too, such as the Muses, who live on Olympus, the nymph Calypso or the witch Circe, each of whom lives in her own island, or Thetis, Achilles' divine mother, wife of the mortal Peleus and sometime consort of Zeus. Thetis, despite being a 'second tier' divinity, has the power to appeal to Zeus and she thus exerts considerable power over the plot of the *Iliad* (see Slatkin 2009).

The world of the gods in Homer is centred around a structured and seemingly well-ordered family, Zeus the father, Hera his wife, Athena his daughter (who was born of Zeus alone, without a mother), Poseidon his brother and so on (see Griffin

1980: 186). The Homeric gods inhabit a 'Panhellenic' (as it has been called) world: They comprise a unified reflection of wider cultural perceptions (see Snodgrass 1971, Nagy 1979) that are more an indication of Homer's place in the cultural and political ideology of Greece than a reflection of actual religion. In real life, Greek religion was often more localized and fragmented, not always as consistent and well rounded as in Homer. In the *Iliad*, the deathless (*athanatoi*) and ageless gods are common to both Greeks and Trojans (Greeks and Trojans share many other beliefs, values and practices), although, significantly, the gods do often take sides. Athena supports the Greeks, Apollo supports the Trojans, Hera seduces Zeus (*Iliad* Book 14) so as to distract him and help the Trojans gain the upper hand. Many gods have their personal favourites among the heroes or otherwise take action which helps one side or the other: Athena has a preference for Diomedes and Odysseus; in battle, Aphrodite rescues Aeneas, her son.

The abodes of the gods in the *Iliad* and *Odyssey* seem secure, calm places compared to the violent spaces of the mortal world. Calypso's island (*Odyssey* Book 5) is a distant, exotic paradise. Olympus is far removed from the mortal sphere and isolated from the elements. At one point in the *Odyssey* (6.42–5), Olympus is described as

> . . . eternally safe.
> It's not battered by the winds, nor drenched
> by rain, snow does not fall near it, but always clear air,
> cloudless, spreads over it, and bright sunlight plays upon it.

Yet beneath the calm facade, more troubling realities lurk. Certainly for mortals, divine space is almost always a place of danger and pain. Calypso's island paradise is also a world of tensions. The union which she hopes for is unwanted by Odysseus, her would-be mortal husband. Odysseus is constantly in tears, pining for a homecoming and for his wife. To Calypso's bitter disappointment, her mortal marriage is also forbidden by Zeus. The island of Circe, the 'fair-tressed' (*eüplokamos*, *Odyssey* 10.136, etc.), likewise seems pleasant at first, but it hides grave dangers for mortals like Odysseus and for his men, whom she turns into pigs. Mortals do not visit Olympus, but its serenity too masks the memory of past hostilities and the potential for future conflict among the gods. Zeus is the 'son of Cronus' (cf. *Iliad* 14.203–4) and heir to a violent dynasty (Cronus usurped and castrated his father Ouranus and swallowed his own children. Cronus is called *ankylomêtis*, 'of the crooked counsel', in the poems. Divine father-and-son relations are thus radically different from their mortal counterparts). Although the gods cannot die, the threat of upheaval lurks in the very narratives that establish the divine order. Zeus is the god 'whose power is the greatest' and thus the one who imposes order on the divine world. Yet the Homeric word for power in this denomination, *kratos*, can equally be translated as 'violence'. Indeed, Zeus sometimes has to threaten the other gods with extreme violence to enforce peace (see, e.g. *Iliad* 1.396–406; 8.2–52; 15.18–24) in his world.

Belief and religion

The Homeric gods do not inspire in mortals quite the kind of reverence, internalized notions of faith or love that characterize attitudes towards the deity in, for example, Abrahamic religions (the act of faith in the Old Testament emerges out of Abraham's commitment to the word of god and his willingness to sacrifice his son). Divine parents and their mortal children do sometimes have a close relationship, as in the case of Thetis and Achilles, and the gods do have their personal favourites who engender stronger sympathy, most prominently Athena in her attitude towards Odysseus. More generally, however, the gods in Homer command a mix of obedient submission, fear and gratitude among mortals, depending on individual circumstances. When, in the first scene in the *Iliad*, Agamemnon scornfully dismisses Chryses, the priest, pacing bitterly by the shore of the 'much-resounding sea' (noisy surroundings for private prayer . . .), appeals to Apollo for help. Chryses invokes his past reverence and a sense of reciprocity between men and gods, which is often manifest elsewhere in the Homeric poems and elsewhere in antiquity (1.37–42):

Hear me, Lord of the Silver Bow, protector of Chryse and sacred Killa, who rules with strength over Tenedos,

Smintheus; if I ever built a temple that has pleased you,
if ever I burned rich thigh pieces for you,
of bulls and rams, then accomplish for me this thing I pray for:
Let the Danaans pay the debt of my tears with your arrows.

As Chryses says and as we often see in both poems (e.g. *Iliad*
1.437ff.; *Odyssey* 3.5ff.), mortals offer sacrifices (of rich fat,
meat and *hecatombs* or 'sacrifices of a hundred oxen' – but the
word can mean simply an elaborate offering) and libations (often
wine or milk) to the gods within a system of exchange.

Apart from prayers, mortals also swear oaths by the gods
(see, e.g. *Odyssey* 14.158–9), observe and interpret dreams (e.g.
Odyssey 19.535–53) and omens (*Odyssey* 20.103) sent by the
gods, and through these omens, sometimes deliver prophecies.
Such prophecies can be spoken by a professional seer or soothsayer
(a *mantis* or *theopropos*) or interpreter of dreams (an *oneiropolos*),
or interpreter of bird omens (an *oiônopolos*) or, on occasion,
perhaps with less conviction, also by 'lay' individuals such as
Odysseus himself, when he interprets Penelope's dream of the geese
(*Odyssey* 19.555–8). Mortals tend to heed the gods, as one would
obey a person of overwhelming power. There are, however, also
cases where mortals act against divine will or contest the gods'
authority, or fail to show the gods due reverence. Such acts are often
described as 'recklessness' (*atasthalia*), and those who commit them
often end up paying a heavy price of their transgressions. This, for
example, is the case with Odysseus' men who slaughter the cattle of
Hyperion and whose 'day of return' is thus taken away from them
or, most famously, on a grand narrative scale in the *Odyssey*, with
Penelope's suitors who pay, through Odysseus' actions for their
irreverence, their disrespect for the laws of hospitality and their
arrogance. In the *Iliad* (2.594–600), the singer Thamyris dares to
challenge the Muses' superiority in singing. As punishment, his
song and skill in playing the lyre are taken away.

Some important aspects of real-life ancient Greek religion,
such as hero-cult practice, are by and large missing from Homer.
However, generally Homer's descriptions of mortal attitudes to the
divine and especially aspects of prayer and sacrifice accord with
'real life' beliefs and attitudes towards the gods and with religious
and cultic practice in ancient Greece (see Dietrich 1979, Burkert
1985, Hitch 2009). The description of such religious practice helps

flesh out a semblance of reality in Homer's world, even though, as we repeatedly stress, the poems are not a depiction of real worlds. Just as the ancient busts of Homer portray the realistic face of an old man (even though that face is different in individual busts), so we can identify an image of religious experience in Homer's portrayal of mortals' relations with the divine.

Contact with 'real world' attitudes to the divine is attested in a different way in the invocations, the appeals by the mortal poet for the Muses' divine help in singing. Although invocations are an integral part of the poems and are composed in the same metre and language, they are set in the present of the performance, indeed, in the present moment of any performance, and they are uttered by a poet who is, we might say, one of the 'men of today' and who is thus sharply distinguished from the heroes of the past. The invocations thus constitute 'non-fictional' yet quintessentially Homeric appeals. Whether such appeals are conventional poetic acknowledgement of the divinity or reflect a deeper sensibility towards the divine, they are situated both *inside* the poems of the past and *outside* the world of the heroes, and are, in this sense, emblematic of Homeric epic's 'liminal' temporal and existential status between past and present.

Divine action

As in other aspects of Homer, in the portrayal of the gods, we often find contradictory practices and characterizations that add up to more than a single picture. Alongside the absolute superiority of immortals, Homer also describes a close, at times irreverent proximity between gods and men. Longinus suggests that 'unless it is to be taken allegorically', Homer's characterization of the gods seems 'downright impious and overstepping the bounds of decency'. Homer, he says, offers us the gods' wounds, their quarrels, acts of revenge, tears, bonds and several other woes so as 'to make the men of the Trojan War, inasmuch as possible, into gods and the gods into men men' (*On the Sublime* 9.7).

Among themselves, the gods do indeed often behave like the ordinary men and women, although such behaviour is not invariably undignified. Like mortals, Gods sit down in the assembly to debate and discuss important issues, as for example, in scenes at the beginning of the *Iliad* and *Odyssey*. When Thetis approaches Zeus on behalf of Achilles in Book 1 of the *Iliad*, her supplication partly resembles, for example, Chryses' plea to Apollo earlier in the book: 'If ever before in word or deed I did you favour among the immortals, now grant me this thing I wish' (*Iliad* 1.503–4). Furthermore, Thetis' supplication relies on physical contact. She embraces Zeus' knees and places her right hand under his chin (1.500–1) using a bodily gesture which a mortal subject might use to approach a mortal king in antiquity. This establishes a clear hierarchy between Thetis and Zeus, but it is not in any way a degrading portrayal. Rather, here, for a brief moment, Homer extracts divine behaviour, social relations and emotion from the otherwise inescapable dichotomy between men and gods, allowing us to escape into a world in which gods and mortals really do share cares and practices.

Nevertheless, Longinus is not entirely mistaken in his judgement. There are many less-dignified and sometimes comical scenes describing divine action in both the *Iliad* and *Odyssey*. We have earlier mentioned Book 14 of the *Iliad*, where the 'wily and scheming' (*dolophroneousa* 14.187) Hera attempts to seduce her husband and brother Zeus (there is no incest taboo on Olympus!), so as to distract him and allow the Trojans to gain ground. Hera asks Aphrodite for the love and desire with which the goddess subdues 'all immortals and mortal men' (14.198–100 – the realm of love is common to all) and borrows Aphrodite's enchanted girdle. Wearing this magical item of clothing, Hera proceeds to seduce her husband. To ensure the success of her plan, she secures the support of Hypnos, Sleep, by means of a bribe. *Post-coitum*, Zeus falls asleep and, with his watchful eyes shut, the Trojans can advance. The scene as a whole is full of domestic humour as well as irony because Hera, the wife who must put up with Zeus' many infidelities (indeed, he woos her with a catalogue of his conquests. See *Iliad* 14.315–28), here, with a bit of outside help, plays the role of an overpowering seductress.

Another prominent example is Demodocus' song in *Odyssey* Book 8, describing the adulterous love affair of Ares and Aphrodite. The song begins as a performance by the Phaeacian bard, but after only a few lines, blends imperceptibly into the main narrative of the poem and takes on what is de facto Homer's voice (8.266–71):

Then, playing the lyre, Demodocus began to sing beautifully
about the love-affair of Ares and the fair-crowned Aphrodite,
how they first lay together in Hephaestus' house,
secretly. Ares gave many gifts, and shamed the bed
of Lord Hephaestus. But straightaway a message came to the
    husband,
from Helios, who recognized the two as they mingled in love.

The cuckold husband Hephaestus, lame craftsman of the gods,
builds a trap of 'unbreakable bonds' for his wife and her lover and
pretends to leave the house. Ares sees him departing and calls out
to Aphrodite, 'Come here, my dear, to bed. Let's lie down and take
our pleasure' (8.295). Hephaestus returns unobserved and ensnares
the adulterers *in flagrante delictu*. The assembled gods witness
the bound lovers and are consumed by 'unquenchable laughter'
(*asbestos . . . gelôs*, 8.326). Apollo banters Hermes, asking if he
too would agree to be bound in return for the pleasure of sleeping
with Golden Aphrodite, and Hermes vigorously asserts that he
would indeed do so. The song is a suitable light-hearted antithesis
to narratives of adventure, martial action and heroic 'imperishable
fame', although it also carries with it sinister overtones. An illicit
amorous affair underpins the plot of the *Iliad*, and the integrity
of marital order is a matter of life and death in the *Odyssey*. The
song of Ares and Aphrodite also contains a kernel of serious
grievance. Hephaestus' complaint to father Zeus rings of legal
argument and raises the question of formal compensation for his
insult (8.317–19):

> . . . my trap and its bonds will hold them fast
> until her father will repay me each and every bridal gift
> I gave him for the sake of his dog-faced ['shameless'] daughter.

There is, furthermore, evidence that a narrative of this kind is not
entirely outside the realm of historical religion. A painting on a
vase fragment from the eighth to seventh century BCE found in the
sanctuary of Hephaestus in Lemnos shows a nude goddess and
a male figure in bonds. Nevertheless, the legal reference, while
introducing a serious practical echo, is itself not entirely free from
humour, since Aphrodite's father in Homer is none other than Zeus
(*Iliad* 5.131), who is also Hephaestus' father.

The gods, both male and female, often take part in fighting, especially in the *Iliad*, for example, in the section of the poem known as the *Theomachy*, 'the battle of the Gods' (*Iliad* 21.331–513), and also in many other pointed scenes (the term *theomachy* can refer to any setting of battle among gods). Gods fight against each other as well as against mortals. In fighting, the boundaries between men and gods are often simultaneously blurred and emphasized. When, in Book 5 of the *Iliad*, Diomedes rushes at Aeneas, Apollo checks him, saying 'take care, son of Tydeus, and stand down. Do not strive to be like the gods in your thoughts, since the race of immortal gods and that of men who walk upon the earth are not the same' (5.440–2; see also comments in Chapter 4, above). It is nevertheless significant that Apollo does not use his superior force but mere words to stop Diomedes. Furthermore, from Apollo's words, it seems that Diomedes aspires, not to the physical state of divinity or immortality, but to make himself 'like the gods *in your thoughts*', as if what separates gods and men is not physical nature, but their consciousness. It is, of course, precisely in valour and 'thoughts' as opposed to bodily strength and fragility that gods and heroes *can* be the same. As one scholar commenting on the general portrayal of the gods in Homer says, 'Homeric theology obviously wanted and got it both ways even at the cost of creating new contradictions' (Dietrich 1979: 136).

Later on in the same book of the *Iliad*, Ares, the god of war, catches sight of Diomedes and casts his spear at the hero. Diomedes is saved by Athena who deflects the missile. Diomedes then casts his own spear at Ares (5.856–7),

> . . . and Pallas Athena pushed it on
> into Ares' lower flank, where he was girt by a waist-band

The wounded god of war bellows with the sound of 9,000 men. He flees to his father, Zeus, shows him the wound and his 'immortal blood' (*ambroton haima* – this divine bodily fluid is elsewhere also called *ichor*) and complains that Zeus always gives his daughter Athena preferential treatment (*Iliad* 5.872–80):

> Father Zeus, when you see these harsh acts, are you not angry?
> We gods always have to bear the most terrible pains
> by each other's will, when we give favour to men.

Because of you we all fight, for you begot this reckless and
destructive
daughter, who is always intent on wicked deeds.
All the rest of us gods on Olympus,
pay heed and submit to you.
Yet you say nothing and do nothing to stop her
Instead, you impel her, since yourself you begot this pestilent
child.

Ares' pride is injured, but his wounds are mere play and his words
are childish – he is a little boy complaining about his sister to
their father. Such levity provides a strong contrast: 'the free and
irresponsible behaviour of the gods in the *Iliad* may have been
the poet's way of throwing the more serious consequences of
comparable human action into stronger relief' (Dietrich 1979:
136). Nevertheless, divine existence in Homer is not without pains.
Thetis' sorrow over Achilles' fate is as deep as that of any mother.
Longinus has a point when he says that the gods are worse off than
mortals since 'when we are unhappy, we have death as a haven from
ills', while the gods Homer portrayed as having 'not the nature of
immortality but eternal misery' (*On the Sublime* 9.7).

Several other domains of activity characterize the interaction
of gods and men in Homer, among them sexual congress. Many
heroes are the issue of mixed divine and mortal provenance.
Sarpedon is the son of Zeus and Laodamia (*Iliad* 6.198–9);
Helen is the daughter of Zeus and Leda (cf. *Odyssey* 11.298–
300); Achilles, of course, is the son of Thetis and Peleus (*Iliad*
18.432–41) and Aeneas is the son of Aphrodite and the Trojan
Anchises (cf. *Iliad* 2.819–21). Significantly, amatory relationships
between gods and mortals are normally restricted to a single
erotic or procreative contact rather than a lasting union (see,
for example, the list of Zeus' lovers in *Iliad* 14.315–28; affairs
by Poseidon, *Odyssey* 11.235–52; Ares, *Iliad* 2.511–15; Apollo,
Iliad 9.559–64). Odysseus' relationship with Calypso lasts for 7
years, but it is a coercive, and, of course, doomed liaison. We
have already seen that normative gender relations in Homer
are structured around the idea of male mastery over the female
subject. A permanent, stable union between a mortal man and a
goddess would have suggested mastery by a mortal, a being 'by
nature' inferior to the gods, over a divine being who is 'by nature'

superior – an intolerable situation. A one-time union between a male god and a mortal woman is in principle easier to accept and stresses the power of divine male beings. But a permanent relationship risks normalizing contact between domains which in essence must be kept apart. The principle that preserves the 'purity' of divine blood is telling: Semi-divine parentage does not endow a hero with immortality nor save the likes of Achilles or Sarpedon from death. Helen's brothers, Castor and Polydeuces (the Dioscuri or 'sons of Zeus') are an unusual exception. They die, but are allowed a curious existence afterwards, alternating between life and death every other day and 'having honour like the gods' (Odyssey 11.303–4).

Gods are anthropomorphic. In essential bodily form, they look like men and women, but they are generally bigger and more beautiful than mortals. The gods eat and drink like mortals, but their drink is immortal nectar (Iliad 1.598, etc.) and their food is ambrosia (Odyssey 5.199, etc.). With partial exceptions during sex and sometimes in battle, gods are often invisible to mortals, or appear in disguise (e.g. Iliad 24.349–469), or in dreams (6.21–4) to mortal eyes, sometimes in a deliberately misleading form. In the lead-up to Hector's death, Athena takes on the semblance of his brother, Deïphobus (Iliad 22.225–47). Athena in particular is a goddess who revels in disguise. It is one of the character traits that she shares with her favourite hero, Odysseus. A few heroes and heroines (Achilles, Helen, Odysseus) sometimes recognize gods facing them, but these are exceptional encounters, reserved for exceptional situations and characters.

Divine guidance, moral responsibility and fate

Whether seen or unseen, the gods play an active, complex and sometimes paradoxical role in guiding the plots of both the Iliad and the Odyssey. The beginning of the Iliad points to the poem as the completion of the will of Zeus (1.5), who, at the end of the poem, also initiates Priam's visit to the Greek camp to ransom Hector's body and sends the message that Achilles should accept Priam's supplication. The Odyssey paints a more ambiguous picture of the relation between Zeus' will and the events of the plot. In the assembly of the gods at the beginning of the poem, Zeus complains, saying 'How mortals blame the gods! We, they say, are the source of their ills, while it is by their own recklessness that they suffer sorrows beyond the measure' (*Odyssey* 1.32–4). Yet Zeus goes on to decree that Odysseus should now return home. At the end of the *Odyssey*, Zeus seems to have it both ways in a different manner. He addresses Athena, seemingly giving her strategic control of the plot, yet asserting his own will (24.479–86):

> Did you not yourself devise this plan,
> that Odysseus should take vengeance on these men when he
>   comes home?
> Do as you will. But I will tell you what is fitting.
> Now that bright Odysseus has taken vengeance on the suitors,
> let the people swear a solemn oath, and let him be king always
> and we shall bring about a forgetting of the killing
> of their sons and brothers and let them love each other
> as before, and let there be great wealth and peace.

Such divinely ordained agreement stands in direct contradiction to the actions of the *Odyssey*'s mortal hero who, shouting horribly, sweeps upon the men of Ithaca 'like an eagle' (24.538 – the eagle is Zeus' bird!). Happily, Zeus sends a thunderbolt and Athena delivers her message of peace, preventing Odysseus from bringing destruction upon his own kingdom and, perhaps with a twist of irony, saving the man who 'was always merciful like a father to the people over whom he ruled' (5.12, etc.) from merciless, self-inflicted bereavement.

Looking at the overall picture, then, it seems difficult to provide a single characterization of the relation between divine will and the action of the poems. The question does not simply concern the control of plot development here or elsewhere in the *Iliad* and *Odyssey*, but also the moral fabric of the Homeric world and the relations between divine will and mortal responsibility. Are men to be held morally accountable for their actions? If so, by what code? The gods are often portrayed as putting ideas in mortal characters' thoughts (*Iliad* 2.5–34, *Odyssey* 21.1–4), as making them aware or unaware of events around them (*Iliad* 19.476–79), or as prompting their decisions. Divine intervention can help or hinder the heroes on the battlefield (*Iliad* 22.273–77; 16.700–12) and in other critical situations. Does Zeus or some other god or divine agency administer justice in Homer? In the last book of the *Iliad*, Achilles speaks of Zeus' two urns, 'an urn of evils and an urn of blessings' (24.528), from which Zeus bestows good fortune and sorrows on mortal. Precisely how the allocation of such gifts is determined, and by what, if any higher principles, is a matter of considerable disagreement that requires long (and often inconclusive) discussion (see Long 1970, Lloyd-Jones 1971, Gagarin 1974, Allan and Cairns 2010). Nor can a single overall picture be drawn of what is 'the right way' (*themis*), 'the right manner of things' (*dikê*), 'the proper measure' (*moros*) or the right action and response to 'wrongful deeds' (*kaka erga*) in Homer. What is, however, beyond doubt is that in both poems there is deep concern for such matters, although by and large, critics agree that these concerns are more pronounced in the *Odyssey*, which also focuses on the actions of fewer gods (Athena, Zeus, Poseidon) who sometimes act more decisively than in the *Iliad*.

As we just noted, Zeus opens the assembly in the first book of the Odyssey by claiming that men bring sorrows upon themselves. They suffer, he says, 'beyond measure' (*hyper moron*, 1.34), by their own reckless folly, himself apparently abdicating both control of the plot and his own moral responsibility. He offers the example of Aegisthus (often cited elsewhere in the poem, as we have seen), who went 'beyond measure' (1.35), when he married Agamemnon's wife and killed the Son of Atreus. Aegisthus, of course, prominently pays for his transgression. We may ask, what this 'measure' is and who exactly is responsible for determining it?

The gods at times seem to behave no differently, or at least without any apparent higher guiding principles than mortals: Gods have their favourites and they often intervene and act on a personal basis. Poseidon at the beginning of the *Odyssey* seems to pursue Odysseus and prevent his homecoming simply because the latter has blinded his son, the Cyclops. The Cyclops' disregard for the laws of hospitality, his cannibalism and asocial existence are not mentioned. The element of personal motivation nevertheless at least sometimes seems to give way to more structured considerations of what should be done (for example, when Zeus decrees that Poseidon shall have to check his wrath and Odysseus will come home, 1.77). Certainly some moments seem to embody more significant principles. Commenting on the end of the *Odyssey* and on Zeus' decision to stop the violence in Ithaca in the passage we have just discussed, one critic suggests that Zeus' action is

> . . . of the greatest importance in the history of ideas: it means nothing less than the abolition of the law of blood-feud, which had hitherto prevailed without qualification; in its place is established a new political order based on justice and law, and validated by the gods, in which a just and benevolent king ensures wealth and freedom. (Heubeck 1992: 412)

Read in this way, the end of the *Odyssey* suggests that the portrayal of divine order and of the behaviour of the gods and of Zeus, *pace* Longinus, is not quite 'impious'. However, if we do follow readings of this type and allow for a principled new order as Zeus decrees, we may need to reframe and reconsider many other scenes in the poems. Does Achilles avenge Patroclus and kill Hector because of a higher moral principle? Does his relentless mistreatment of Hector's corpse operate, perhaps as a negative example, within a principled moral universe? Does Achilles eventually take pity on Priam because he has recognized what is just? Zeus' inauguration of a new age of wealth and peace at the end of the *Odyssey* and a 'forgetting of the killing' of the suitors (24.484–85) may force us to remember and contemplate many earlier killings in Homer and more generally the 'countless woes' (*Iliad* 1.2) of the heroic past. There is no open-and-shut way to read the poems as moral paradigms, and it is precisely the remembering and not-forgetting of the killing and pain preserved in the poems and the acknowledgement of 'imperishable fame' that accompanies death that are the essence of heroic poetry.

No matter how exactly we interpret elements of justice and moral and legal principles in the Homeric poems, we must always allow for the possibility that such elements are not evenly or consistently distributed. Furthermore, there remains, in both the *Iliad* and the *Odyssey*, the inevitability of fate, marked by the words *moira*, one's 'share', 'portion', or 'lot', and *aisa*, one's 'dispensation', or 'share'. Fate brings death to all mortals (see, e.g. *Iliad* 16.849; 18.119–21 and elsewhere). Even Zeus cannot ultimately save a hero from death, not even when the hero is his own mortal son Sarpedon (see *Iliad* 16.431–61). In the *Odyssey*, because it is a poem of human survival, a man's fate or 'share' is seen to affect not only his death but also his life. Hermes tells Calypso that 'it is not his [Odysseus'] *aisa* to perish far away from his loved ones, but it is still his *moira* to see his loved ones and reach his high-roofed house and fatherland' (5.113–15). In later Greek literature, fate, or rather the Fates, are often personified. In Homer, the personification is weaker, although sometimes we do find 'harsh Moira' spinning the thread, for example, of Hector's life (in Hecuba's words, see *Iliad* 24.209–10).

Being immortal and deathless, the Homeric gods are not subject to fate in the manner of men, and, paradoxically, they seem to have little to look forward to in their lives, relative to mortals. They suffer their light wounds, take part in petty quarrels, trick and seduce each other, choose their mortal favourites and put ideas into their heads, help them in battle or doom them and grieve for their favoured heroes when these heroes die. Yet, although the gods are central to the action and thought of the poems, although we cannot imagine Homeric epic without the gods, immortal beings are, we might almost say, 'outsiders' to the poems. When Achilles and Hector in their final, mortal combat circle the walls of Troy, 'all the gods gazed upon them' (*Iliad* 22.166). The gods, as Jasper Griffin points out, are like spectators at a sporting event. Unlike most spectators (but like spectators in a gladiatorial show – the analogy and its cruelty are significant), they do have some power to affect the outcome of the spectacle. As the two tragic heroes of the *Iliad* fight, Zeus proposes to the gods that they should take counsel and consider 'whether to save Hector or to slay him at Achilles' hands'. Yet, because of their freedom from death, the gods can never fully enter the realm of mortal action or motivation, even when they guide it. The Greeks and the Trojans, Achilles, Agamemnon and Odysseus do not fight, live or die for the glory of Zeus, Athena or Apollo – certainly not in the same way that, for example, major figures in the Old Testament such as Joshua, Saul or David fight *for* Yahweh (and for what we might perhaps call Yahweh's 'plan'), not in the way that the Knights of the Round Table fight for the Holy Grail or in the way St Joan fights for God. In the end, the mortal heroes of the *Iliad* and *Odyssey* fight, struggle and strive for mortal women, for prizes and for recognition and glory among their peers and among the men and women of the future. Heroes are motivated, above all, by the knowledge that death is fated and certain. Inasmuch as the centre of Homeric experience is the mortal condition, a condition outside of the realm of immortal experience, the gods must live 'vicariously' through the fortunes of heroes. We, the audiences and readers of the Homeric poems, are mortal, yet we too, like the gods, can live vicariously through the poems. Our vicarious experience may thus, to give Longinus' words a different twist, not merely bring gods closer to ourselves but perhaps allow ourselves to look upon the world of the heroic past from the perspective of the gods.

Envoi

In a book about Homer, perhaps the most difficult part to write is the end. Homer, as we have been trying to show throughout this book, and as many scholars have argued, resists the kind of closure that allows us, for example, to sum up his two poems as a simple unity, his relation to history and historical eras as a simple association with the Bronze Age or the Iron Age, his identity as a poet simply as a genius individual or even as a straightforward tradition, be it 'oral' or written, or somewhere in-between. The transmission of the Homeric poems is likewise not a simple act of memory or committal to script. In terms of contents, the poems celebrate the hero and martial achievements, and the preservation of past glory. They bring together lament, an awareness of irretrievable loss, of the fleeting moment and of the relentless passage of time, but equally of an exuberant sense of being, a recognition of otherness, an optimism of the will and a portrayal of the true force of human emotion and trust. The *Iliad* and *Odyssey* are poems by a man (or what seems to be a tradition of male singers), about men, and perhaps, for men, but we have seen that women play key and often leading roles in both the *Iliad* and the *Odyssey* in every sense, and the characterization of gender and other basic dividing categories cannot be confined within a simple relationship of those who hold power and exercise control and those who do not. Homeric poetry is, without doubt, poetry that portrays the close interaction of gods and men, and the poems, both in their detailed language and in their broader themes, take mortal heroes almost to the point of immortality, yet the gulf between gods and men, the finitude of the mortal condition and the centrality of the fact of death are never clearer anywhere than in the *Iliad* and in the *Odyssey*. We have suggested, at the beginning of this short book, that Homer and Homeric poetry continue to live through their receptions, not least in modern traditions. We have also seen that such traditions change the poems, their settings, their themes and concerns almost beyond recognition. Yet the links between such changed versions of the *Iliad* and *Odyssey* and the Homeric 'source' remain as close and as distinct as ever. There are, it is true, no absolute beginnings (with the exception, perhaps, of a Biblical *fiat*! ['Let there be light!'] in religious narratives or the so-called Big Bang in scientific histories of the universe), but even Aristotle, when he says that a beginning is that before which there is nothing, knows that this is not a literal, material fact, but rather a 'phenomenological' element of the truth of our understanding and perception: A 'beginning' is that which we acknowledge, within a certain set of conventions, contexts and beliefs, before which there is nothing that 'belongs' to our plot. In this sense, Homer is indeed, the beginning of the literary tradition of the West, a tradition that is always changing, adapting and in various ways acknowledging other traditions and ways of looking at the world. Homer, being, as we might say, one of the continuing elements of change, is an important part of this process, and it is for this reason, as we have tried to suggest, that he remains a vital, vibrant part of our cultural consciousness.

The title of the series within which this book is published, *Guides for the Perplexed*, is drawn, in fact, from a tradition which has sometimes been seen as contrastive, perhaps even antagonistic to the culture of the Greeks and of Greco-Roman classical antiquity. *Guide for the Perplexed*, *Dalalatul Hairin* (the original title in Arabic), the *Moreh Nevuchim* (its translation in Hebrew), is originally the name of an important critical-philosophical work by the great twelfth-century Jewish scholar Moses Maimonides ('the Son of Maimon') who was born in Spain and who was active mainly in Egypt and in Morocco. Have we, then, stretched our links too far when we called our book 'Homer'? Should this title be read without any of its historical and cultural resonance? Is it merely a pretty catchphrase? Maimonides, let us not forget, was a scholar of Judaic and Rabbinic thought. Yet he was equally well-versed in the Greek philosophical tradition, and especially Aristotelian scholarship, as it came to him through its great medieval Arabic commentators. The main effort of Maimonides' *Guide for the Perplexed* was to build a meaningful dialogue between these two ancient rival traditions, Judaic and Hellenic. In this cross-cultural dialogue, Arabic culture and traditions played the role of a moderator. Together, all three traditions (interspersed with many other elements woven into the 'text' with the benefit of Maimonides' enormous erudition) were drawn in, not in a homogenous mix, but working together to provide, precisely, a 'guide' for the 'perplexed'. A book on Homer, then, in a series that borrows its title from a source of this type, may have some hope of offering the reader at least the beginning of a many-voiced conversation. Beyond which, of course, it is up to the reader to ask the questions and to seek answers in greater depth.

Suggestions for further reading

The bibliography on Homer ranges from general studies for the absolute beginner to more advanced overviews (like the present volume) and extends to numerous specialized studies of every aspect of Homeric poetry. Wherever possible, studies that are more accessible to the general engaged reader are listed below, but a few specialized studies are also cited (including works noted in the main text, particularly where no more-general work is available. Full publication details are given in the bibliography).

Translations

Among the most widely read translations of Homer are those in verse by Richmond Lattimore (originally 1951, 1965), which follow the original closely, and by Robert Fitzgerald (1961, 1974), which claim greater poetic freedoms. Robert Fagles' version (1990, 1996) is also noteworthy, as is Stanley Lombardo's verse translation (1997, 2000), which are both resonant and attentive to the original. More recent (2011) is Verity's translation of the *Iliad*. E. V. Rieu's prose translations for Penguin Classics (originally 1946, 1950) have been a favourite for many years. More recent is W. Shewring's prose version of the *Odyssey* (1980). There are many other classic translations, in both verse and prose. Perhaps, the best known is Alexander Pope's poetic version (1715, 1725), but others that merit mention include those by George Chapman (1611, 1615), Thomas Hobbs (1616, 1675), John Dryden

(1700), Matthew Arnold (1861), Samuel Butcher and Andrew Lang (1879) all available in numerous reprints and editions, and T. E. Lawrence ('Lawrence of Arabia', 1932). A bilingual ancient Greek and English text with prose translations by A. T. Murray (1919, 1924–5) can be found in the *Loeb Classical Library* series. George Steiner's *Homer in English* (1996) provides a useful survey. Many translations contain helpful introductory comments. *The Chicago Homer* (http://digital.library.northwestern.edu/homer/) is an online text with the original Greek and English and German translations, as well as Latin-character transliterations of the Greek and various analysis and study tools and commentaries. A basic online text of Homer (and most other major other classical and other texts, in translation and in the original languages) can also be found at the *Perseus Digital Library* site (http://perseus.tufts.edu/hopper/). Translations of Homer are also available as electronic files and in many e-reader formats. There are countless more-free adaptations of Homer, for example, by poets Christopher Logue (2001), Simon Armitage (2006), Alice Oswald (2011) and Miller (2012).

General reference books on Homer

See *The Homer Encyclopedia* (Finkelberg 2010), a three-volume compendium containing short entries on all major topics in Homer. Three general handbooks, Fowler (2004), Morris and Powell (1997) and Wace and Stubbings (1963, older, but still useful), provide essays on main themes in Homer. Basic introductions can be found in Silk (2004), Griffin (1987), Mueller (2009) and elsewhere. Edwards (1987) is a little more detailed. Many online resources are excellent (especially those within the university domains '.edu' and '.ac'), but the quality of online material is not uniform and caution is still sometimes required (especially in more-commercial sites).

Detailed commentaries on Homer

For comments on specific passages, see Willcock (1976) and Pothlethwaite (2002) on the *Iliad*, and Jones (1990) on the

Odyssey, all based on Richmond Lattimore's translation. See also commentaries based on Fitzgerald's translation by Hogan (1979) for the *Iliad* and Hexter (1993) for the *Odyssey*, and further commentaries on the *Iliad* in translation in Jones (2003) and Graziosi (in Verity 2011, based on a new translation by Verity). The standard commentaries for specialists in English are the ones on the *Iliad* under the general editorship of Geoffrey Kirk (with contributions by several other scholars. In six volumes, 1985–93), and on the *Odyssey*, by Alfred Heubeck and others (in three volumes, 1988–92). These works contain much valuable information, as do several volumes in the 'Cambridge Greek and Latin Classics' commentary series covering some, but not all books of the *Iliad* and *Odyssey*. There is a 'narratological' commentary on the *Odyssey* by de Jong (2001) which places emphasis on questions of narrative and narration in the poem, but which covers many other major topics. Advanced commentaries and other studies generally assume knowledge of the original Greek and can be difficult for general readers. The *Chicago Homer* is a comprehensive online resource that contains some commentary materials, translations and transliterations that allow both readers with no knowledge of the language or of Homer and advanced researchers access to many aspects of Homer and Homeric poetry.

Chapter 1

On the reception of Homer, see Graziosi and Greenwood (2007), the section 'Homeric Receptions' in Fowler (2004), Hall (2008) and Finkelberg (2010, under several headings that deal with 'Reception'). For the idea of 'many Homers', see Porter (2004) and Nagy (1996). For the *Epic Cycle*, see Burgess (2001). Many of the specific issues mentioned in this introductory chapter are discussed in greater detail in the following chapters.

Chapter 2

For Homer and the ancient historians, see Rengakos (2005). For the question of Homer and History in general, see, for example, Raaflaub (2005) and Grethlein (2010). On Homeric geography (real and imagined), see Luce (1998) and Dickinson (2007). On the historical aspects of Homer, there is much useful material in Morris and Powell (1997). For Troy and Homer, see Latacz (2004) and, from an archaeological point of view, Korfmann (2004), as well as significant reservations and opposition by Raaflaub (1998, where much other work is cited, too). More generally on Troy, see Michael Wood (1987). For the remains on the site of Troy, see Rose (1997). Allen (1999) is useful on the work of Heinrich Schliemann. On the Archaic Age, see Raaflaub and van Wees (2009). On the eighth century specifically, see Morris in the same. For Linear B, see Chadwick (1958). On the representation of social reality in Homer, see Osborne (2004).

Chapter 3

For the figure of the poet in antiquity, see Graziosi (2002). For poets and poetry in Homer, see Ford (1992) and McLeod (1983). For Homer in ancient scholarship, see Pfeiffer (1968). For Homer in modernity since Vico and for the so-called Homeric Question, see Turner (1997). Milman Parry's work, collected after his death by his son Adam, who was also a prominent Homer scholar (Parry 1971), is of fundamental importance. Albert Lord's work (Lord 1960) provides a wider sweep and is accessible to general readerships. Paul Zumthor (1990) offers a good introduction to oral poetry, and John Foley's studies of orality (e.g. 1991) are also very useful. An excellent (but difficult) summary of the question of the formula can be found in Russo (1997).

Chapter 4

The details of Homeric poetic form, their effects and their relations to orality and to the creation of the poems are highly technical matters. Readers at all levels, including those with no prior knowledge whatsoever, can read the text in English with direct and easy access to many features of Homeric language and its unique repetitions using the Chicago Homer (http://digital .library.northwestern.edu/homer/). In English, the classic early study of the arrangement of motifs and of typical scenes in Homeric narrative is by Fenik (1968). Edwards (1992) is also helpful. Mary Douglas' recent general work (2007) on ring composition is important for an overall understanding of this key feature of literature in general; in the context of Homer and Homeric orality, see Nimis (1998). More detailed references can be found in Edwards (1987). For accessible information on metaphor and simile, see Scott (2009), Lonsdale (1990), Minchin (2001) and Edwards (1987).

Chapter 5

For the narrator in Homer, see Richardson (1990). There are many specialized studies of the proems of the *Iliad* (e.g. Redfield [1979]) and the *Odyssey* (e.g. in Pucci [1998] and in de Jong [2001]). For the Muses, see Ford (1992) and in general Spentzou and Fowler (2002). For Homer and Aristotle, see Halliwell (1986). For plot structures, see Schein (1997) and Latacz (1998) for the *Iliad* and Tracy (1997) for the *Odyssey*.

Chapters 6 and 7

For pointed issues, see references in the chapters themselves and also in the translation-based commentaries listed above (Willcock [1976], Jones [1990, 2003], Hogan [1979] and Hexter [1993]). For some influential and eloquent overall studies, see, among the very many worthy books, Whitman (1958), Austin (1975), Nagy (1979), Griffin (1980), Schein (1984), Pucci (1987), Peradotto (1990), Scodel (2008) and Burgess (2009).

Chapter 8

Gender has been one of the most productive topics of study in Homer in recent decades. For general questions, see essays in Arthur (1973), Halperin et al. (1990), also McLure (2002). For gender in Homer, and for such figures as Penelope and Helen, see, for example, Foley (1978), Katz (1991), Felson (1994), Zeitlin (1995) and Cohen (1995). Said (2011) is a general survey, but it has a useful new long survey chapter on women in the *Odyssey*.

Chapter 9

For Greek religion in general, see Burkert (1985). For the gods in Homer, see Emlyn-Jones (1992). Griffin (1980) offers a perspective with powerful literary intuitions. See also Dietrich (1979) and Hitch (2009). For questions of morality and ethics in Homer, see Adkins (1960), an incisive and influential work whose premises about historical development are now challenged, for example, in Williams (1993). On the question of justice and law in Homer, see (among many important works) Long (1970), Lloyd-Jones (1971), Gagarin (1986) and Allan and Cairns (2010).

BIBLIOGRAPHY

Adkins, A. W. H. 1960. *Merit and Responsibility: A Study in Greek Values.* Oxford: Oxford University Press.

Alcock, S. E. 1993. *Graecia Capta: The Landscapes of Roman Greece.* Cambridge: Cambridge University Press.

Allan, W. and Cairns, D. L. 2010. 'Conflict and Community in the *Iliad*', in N. R. E. Fisher and H. van Wees (eds), *Competition in the Ancient World.* Swansea: The Classical Press of Wales, pp. 113–46.

Allen, S. H. 1999. *Finding the Walls of Troy: Frank Calvert and Heinrich Schliemann at Hisarlik.* Berkeley: University of California Press.

Arend, W. 1933. *Die typischen Szenenen bei Homer.* Berlin: Weidmann.

Armitage, S. 2006. *Homer's Odyssey.* London: Faber and Faber.

Arthur, M. B. 1973. 'Early Greece and the Origins of Western Attitudes towards Women', *Arethusa* 6: 7–58.

Austin, N. 1975. *Archery at the Dark of the Moon.* Berkeley: University of California Press.

—. 1966. 'The Function of Digressions in the *Iliad*', *Greek, Roman, and Byzantine Studies* 7: 295–312.

Bakker, E. J. and Kahane, A. (eds). 1997. *Written Voices, Spoken Signs: Tradition, Performance and the Epic Text.* Cambridge, MA: Harvard University Press.

Beck, D. 2005. *Homeric Conversations.* Washington, DC: Center for Hellenic Studies.

Becker, A. S. 1995. *The Shield of Achilles and the Poetics of Ecphrasis.* Lanham, MD: Rowman and Littlefield.

Bennet, J. 1998. 'The Linear B Archives and the Kingdom of Nestor', in J. Davies (ed.), *Sandy Pylos: An Archaeological History from Nestor to Navarino.* Austin: University of Texas Press, pp. 111–33.

Bergren, A. 1981. 'Helen's "Good Drug"', in S. Kresic (ed.), *Contemporary Literary Hermeneutics and Interpretation of*

Classical Texts. Ottawa: Editions de l'Universite, pp. 201–14 (Repr.
  in A. Bergren. 2008. *Weaving Truth: Essays on Language and the
  Female in Greek Thought*. Washington, DC: Center for Hellenic
  Studies).
Bittlestone, R. 2005. *Odysseus Unbound: The Search for Homer's
  Ithaca*. Cambridge: Cambridge University Press.
Blegen, C. 1963. *Troy and the Trojans*. London: Thames and Hudson.
Blundell, M. W. 1991. *Helping Friends and Harming Enemies*.
  Cambridge: Cambridge University Press.
Burgess, J. S. 2009. *The Death and Afterlife of Achilles*. Baltimore:
  Johns Hopkins University Press.
—. 2001. *The Tradition of the Trojan War in Homer and the Epic Cycle*.
  Baltimore and London: Johns Hopkins University Press.
Burkert W. 1985. *Greek Religion: Archaic and Classical* (trans. G.
  Raffan). Cambridge, MA: Harvard University Press.
Calder, W. W. 1986. 'A New Picture of Schliemann', in W. M Calter
  III and D. A. Traill (eds), *Myth, Scandal and History: The Heinrich
  Schliemann Controversy and a First Edition of the Mycenean Diary*.
  Detroit: Wayne State University Press, pp. 17–47.
Chadwick, J. 1958. *The Decipherment of Linear B*. Cambridge:
  Cambridge University Press.
Clark, M. 2004. 'Formulas, Metre, and Type Scenes', in R. L. Fowler
  (ed.), *The Cambridge Companion to Homer*. Cambridge: Cambridge
  University Press, pp. 117–38.
Clay, J. S. 1983. *The Wrath of Athena: Gods and Men in Homer's*
  Odyssey. Princeton: Princeton University Press (2nd edn, 1997).
Clayton, B. 2004. *A Penelopean Poetics: Reweaving the Feminin in
  Homer's* Odyssey. Lanham, MD: Rowman and Littlefield.
Cohen, B. (ed.). 1995. *The Distaff Side: Representing the Female in
  Homer's* Odyssey. Oxford and New York: Oxford University Press.
de Jong, I. J. F. 2001. *A Narratological Commentary on the* Odyssey.
  Cambridge: Cambridge University Press.
Detienne, M. 1996. *The Masters of Truth in Archaic Greece* (trans. J.
  Lloyd). New York: Zone Books.
Dickinson, O. 2007. 'Aspects of Homeric Geography', in S. P. Morris
  and R. Laffineur (eds), *EPOS. Reconsidering Greek Epic and Aegean
  Bronze Age Archaeology*. Liege: University of Liege, pp. 233–8.
Dietrich, B. C. 1979. 'Views of Homeric Gods and Religion', *Numen* 26:
  129–51.
Dimock, G. 1963. 'The Name of Odysseus', in C. H. Taylor (ed.), *Essays
  on the* Odyssey. Bloomington: Indiana University Press, pp. 54–72.
Douglass, M. 2007. *Thinking in Circles: An Essay on Ring
  Composition*. New Haven, CT: Yale University Press.

Dué, C. and Ebbott, M. 2010. *Iliad 10 and the Poetics of Ambush: A Multitext Edition with Essays and Commentary*. Washington, DC: Center for Hellenic Studies.

Easton, D. F. 2002. *Schliemann's Excavations at Troia* 1870–1873. Mainz: von Zabern.

Edwards, M. W. 1992. 'Homer and Oral Tradition: The Type-Scene', *Oral Tradition* 7: 284–330.

—. 1987. *Homer: Poet of the Iliad*. Baltimore and London: Johns Hopkins University Press.

—. 1980. 'The Structure of the Homeric Catalogue', *Transactions of the American Philological Association* 110: 81–105.

Emlyn-Jones, C. 1992. 'The Homeric Gods: Poetry, Belief, and Authority', in C. Emlyn-Jones, L. Hardwick and J. Purkis (eds), *Homer: Readings and Images*. London: Duckworth and the Open University, pp. 91–104.

Fagles, R. 1990. *The Iliad/Homer*. New York: Penguin.

—. 1996. *The Odyssey/Homer*. New York: Penguin.

Felson, N. 1994. *Regarding Penelope: From Character to Poetics*. Princeton: Princeton University Press.

Fenik, B. 1968. *Typical Battle Scenes in the Iliad: Studies in the Narrative Technique of Homeric Battle Description*. Wiesbaden: Steiner.

Finkelberg, M. (ed.) 2010. *The Homer Encyclopedia*. Malden, MA and Oxford: Wiley-Blackwell.

Finley, M. I. 1978 [1954]. *The World of Odysseus* (2nd edn). New York: Viking Press (Repr. 2002 with a new introduction by S. Hornblower).

Finley, M. I., Caskey J. L., Kirk G. S. and Page D. L. 1964. 'The Trojan War', *Journal of Hellenic Studies* 84: 1–20.

Fitzgerald, R. 1974. *Homer: The Iliad*. Oxford: Oxford University Press.

—. 1961. *Homer: The Odyssey*. Garden City: Anchor Press/Doubleday.

Foley, H. 1978. '"Reverse Similes" and Sex Roles in the Odyssey', *Arethusa* 11: 7–26.

Foley, J. M. (ed.). 2005. *A Companion to Ancient Epic*. Oxford: Blackwell.

—. 1991. *Immanent Art: From Structure to Meaning in Traditional Oral Epic*. Bloomington: Indiana University Press.

Ford, A. 1992. *Homer: The Poetry of the Past*. Ithaca and London: Cornell University Press.

Foucault, M. 1977. 'What is an Author?' in D. F. Bouchard (ed.), *Language, Counter-Memory, Practice: Selected Essays and Interviews*. Ithaca: Cornell University Press, pp. 113–38.

Fowler, R. (ed.). 2004. *The Cambridge Companion to Homer*. Cambridge: Cambridge University Press.

Gagarin, M. 1986. *Early Greek Law.* Berekeley: University of California Press.

—. 1974. 'Dike in Archaic Greek Thought', *Classical Philology* 69: 186–97.

Gill, C. 1996. *Personality in Greek Epic, Tragedy and Philosophy.* Oxford: Oxford University Press.

Glenn, J. 1971. 'The Plyphemus Folktale and Homer's Kyklopeia', *Transactions of the American Philological Association* 102: 133–81.

Graziosi, B. 2002. *Inventing Homer: The Early Reception of Epic.* Cambridge: Cambridge University Press.

Graziosi, B. and Greenwood, E. (eds). 2007. *Homer in the Twentieth Century: Between World Literature and the Western Canon.* Oxford: Oxford University Press.

Grethlein, J. 2010. 'From "Imperishable Glory" to History: The *Iliad* and the Trojan War', in D. Konstan and K. A. Raaflaub (eds), *Epic and History.* Malden, MA and Oxford: Wiley-Blackwell.

Griffin, J. 1987. *Homer: The* Odyssey. Cambridge: Cambridge University Press.

—. 1980. *Homer on Life and Death.* Oxford: Oxford University Press.

—. 1977. 'The Epic Cycle and the Uniqueness of Homer', *Journal of Hellenic Studies* 97: 39–53.

Hall, E. 2008. *The Return of Ulysses: A Cultural History of Homer's Odyssey.* London: I. B. Tauris.

Halliwell, S. 1986. *Aristotle: Poetics.* London: Duckworth.

Halperin, D., Winkler, J. J., and Zeitlin, F. (eds). 1990. *Before Sexuality: The Construction of Erotic Experience in the Ancient Greek World.* Princeton: Princeton University Press.

Hammer, D. 2002. *The Iliad as Politics: The Performance of Political Thought.* Norman, OK: University of Oklahoma Press.

Hardwick, L. 2003. *Reception Studies.* Oxford: Oxford University Press.

Hardwick, L. and Gillespie, C. (eds.) 2007. *Classics in Post-Colonial Worlds.* Oxford: Oxford University Press.

Hardy, T. 1998 [1886]. *The Mayor of Casterbridge.* London: Penguin Classics.

Herman, G. 1987. *Ritualized Friendship and the Greek City.* Cambridge: Cambridge University Press.

Heubeck, A. et al. 1988–92. *A Commentary on the* Odyssey (vols I–III). Oxford: Oxford University Press.

Hexter, R. 1993. *A Guide to the Odyssey: A Commentary on the English Translation by Robert Fitzgerald.* New York: Vintage Books.

Higbie, C. 1990. *Measure and Music: Enjambement and Sentence Structure in the Iliad.* Oxford: Clarendon Press.

Hitch, S. 2009. *The King of Sacrifice: Ritual and Royal Authority in the Iliad.* Cambridge, MA: Harvard University Press.

Hobsbawm, E. and Ranger, T. 1992. *The Invention of Tradition.* Cambridge: Cambridge University Press. Vintage.

Hogan, J. C. 1979. *A Guide to the Iliad: Based on the Translation by Robert Fitzgerald.* New York: Anchor Books.

Holoka, J. 1983. '"Looking Darkly" (ΥΠΟΔΡΑ ΙΔΩΝ): Reflections on Status and Decorum in Homer', *Transactions of the American Philological Association* 113: 1–16.

Jones, P. V. 2003. *Homer's Iliad: A Commentary on Three Translations.* London: Bristol Classical Press.

—. 1990. *Homer's Odyssey: A Companion to the English Translation of Richmond Lattimore.* London: Bristol Classical Press.

Kahane, A. 2005. *Diachronic Dialogues: Authority and Continuity in Homer and the Homeric Tradition.* Lanham, MD: Rowman and Littlefield.

Kakridis, J. T. 1949. *Homeric Researches.* Lund: Karl Bloms Boktryckeri.

Katz, M. A. 1991. *Penelope's Renown: Meaning and Indeterminacy in the* Odyssey. Princeton: Princeton University Press.

Kirk, G. et al. 1985–93. *The Iliad: A Commentary* (vols. I–VI). Cambridge: Cambridge University Press.

Korfmann, M. O. 1997. 'Troia, an Ancient Anatolian Platial and Trading Centre: Archaeological Evidence for the Period of Troia VI/VII', in D. Boedeker (ed.), *The World of Troy: Homer, Schliemann and the Treasures of Priam.* Washington, DC: Society for the Preservation of the Greek Heritage, pp. 51–73 (Repr. in *Classical World* 91 [1988]: 369–85).

—. 2004. 'Was There a Trojan War?' *Archaeology* 57 (3): 36–41.

Kulmann, W. 1984. 'Oral Poetry Theory and Neoanalysis in Homeric Research', *Greek, Roman and Byzantine Studies* 25: 307–23.

Lachmann, K. 1847. *Betrachtungen über Homers Ilias.* Berlin: G. Reimer.

Latacz, J. 1998. *Homer: His Art and His World* (trans. J. P. Holoka). Ann Arbor: University of Michigan Press.

—. 2004. *Troy and Homer: Towards a Solution of an Old Mystery* (trans. K. Windle and R. Ireland). Oxford: Oxford University Press.

Lateiner, D. 2004. 'The *Iliad*: An Unpredictable Classic', in R. Fowler (ed.), *The Cambridge Companion to Homer.* Cambridge: Cambridge University Press, pp. 11–30.

Lattimore, R. 1951. *The Iliad of Homer.* Chicago: University of Chicago Press.

—. 1965. *The Odyssey of Homer.* New York: Harper and Row.

Lawrence, T. E. 1932 [1991]. *The Odyssey of Homer*. Oxford: Oxford University Press.

Leach, E. R. 1982. 'Critical Introduction', in M. I. Steblin-Kamenskij, *Myth* (trans. M. P. Coote). Ann Arbor: Karoma, pp. 1–20.

Lessing, E. G. 1984 [1766]. *Laocoon: An Essay on the Limits of Painting and Poetry* (trans. E. A. McCormick). Baltimore: Johns Hopkins University Press.

Lévi-Strauss, C. 1969. *The Elementary Structures of Kinship* (trans. J. H. Bell, J. R. Von Sturmern and R. Needham). Boston: Beacon Press.

Lloyd-Jones, H. 1971. *The Justice of Zeus*. Berkeley: University of California Press (revised edn 1983).

Logue, C. 2001. *War Music: An Account of Books 1–4 and 16–19 of Homer's Iliad* (new edn). London: Faber and Faber.

Lombardo, S. 2000. *The Iliad/Homer*. Indianapolis: Hackett Publishing Co.

—. 1997. *The Odyssey/Homer*. Indianapolis: Hackett Publishing Co.

Long, A. A. 1970. 'Morals and Values in Homer', *Journal of Hellenic Studies* 103: 87–102.

Longfellow, H. W. 1992. *Henry Wadsworth Longfellow: Selected Poems*. New York: Random House (Penguin Classics).

Lonsdale, S. H. 1990. *Creatures of Speech: Lion, Herding, and Hunting Similes in the Iliad*. Stuttgart: Teubner.

Lord, A. B. 1960. *The Singer of Tales*. Cambridge, MA: Harvard University Press.

Lorrimer, H. L. 1950. *Homer and the Monuments*. London: MacMillan and Co.

Lowenstam, S. 2000. 'The Shroud of Laertes and Penelope's Guile', *Classical Journal* 95: 333–48.

Luce, T. V. 1998. *Celebrating Homer's Landscapes: Troy and Ithaca Revisited*. New Haven: Yale University Press.

Lynn-George, M. 1988. *Epos: Word, Narrative and the Iliad*. Basingstoke: Macmillan.

Lyons, D. 2003. 'Dangerous Gifts: Ideologies of Marriage and Exchange in Ancient Greece', *Classical Antiquity* 22: 93–134.

Mackie, H. 1997. 'Song and Storytelling: An Odyssean Perspective', *Transactions of the American Philological Association* 127: 77–95.

Maronitis, D. N. 2004. *Homeric Megathemes: War-Homilia-Homecoming*. Lanham, MD: Rowman and Littlefield.

Martin, R. P. 1993. 'Telemachus and the Last Hero Song', *Colby Quarterly* 29: 222–40.

—. 1989. *The Language of Heroes: Speech and Performance in the Iliad*. Ithaca: Cornell University Press.

—. 2000. 'Wrapping Homer Up: Cohesion, Discourse, and Deviation', in A. Sharrock and H. Morales (eds), *Intratextuality: Greek and Roman Textual Relations*. Oxford: Oxford University Press, pp. 43–65.

McLeod, C. 1983. 'Homer on Poetry and the Poetry of Homer', in idem, *Collected Essays*. Oxford: Oxford University Press, pp. 1–15.

McLure, L. K. (ed.) 2002. *Sexuality and Gender in the Classical World, Part I: Greece*. Oxford: Oxford University Press.

Miller, M. 2012. *The Song of Achilles*. London: Bloomsbury.

Minchin, E. 2001. *Homer and the Resources of Memory: Some Applications of Cognitive Theory to the Iliad and the Odyssey*. Oxford: Oxford University Press.

Montanari, F. and Rengakos, A. (eds). 2005. *La Poésie épique grecque: Métamorphoses d'un genre litéraire*. Vandoeuvres, Geneva: Fondation Hardt.

Morris, I. 2009. 'The Eighth-Century Revolution', in K. Raaflaub and H. van Wees (eds), *A Companion to Archaic Greece*. Malden, MA and Oxford: Wiley-Blackwell, pp. 64–80.

Morris, I. and Powell, B. (eds). 1997. *A New Companion to Homer*. Leiden: Brill.

Most, G. 2004. 'How Many Homers?' in A. Santoni (ed.), *L'Autore Multiplo*. Pisa: Scuola Normale Superiore, pp. 1–14.

Mueller, M. 2009 [1984]. *The Iliad* (2nd edn). Bristol: Bristol Classical Press.

Murnaghan, S. 1987. *Disguise and Recognition in the* Odyssey. Princeton: Princeton University Press.

Murray, A. T. 1924–25 [1999]. *The Iliad: Volume I, Books 1-12; Volume II, Books 13–24* (2nd edn, rev. W. F. Wyatt. Loeb Classical Library). Cambridge, MA: Havard University Press.

—. 1919 [1995]. *The Odyssey: Volume I, Books 1–12; Volume II, Books 13–24* (2nd edn, rev. W. F. Wyatt. Loeb Classical Library). Cambridge, MA: Harvard University Press.

Nagler, M. N. 1974. *Spontaneity and Tradition: A Study in the Oral Art of Homer*. Berkeley: University of California Press.

Nagy, G. 1999 [1979]. *The Best of the Achaeans: Concepts of the Hero in Archaic Greek Poetry* (2nd edn). Baltimore and London: Johns Hopkins University Press.

—. 1990. *Greek Mythology and Poetics*. Ithaca: Cornell University Press.

—. 1996. *Homeric Questions*. Austin: University of Texas Press.

Nimis, S. 1998. 'Ring Composition and Linearity in Homer', in E. A. Mackay (ed.), *Signs of Orality: The Oral Tradition and Its Influence in the Greek and Roman World*. Leiden: Brill, pp. 65–78.

Olson, S. D. 1995. *Blood and Iron: Stories and Storytelling in Homer's Odyssey*. Leiden: Brill.

Osborne, R. 2004. 'Homer's Society', in R. Fowler (ed.), *The Cambridge Companion to Homer*. Cambridge: Cambridge University Press, pp. 206–19.

Oswald, A. 2011. *Memorial*. London: Faber and Faber.

Parry, M. 1971. *The Making of Homeric Verse* (ed. A. Parry. New edn 1988). Oxford: Oxford University Press.

Peradotto, J. 1990. *Man in the Middle Voice: Name and Narration in the* Odyssey. Princeton: Princeton University Press.

Pfeiffer, R. 1968. *History of Classical Scholarship from the Beginnings to the End of the Hellenistic Age*. Oxford: Oxford University Press.

Porter, J. I. 2004. 'Homer: The History of an Idea', in R. Fowler (ed.), *The Cambridge Companion to Homer*. Cambridge: Cambridge University Press, pp. 324–43.

—. 2010. 'Wolf, Friedrich August', in M. Finkelberg (ed.), *The Homer Encyclopedia*. vol. III, London: Wiley-Blackwell, pp. 937–9.

Pothlethwaite, N. 2002. *Homer's Iliad: A Commentary on the Translation of Richmond Lattimore*. Exeter: University of Exeter Press.

Powell, B. B. 2007. *Homer* (2nd edn). Malden, MA and Oxford: Wiley-Blackwell.

—. 1991. *Homer and the Origin of the Greek Alphabet*. Cambridge: Cambridge University Press.

Pucci, P. 1987. *Odysseus Polytropos: Intertextual Readings in the* Odyssey *and the Iliad*. Ithaca: Cornell University Press.

—. 1998. *The Song of the Sirens*. Lanham, MD: Rowman and Littlefield.

Raaflaub, K. A. 2005. 'Epic and History', in J. Foley (ed.), *A Companion to Epic*. Oxford: Blackwell, pp. 55–70.

—. 1998. 'Homer, the Trojan War, and History', *Classical World* 91: 387–403.

—. 1997. 'Homer, the Trojan War, and History', in D. Boedeker, *The World of Troy: Homer, Schliemann, and the Treasures of Priam*. Washington, DC: Society for the Pre servation of the Greek Heritage, pp. 76–99.

Raaflaub, K. A. and van Wees, H. (eds). 2009. *A Companion to Archaic Greece*. Malden, MA and Oxford: Wiley-Blackwell.

Redfield, J. 1975 [1994]. *Nature and Culture in the Iliad: The Tragedy of Hector* (expanded edn). Durham, NC: Duke University Press.

—. 1979. 'The Proem of the *Iliad*: Homer's Art', *Classical Philology* 74: 95–110.

Rengakos, A. 2005. 'Homer and the Historians: The Influence of Epic Narrative Technique on Herodotus and Thucydides', in F. Montanari and A. Rengakos (eds), *La Poésie épique grecque: Métamorphoses d'un genre littéraire*. Vandoeuvres, Geneva: Fondation Hardt, pp. 183–214.

Richardson, S. 1990. *The Homeric Narrator*. Nashville, TN: Vanderbilt University Press.

Rieu, E. V. 1950 [2003]. *Homer: The Iliad* (revised edn. w. notes, by P. V. Jones and D. C. H. Rieu). London: Penguin.

—. 1946 [2003]. *Homer: The Odyssey* (revised translation by D. C. H. Rieu, w. notes by P. V. Jones). London: Penguin.

Rose, C. B. 1997. 'Troy and the Historical Imagination', in D. Boedeker, *The World of Troy: Homer, Schliemann, and the Treasures of Priam*. Washington, DC: Society for the Preservation of the Greek Heritage, pp. 100–10.

Ruijgh, C. J. 1985. 'Le mcénien et Homère', in A. Morpurgo Davies and Y. Dohous (eds), *Linear B: A 1984 Survey*. Louvaine: Cabay, pp. 143–90.

Russo, J. 1997. 'The Formula', in I. Morris and B. Powell (eds), *A New Companion to Homer*. Leiden: Brill, pp. 238–60.

Said, S. 2011. *Homer and the* Odyssey. Oxford: Oxford University Press.

Sammons, B. 2010. *The Art and Rhetoric of the Homeric Catalogue*. Oxford: Oxford University Press.

Schadewaldt, W. 1965. *Von Homers Welt und Werk: Ausätze und Auslegungen zur Homerischen Frage* (4th edn). Stuttgart: K. F. Koehler.

Schein, S. L. 1997. 'The *Iliad*: Structure and Interpretation', in I. Morris and B. Powell (eds), *A New Companion to Homer*. Leiden: Brill, pp. 345–59.

—. 1984. *The Mortal Hero: An Introduction to Homer's Iliad*. Berekeley: University of California Press.

Scodel, R. 2008. *Epic Facework: Self-Presentation and Social Interaction in Homer*. Swansea: The Classical Press of Wales.

Scott, W. C. 2009. *The Artistry of the Homeric Simile*. Lebanon, NH: University Press of New England (Dartmouth College Press).

Segal, C. 1994. *Singers, Heroes, and Gods in the* Odyssey. Ithaca: Cornell University Press.

Shewring, W. 1980. *The Odyssey/Homer*. Oxford: Oxford University Press.

Shive, D. 1987. *Naming Achilles*. Oxford: Oxford University Press.

Silk, M. 2004. *Homer: The Iliad*. Cambridge: Cambridge University Press.

Simpson, R. H. and Lazenby, J. F. 1970. *The Catalogue of Ships in Homer's Iliad*. Oxford: Oxford University Press.

Slatkin, L. 1991 [2009]. *The Power of Thetis: Allusion and Interpretation in the Iliad* (2nd edn). Berkeley: University of California Press.

Snell, B. 1953. *The Discovery of the Mind: The Greek Origins of European Thought* (trans. T. G. Rosenmeyer). Cambridge: Cambridge University Press.

Snodgrass, A. M. 1971 [2000]. *The Dark Age of Greece* (2nd edn). Edinburgh: Edinburgh University Press.

Spentzou, E. and Fowler, D. (eds). 2002. *Cultivating the Muse: Struggles for Power and Inspiration in Classical Literature.* Oxford: Oxford University Press.

Stanley, K. 1993. *The Shield of Homer: Narrative Structure in the Iliad.* Princeton: Princeton University Press.

Steiner, G. 1996. *Homer in English.* London. Penguin.

Taplin, O. 1992. *Homeric Soundings: The Shaping of the Iliad.* Oxford: Oxford University Press.

Thalmann, W. 1992. *The* Odyssey: *An Epic of Return.* New York: Twayne Publishers.

Tracy, S. V. 1990. *The Story of the Odyssey.* Princeton: Princeton University Press.

—. 1997. 'The Structures of the *Odyssey*', in I. Morris and B. Powell (eds), *A New Companion to Homer.* Leiden: Brill, pp. 360–79.

Turner, F. M. 1997. 'The Homeric Question', in I. Morris and B. Powell (eds), *A New Companion to Homer.* Leiden: Brill, pp. 123–45.

van Wees, H. 1992. *Status Warriors: War, Violence and Society in Homer and History.* Amsterdam: Gieben.

Verity, A. 2011. *Homer: The Iliad.* Oxford: Oxford University Press.

Vico, G. 2005 (1725). *New Science: Principles of the New Science Concerning the Common Nature of Nations.* London: Penguin.

Vivante, P. 1982. *The Epithets in Homer: A Study in Poetic Values.* New Haven: Yale University Press.

Wace, A. J. B. and Stubbing, F. H. (eds). 1963. *A Companion to Homer.* London: MacMillan and Co.

Walcott, Derek. 1990. *Omeros.* New York: Farrar, Straus and Giroux.

Whitman, C. H. 1958. *Homer and the Heroic Tradition.* Cambridge, MA: Harvard University Press.

Willcock, M. M. 1976. *A Companion to the Iliad: Based on the Translation by Richard Lattimore.* Chicago: University of Chicago Press.

Williams, B. 1993 [2008]. *Shame and Necessity.* Berkeley: University of California Press.

Wolf, F. A. 1985. *Prolegomena to Homer, 1795* (trans. A. Grafton, G. W. Most and J. E. G. Zetzel). Princeton: Princeton University Press.

Wood, Michael. 1987. *In Search of the Trojan War.* New York: New American Library.

Younger, J. G. 1998. *Music in the Aegean Bronze Age.* Jonsered: P. Åström.

Zeitlin, F. I. 1995. 'Figuring Fidelity in Homer's *Odyssey*', in F. Zeitlin (ed.), *Playing the Other: Gender and Society in Classical Greek Literature.* Chicago: University of Chicago Press, pp. 19–52.

Zumthor, P. 1990. *Oral Poetry: An Introduction.* Minneapolis: University of Minnesota Press.

GENERAL INDEX

INDEX OF HOMERIC CHARACTERS

INDEX OF SELECTED GREEK WORDS AND HOMERIC EXPRESSIONS AND PHRASES

www.ingramcontent.com/pod-product-compliance
Ingram Content Group UK Ltd.
Pitfield, Milton Keynes, MK11 3LW, UK
UKHW020734280225
455688UK00012B/646